NEWS FROM THE FRONT

To the memory of
15955 Private Benjamin Woodhead
1895–1916

NEWS FROM THE FRONT

WAR CORRESPONDENTS ON THE WESTERN FRONT 1914–18

MARTIN J. FARRAR

SUTTON PUBLISHING

First published in 1998 by Sutton Publishing Limited
Phoenix Mill · Thrupp · Stroud · Gloucestershire · GL5 2BU

Paperback edition first published 1999

British Library Cataloguing in Publication Data
A catalogue record for this book is available from the British Library

ISBN 0-7509-2326-1

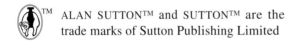
Typeset in10/12 pt Times.
Typesetting and origination by
Sutton Publishing Limited.
Printed in Great Britain by
Redwood Books Limited,
Trowbridge, Wiltshire.

CONTENTS

LIST OF ILLUSTRATIONS

ACKNOWLEDGEMENTS

I am indebted to the following people without whose support this book could not have been completed:

Hilary Farrar, who gave of her valuable time to proofread the script. Jo Thatcher, for the use of her living room floor during the months of research. Sarah Kidner and her picture researching skills. Penny and Alan Savage and their computer. Andy Brooks and Sue Hughes for believing in me, and Nigel Mace, my college lecturer. Family members in Yorkshire, for their help in tracing the history surrounding the life of my great uncle, Benjamin Woodhead, and for loaning documents and personal photographs. Thanks also go to my family and friends for the encouragement and moral support they have given me during this project.

Much information and many sources of research were available thanks to the helpful staff of the following institutions:

The British Newspaper Library, Colindale; The Imperial War Museum; The Commonwealth War Graves Commission; The Ministry of Defence – Army Records Centre; The King's Own Yorkshire Light Infantry Regimental Museum at the Doncaster Museum and Art Gallery; J.S. Cowley, Regimental Secretary with the Light Infantry Office in Pontefract; the Public Record Office at Kew; the public libraries of Milton Keynes and Stony Stratford.

INTRODUCTION

The Allies at Germans lunged,
And won a fight at name – expunged.
But the French's army was defeated,
Upon the field of place – deleted.
From Town-Blue-Pencilled, lovely spot,
The unions galloped, fierce and hot,
But hundreds bit the dust and grass,
In the place-Press-Bureau-Would-Not-Pass.
The hottest work in the field,
Burst around locality-concealed.[1]

The reality of what actually happened on the First World War battlefields at Mons, Ypres, Neuve Chapelle, Loos, the Somme and Passchendaele, was not widely known in Britain until the 1920s. How could this have happened? How clear were the facts emerging a decade later, which form the foundations of how people view the First World War today, compared to the reality of 1914–18?

Books like *The First Day of the Somme*[2] by Martin Middlebrook, Lyn Macdonald's *They Called it Passchendaele*[3] and *The Donkeys*[4] by Alan Clark offer the reader of the late twentieth century a first-hand account of the First World War battles on the Western Front. These authors provide the reader with knowledge of the heavy casualties which resulted from these offensives and the idea that these battles were arguably the British Army's most costly in terms of human life and suffering.

However genuine this picture is of the events on the Western Front, eighty years later it is difficult to believe that at the time the people on the Home Front had little notion of what was happening there. Commenting on the Battle of the Somme, John Terraine remarked on its repercussions, which still haunt us today:

It was a long time before the grisly facts about July 1st penetrated the British Consciousness. . . . But when at last the British public learned what the loss of life had been in that short span of time, the paroxysm was tremendous. Its effects were felt all through the Second World War, influencing British strategy; they are still felt in Britain today.[5]

This book examines the styles of reporting output from the war correspondents and pinpoints their role within the propaganda processes in place during the different stages of the war. From this point the changing images of war can be traced as they passed into history and became the familiar concepts we know today.

It appears that at the start of the First World War the role of the war correspondent was almost non-existent, but as the conflict developed into an endurance test so the importance of news reporting increased in an effort to keep the Home Front fully supportive of the struggle. In 1914 Kitchener had branded war correspondents as outlaws and liable to arrest if found anywhere near the Western Front in France. However, by 1918 they had become fully integrated into the military system and were even rewarded for their role in the war with five correspondents becoming Knights of the Order of the British Empire in 1920.

The role of the correspondent during the war was directly linked to the alliance which the Government and military had developed and needed to maintain their popularity. The relationship between the military and the newspapers changed in three dramatic phases which were closely related to action on the Western Front and the Home Front's reaction to it. Accordingly, the dispatches of the news from the Western Front were adjusted to suit the access given to the war correspondents at the time. Over four years the image of the war correspondent as outlaw changed to that of knight, and this is the pattern of development which Beach Thomas records in his book *A Traveller in News*. This model can be used to examine the reasons for these changes and how they affected the style of reporting from the British-held Western Front, supported with examples of war correspondents' dispatches.

From the outbreak of war in August 1914 until May 1915 Kitchener made the correspondents' job as difficult as possible, by banning their entry into the Western Front Zone. Philip Gibbs said of the early newspaper reporting on the war:

> Reading the English newspapers in those early days of the war, with their stories of starving Germany, their atrocity-mongering, their wild perversions of truth, a journalist proud of his profession must blush for shame at its degradation and insanity.[6]

Between May 1915 and April 1917 the military warmed to the idea of official correspondents on the Western Front. However, this was still only a military exercise in time wasting, as the war correspondents saw very little of the real battles and were closely controlled. During the last phase, between April 1917 and the armistice in late 1918, there was a thawing of relations and the complete surrender of the Army and War Office to the needs of the war correspondent. By this stage the war correspondent had been fully developed by the military as another weapon of propaganda dissemination.

At the time of the First World War the general population was aware that the true picture of the events on the Western Front was not reaching them. This was a time when newspapers were the main source of information with up to three daily editions. The only other forms of communication available to the Home Front were the telegram and word of mouth, which often led to the spreading of rumours and lies.

In her diary entry for 2 August, as the prospect of war became more likely, Vera Brittain wrote of the problems in acquiring news on the current situation.

> Mother tried to get a paper when she went down to the baths, but they were all sold up; however the Ellingers lent us theirs. But it was not so much what was in the paper that caused excitement as the rumours that were spreading about all day.[7]

Again on 3 August much of Vera Brittain's time was spent just trying to find out the latest news. Rumours formed a large part of her daily diet of news during the early part of the First World War. It was very much a time of uncertainty, which was not alleviated by the military and Government institutions' hold over how news was to be reported.

> I sat this morning after breakfast reading various newspapers for about two hours. A rumour is going round to-night that England has declared to Germany that if a German sets foot in Belgian territory her [England's] navy will immediately act.
>
>   I should think this must be the blackest Bank Holiday within memory. Pandemonium reigned in the town. What with holiday-trippers, people struggling for papers, trying to lay in stores of food & dismayed that the price of everything had gone up, there was confusion everywhere.[8]

Who was to blame for this lack of knowledge of the events in France and of news of the war in general? Philip Knightley believed this had much to do with the war correspondents.

> They were in a position to know more than most of the nature of the war of attrition on the Western Front, yet they identified themselves absolutely with the armies in the field; they protected the high command from criticism, wrote jauntily about life in the trenches, kept an inspired silence about the slaughter, and allowed themselves to be absorbed by the propaganda machine.[9]

However, this was not the whole picture and was only partly true from May 1915, when war correspondents were allowed to join the British Army on the Western Front.

The soldiers at the Front blamed the newspapers. In the *Kemmel Times* for Monday 3 July 1916, a newspaper produced by soldiers in the Front line asks under a heading,

> Things we want to know:
> Whether the London press are aware there are a few British troops on the Western Front???[10]

After the Battle of Neuve Chapelle in March 1915 the *Daily Mail*'s war correspondent attacked the censorship of information by the authorities and especially how the costs of battle were being hidden from the public.

> WHY NOT TRUST THE PEOPLE? . . . When the big advance comes, the big advance that would have started at Neuve Chapelle had things gone well as was hoped, losses will be much greater. The nation will not shrink back. But our authorities would be well advised not to try to blind the public, even for a time, by telling of victories and glossing over reverses.[11]

However large this information gap was, one wonders why it took so long for the public to realize it existed. Maybe they needed to block out the truth, so they had time to absorb the magnitude of the situation and consequences which war brought.

In Vera Brittain's case, as with many on the Home Front, she could only guess what events were taking place in France. After the Battle of Neuve Chapelle she speculated that all was not going to plan because of the numbers of casualties returning to Britain.

> As usual the Press had given no hint of that tragedy's dimensions, and it was only through the long casualty lists, and the persistent demoralising rumours that owing to a miscalculation in time thousands of our men had been shot down by our guns, that the world was gradually coming to realise something of what the engagement had been.[12]

This book examines the work of the war correspondents who became accredited to British General Headquarters (GHQ) from May 1915, and attempts to experience the war through their eyes and ears. These five were William Beach Thomas,[13] Philip Gibbs,[14] Percival Phillips,[15] Perry Robinson[16] and Herbert Russell,[17] who all spent most of the four years reporting from and around the British Western Front. Their information was what the Home Front craved on a daily basis, and their dispatches shaped the public's image of war on the Western Front. Reading these accounts and understanding the influences under which they were written enables us to grasp a real sense of that period of our very recent history.

It is helpful to appreciate the nature and influence of propaganda at the time of the First World War.

> If the truth were told from the outset, there would be no reason and will for war.[18]

The First World War was the first total war, and it ceased to be the sole privilege of the military authorities because it involved civilians of all the combatant nations. War was no longer some secret distraction of the military generals somewhere in the distant Empire, it now absorbed the Home Front and demanded their total commitment.

> The truth was that the military mind was obsessed with the necessity of fighting this war – 'our war' as the regulars called it – in the dark, while the non-military mind knew that such a policy was impossible, and might be disastrous.[19]

Because of the nature of this war it was impossible to exclude the Home Front from the impact of battle as they were suffering in a direct way never experienced before. During the Somme and other major offensives the Home Front in the south-east and London could hear the guns roaring and feel the mines exploding which preceded battle. The after-effects of war in the form of casualties returning to Britain to be nursed and the dreaded telegrams dropping into homes all around the country informing families of relatives who had died also had a great impact on morale.

Shortages owing to the German U-boat blockade of Britain, especially of food, seemed to both Vera Brittain and Siegfried Sassoon[20] the main preoccupation of the Home Front, even more so than the fighting in France.

However, for the Government and the military leaders this was the least of their worries, as the Home Front became a major target of the German war machine in the form of the Zeppelin raid. It would appear that by the end of May 1916 at least 550 British civilians had been killed by German Zeppelin attacks and these were not just focused on London.[21] Many places suffered from Zeppelin raids including Yarmouth, King's Lynn, Gravesend, Sunderland, Edinburgh, the Midlands and the Home Counties.

When compared with the first day of the Somme, the 550 civilians to 60,000 soldiers would be little for the Government and military generals to worry about. Yet because of the way rumours spread around Britain concerning the fear of Zeppelin raids, and later German seaplane attacks, if not checked by the military and Government they could have cut the war short through a lack of support from the Home Front. Propaganda became a vital tool in the bid to keep the Home Front sustaining the war effort.[22] As it became necessary for the authorities to control information on the war a structured and organized propaganda machine was developed on a large scale.

Propaganda is a weapon used in warfare where information is intentionally distorted to create an image which can be employed to beguile the general public, allure allies and deceive the enemy. Cate Haste identifies the process of propaganda in her book *Keep the Home Fires Burning*.

> The essence of propaganda is simplification. Through the methods adopted by the media and organizations engaged in propaganda, a fabric of images about war was gradually built up, by eternal repetition over a long period, to provide indisputable justification for the fighting.[23]

The ingredients for successful propaganda are plenty of raw material, a public whose access to the truth is severely restricted and a controlled means of disseminating information, such as the press. Mixed together, the machinery of the propaganda process churns out 'information' which is designed to justify the war and boost recruitment. Types of propaganda are identified in Ponsonby's book *Falsehood in Wartime* and include patriotism, lies heard, omissions, exaggerations, truth concealment, faked photography, film, forgery and mistranslation.[24]

The Defence of the Realm Act was passed in 1914 and is significant in the evolution of propaganda. Although the Act was not principally drafted to control public opinion, its after-effects did. The act of publishing information that was calculated to be indirectly or directly of use to the enemy became an offence and accordingly punishable in a court of law. This included information on any troop and naval movement, any description of war and any news that was likely to cause a rift between the public and military authorities.[25]

Owing to the vagueness of the Act just about everything in wartime could be seen as useful to the enemy – a weather report, a role of honour and even chess problems sent to newspapers from a foreigner could be thought of as some sort of secret code to enemy powers.[26] There is cause to question who were the true enemies of the military generals – was it the Germans across no man's land or could it be the people on the Home Front who had the power to bring war to an end if their support failed?

Justification is a large part of the aim of propaganda, to vindicate the fighting to both soldiers and the Home Front. Tactics were to bond the appeal of sacrifice to the image of war, to promote the idea that Britain was indeed fighting a moral crusade in the name of civilization.

> The British soldier had gone to war full of patriotism and enthusiasm. He had been led to believe that the German was a barbarian who had trampled over half of Europe, raped women, murdered babies and committed every possible atrocity. He believed, also, that Britain had the most capable generals and people at home were solidly behind him. To many it was more like a crusade than a political war.[27]

The effects on the Home Front of these stories of atrocity can also be noted in Vera Brittain's accounts of her first experiences of nursing wounded German prisoners of war alone while in France.

> . . . into the midst of thirty representatives of the nation which, as I had repeatedly been told, had crucified Canadians, cut off the hands of babies, and subjected pure and stainless females to unmentionable 'atrocities'. I didn't think I had really believed all those stories, but I wasn't quite sure. I half expected that one or two of the patients would get out of bed and try to rape me, but I soon discovered that none of them were in a position to rape anybody. . . .[28]

By 1915 the war was one of military stalemates in the trenches and alarming casualty rates, and it had become a test of staying power to the bitter end. Gone were the days of enthusiasm for the war: they had been replaced by war weariness and exhaustion. Recruitment had remained the dominant focus of the domestic propaganda in Britain until the introduction of conscription in January 1916. From this point the machinery's course had to be changed to target the war-fatigued Home Front. The dangers of a long war were beginning to take effect as the images of battle became progressively less convincing.

> People must never be allowed to become despondent; so victories must be exaggerated and defeats, if not concealed, at any rate minimized, and the stimulus of indignation, horror and hatred must be assiduously and continuously pumped into the public minds of 'propaganda'.[29]

This quote is from Ponsonby's book, *Falsehood in Wartime*, and it must be noted that this book was published some time after the war in 1928. By this time ordinary people were becoming aware of some of the truths of the First World War, such as the casualty figures of the Battle of the Somme. There was a backlash against the Government power – people felt betrayed because of the war and consequently were very cynical.

One of the direct consequences of the concentration of propaganda on raising civilian morale was the introduction of the accredited war correspondents to the Western Front in May 1915. The press probably had the greatest influence in moulding attitudes towards the war and in the public's eyes it was their responsibility to provide accurate information on the war. However, the reporting of the truth was turned by the propaganda machine into an obligation to promote patriotic duty and to inspire hatred of the enemy. Control of the press utilized the negative propaganda form of censorship, which meant restricting access to information concerning the war. What actually happened was that because so little information was released the Home Front had insufficient knowledge of the true nature of war. This led to a gap in the understanding of why the war was being fought and any information which reached Britain became twisted and exaggerated; an effective and yet simple way to exploit the fears and patriotism of the Home Front.

The effects of the policy of news censorship by High Command, the Army and the war correspondents were far reaching, lasting long after the fighting had ended as John Terraine explained.

> The British people, between 1914 and 1918, displayed great fortitude; enough to make one feel that a little more truth, a little more reality (even at the cost of giving some small comfort to the enemy at times) would not have been beyond their power to bear, and could have saved them the worst of the penalty they later incurred, the dire sickness of Disillusion.[30]

Both soldiers' letters from the trenches to the Home Front and the war correspondents' dispatches contained censorship which was to create a reality gap between those fighting and the British people. This censorship took two forms: one was the official censorship of the Army which would not allow Allied plans or names of battalions and battles to be directly disclosed, and the other was the self-censorship of the British 'stiff upper lip' kind.

Hawkin Mundy, a soldier with the Bucks Territorials during the First World War, talked in his book about how letters home from the Front did not express combatants' true feelings about battle. He was about to go over the top and at the time was writing home; the advice from senior officers was not to write about what was about to happen.

> Mine was just an ordinary letter to me mother, in any case I shouldn't have wrote and said 'I'm going into battle tomorrow morning.' That's natural, when you write to your mother you don't want to upset her. . . . You try to write a cheerful letter home, you don't write and say 'Oh Hell! I'm going into battle tomorrow and I'm frightened to death.' You wouldn't dream of that, or shouldn't do then.[31]

Many letters home talked of war as if it was matter of fact and completely normal. Paul Fussell sees this as the British phlegmatic character, that in many letters from the Western Front there is a refusal by the men to say anything and a tendency to be entirely unflappable about the events which surrounded them.[32] This was also true of the war correspondents and the ethical problem of self-censorship.

During the First World War, editors and proprietors faced the problem of what to leave out and how to interpret events 'in the national interest'.[33]

The war correspondents' dispatches were collected together and published in book form during the war, part of mass instant history. These came from the likes of William Beach Thomas,[34] Perry Robinson,[35] Lt-Col Repington[36] and Philip Gibbs[37] who went on to write about the role they played in the war. Such works document their changing attitudes to the reporting of warfare.

Higher up the scale the historian can study the thoughts of Sir Douglas Haig and the generals with regard to the relationship between the Army and the role of the war correspondents found in their private papers and books written from their diaries of the conflict. Another major source is the actual film footage available from the film *The Battle of the Somme* (1916).[38] This contains some of the best-remembered imagery of war produced in the twentieth century, which has become the myth of the Somme. Lastly there are many histories written about the First World War based on accounts of soldiers on both sides of no man's land.

It is important to understand why the Army allowed correspondents to the Front in May 1915 for the first time and to investigate how they were subsequently controlled to produce reports which enhanced and sensationalized the British position. What form did the censorship placed upon the war correspondents in the field take? This was performed by the state institutions, by employers and by self control. A body to supervise the press and news was not set up until 1917, when the Department of Information was established. But how did the war correspondents justify their part in the propaganda process which led to the myth of the First World War?

Why were the newspaper proprietors of the day such as Lord Northcliffe so willing to accept this censorship and to play such a crucial part in this propaganda machine? It is meaningful to study their relationship with the people in charge and to ask what were their interests in playing the propaganda game for the war effort. Their actions not only affected the mass media's credibility at the time, but also had serious consequences in terms of whether the truth of the war could have brought peace earlier than 1918.

NOTES

1. First published in the *Sphere*, 7 November 1914, an American poem called *News from the Front* which describes the official censors.
2. M. Middlebrook, *The First Day of the Somme* (Penguin Books, 1971).
3. L. Macdonald, *They Called it Passchendaele* (Papermac, 1984).
4. A. Clark, *The Donkeys* (Pimlico, 1991).
5. J. Terraine, *The First World War, 1914–18* (Papermac, 1984), p. 117.
6. P. Gibbs, *Adventures in Journalism* (Heinemann, 1923), p. 217.
7. A. Bishop, *Chronicle of Youth, Vera Brittain's War Diary, 1913–1917* (Victor Gollancz, 1981), p. 83.
8. Bishop, *Chronicle of Youth*, pp. 84–5.
9. P. Knightley, *The First Casualty* (Quartet Books, 1982), p. 65.
10. P. Beaver, *The Wipers Times* (Papermac, 1988), p. 105.
11. L. Macdonald, *1915, The Death of Innocence* (Headline Book Publishing, 1993), p. 149.
12. V. Brittain, *Testament of Youth* (Virago Press, 1978), p. 136.

13. Represented the *Daily Mail* and the *Daily Mirror*.

14. Represented the *Daily Chronicle* and the *Daily Telegraph*.

15. Represented the *Daily Express* and the *Morning Post*.

16. Represented the *Daily News* and *The Times*.

17. Represented the Reuters agency.

18. A. Ponsonby, *Falsehood in Wartime* (George Allen and Unwin, 1928), p. 27.

19. Gibbs, *Adventures*, p. 227.

20. Brittain, *Testament of Youth*, p. 401; in a letter from home Vera Brittain noted the mood of the Home Front and the food shortages. S. Sassoon, *Memoirs of an Infantry Officer* (Faber and Faber, 1930); a lack of sugar seems to be a main conversation point on the Home Front when Mr Sherston returns from France on leave in Siegfried Sassoon's semi-autobiographical book.

21. M. Gilbert, *First World War* (HarperCollins, 1995), p. 230.

22. For accounts of air attacks in progress refer to Vera Brittain's description of an assault on Kensington High Street or Siegfried Sassoon's assessment of the strike on Liverpool Street station. Brittain, *Testament of Youth*, p. 365; Sassoon, *Memoirs*, p. 197.

23. C. Haste, *Keep the Home Fires Burning* (Allen Lane, 1977), p. 3.

24. Ponsonby, *Falsehood in Wartime*, pp. 13–31.

25. Knightley, *First Casualty*, p. 64.

26. Haste, *Home Fires*.

27. Middlebrook, *First Day*, p. 49.

28. Brittain, *Testament of Youth*, p. 374.

29. Ponsonby, *Falsehood in Wartime*, p. 14.

30. J. Terraine, *Impacts of War, 1914 & 1918* (Leo Cooper, 1993), p. 108.

31. H. Mundy, *No Heroes, No Cowards* (The People's Press of Milton Keynes, 1981), p. 54.

32. P. Fussell, *The Great War and Modern Memory* (Oxford University Press, 1975), p. 181.

33. C. Lovelace, 'British Press Censorship During the First World War', Boyce, Carran, & Wingate, *Newspaper History: From the 17th Century to the Present Day* (Constable & Company, 1978), p. 317.

34. W.B. Thomas, *With the British on the Somme* (Methuen, 1917).

35. H.P. Robinson, *The Turning Point; The Battle of the Somme* (William Heinemann, 1917).

36. C. Repington, *The First World War, 1914–1918. Personal Experiences* , volume I (Constable & Company, 1920).

37. P. Gibbs, *The Battles of the Somme* (Heinemann, 1917).

38. G. Mallins & J.B. McDowell, *The Battle of the Somme* (WO Films Committee, 1916).

Section One

OUTLAWS AND 'EYEWITNESS', AUGUST 1914 TO MAY 1915

OUTLAWS AND 'EYEWITNESS'

At a conference between the press, the War Office and the Admiralty on 27 July 1914 the press assented to a voluntary code of censorship with regard to the reporting of the movements of troops and shipping which might prove harmful to the country's security. By 29 July the British First Fleet had orders to mobilize and to form up in the safe waters of the North Sea. In Britain the wheels of the war machine had already started to turn and at this early stage the role of the press and censorship were still being discussed.

In Fleet Street there was a hive of activity as each of the newspapers prepared to provide the best coverage of the impending crisis on the European continent. Journalists were all desperate to acquire the role of war correspondent for their respective newspapers as it was a way of becoming a household name almost over night – the Boer War had proved that.

> Special correspondents, press photographers, the youngest reporters on the staff, sub-editors emerging from the little dark rooms with a new excitement in eyes that had grown tired with proof correcting, passed each other on the stairs and asked for their chance. It was a chance of seeing the greatest drama in life with real properties, real corpses, real blood, real horrors with a devilish thrill in them. It was not to be missed by any self-respecting journalist to whom all life is a stage play which he describes and criticises from a free seat in the front of the house.[1]

As the British First Fleet moved into position, so the war correspondents were assembling in France and at the War Office to witness this fracas which most considered would be over before Christmas. Philip Gibbs was on his way and doubted the enormity of the developing crisis.

> 'I shall be back in a few days. Armageddon is still a long way off. The idea of it is too ridiculous and too damnable!'[2]

Philip Gibbs was thirty-seven in 1914, the son of Henry James Gibbs, a civil servant at the Board of Education and the fifth of seven children. Owing to a lack of funds, Philip had been unable to attend public school and had been educated by his father for much of his early life. At the age of twenty-two he began work at the publishers Cassell, earning a wage of £2 10s a week; his first book was published in 1899. Three years later Philip was working in Fleet Street as the literary editor at the *Daily Mail*, then moved to the *Daily Express* for a brief period before joining the *Daily Chronicle* in 1908.

Mr J. Irvine, *Morning Post* (centre), and Mr P. Gibbs, *Daily Chronicle* (right), watch an aerial combat from a trench,17 September 1916.

It was with the *Daily Chronicle* that Gibbs proved himself as a reporter with his eyewitness accounts of the headline stories at the time. In 1911 he reported from the prisons of Portugal at the request of Lord Lytton and in the following year he became war correspondent for the *Daily Graphic*, reporting with the Bulgarian Army in the Balkan War. This experience enabled him to develop his skills as a war correspondent, which he would draw on throughout the First World War. During 1913 and the early part of 1914 Gibbs was in Germany reporting for the *Daily Chronicle* on a tour of inquiry. *The Times* described Gibbs as he set off for adventure in 1914.

> In early August of that year – clad, so it was said, in a lounge suit and carrying a walking stick – he started off for France.[3]

On 3 August the *Daily Express* announced to its readers how it intended to report the news of the impending European conflict. Percival Phillips was on standby in Brussels 'Waiting for the onslaught' as Britain held its breath.

> The Express has made the fullest possible arrangements for a complete service of news from all parts of Europe. Special correspondents are now at their posts with instructions to spare no expense in furnishing our readers with the fullest and latest information.[4]

Percival Phillips was an experienced war correspondent having spent many years reporting from trouble spots around the world. Born in 1877 in Brownsville, Pennsylvania, USA, he spent his early career with various American daily newspapers which gave him his first taste of war correspondence. He reported from the Greek-Turkish War of 1897, where he was attached to the Greek Army, and the Spanish-American War in 1898. The turning point in Percival Phillips' career came in 1901 when he moved to England and joined the staff of the *Daily Express*. From this point until the outbreak of the First World War he reported from many major trouble spots including the Jamaican earthquake of 1907, revolutions in Catalonia in 1909 and Portugal in 1910, the Italian expedition to Tripoli in 1911, and an imperial tour of India, 1911–12. During the first Balkan campaign of 1912 to 1913 he was attached to the Bulgarian General Staff. By August 1914 Percival Phillips was with the Belgium Field Army ready to report on Germany's next move.

In London at the War Office provision for correspondents to accompany the British Army was set out in the 'Regulations for Press Correspondents Accompanying a Force in the Field'. This comprised 'three parts, thirty-seven paragraphs, and six appendices' according to Henry W. Nevinson[5] and resulted in the creation of a register of approved correspondents who could travel with the Army. The object of this was to limit the number of correspondents, choosing those who were most likely to toe the official line and to protect the military from possible betrayal of information into enemy hands.

After consultation between the press and War Office all prospective correspondents had to be approved by the Army Council before a licence was granted and their name was added to the register. For a licensed correspondent this meant that he was now subject to military law and the Chief Field Censor attached to General Headquarters became their commanding officer.

Each correspondent was only allowed to take one servant and one horse with him. Their personal baggage was not to exceed more than 110 lb and they could draw the ordinary army rations, which was all at their own paper's expense. Correspondents were not allowed runners or dispatch riders and were banned from bringing motor vehicles. Any communications would have to be submitted in duplicate to the Press Officer who would accompany the correspondents, and he in turn submitted them to the Chief Field Censor for authorization. There were strict rules about what could and could not be included in a correspondent's dispatch. No reference could be made to the morale of troops, casualties, troop movements, their strength, location or composition and criticism or praise of a personal nature was also forbidden. Once on the register and licensed the correspondent had to wait in London, horse and servant at the ready for his call-up by the War Office.

At 4 p.m. on 4 August 1914 orders were issued by the British Government for the mobilization of the Army. By 12.15 a.m. the following day the Foreign Office issued the statement that Britain had declared war on Germany.

Owing to the summary rejection by the German Government of the request made by His Majesty's Government for assurances that the neutrality of Belgium will be respected, His Majesty's Ambassador at Berlin has received his passports and

Horatio Herbert Kitchener, First Earl of Khartoum (1850–1916), Secretary of State for War and Head of the War Office (August 1914–June 1916). He was drowned en route to Russia in June 1916.

His Majesty's Government have declared to the German Government that a state of war exists between Great Britain and Germany as from 11 p.m. on August 4.[6]

Apart from being the day that Britain committed itself to the crisis taking place on the continent, 5 August saw the appointment of Kitchener to the post of Secretary of War. It was his policies and decisions which shaped and moulded the role of the war correspondent during this early part of the hostilities. Under Kitchener, the war correspondent was banned from entering a set military zone around the British Expeditionary Force and any dispatches from France were to be examined by the War Office before being published in the general press. The war correspondents already waiting at the War Office were informed by Kitchener that they would not be joining the British Army until the French General Staff had sent for its own French correspondents.

In place of the war correspondent the War Office set up the Press Bureau under F.E. Smith (later Lord Birkenhead) in order to censor news and telegraphic reports from the British Army and to issue this information to the press waiting in London and throughout the world. Any news that was not thought to be in the national interest was withheld and the bureau also became a consultative panel for the editors of newspapers. On 11 August 1914 the Press Bureau circulated its first communiqué which did very little to satisfy the appetite of the news hungry public and newspapers. *The Times* pointed out that material in the communiqué was already well known and published by the newspaper before the Press Bureau's release.

The following communiqués were issued yesterday by the newly-established official Press Bureau. It will be noticed that much of the information has already appeared in the Press:–

Noon:– About two German Cavalry divisions are reported in the neighbourhood of Tongres; three German corps are still opposite Liège: other German troops are reported to be entrenching the line of the river Aisne.

The large German force is moving through Luxembourg, and the advanced troops are now on the Belgian frontier. . . .

GERMANS SHORT OF FOOD
12.30 p.m.– Several individuals from German patrols have been captured both in France and Belgium. In all cases they are reported to be short of food for both men and horses and to have made no resistance.[7]

The Press Bureau was created to remove the need for war correspondents to be stationed at the Front and to duplicate information already being sent by the military authorities themselves to the Home Front and press. During this phase of the war the lack of a role for the war correspondent was directly linked to the personality of the man in charge at the War Office.

However, Kitchener's policies and distrust of the war correspondent were evident before his arrival at the War Office in August 1914; his attitude had arisen out of his own personal experience of the press during the Boer War. As a result of the fighting in Africa against the Boers and Zulu the British military resisted the war correspondent.

The Boer War has been described as Britain's first mass media war, created by a number of factors that made the news of warfare easily accessible to the Home Front. These included the establishment of the first mass-circulation newspapers such as the *Daily Mail*, film coverage of the war, and an increasingly speedy communication system through field telephones and wireless telegraphy. The war correspondents brought back to Britain in their dispatches a new kind of journalism which was to change the focus of their reporting. The human interest side of war evolved and became as important as the tactical details of battle. The likes of Edgar Wallace at the *Daily Mail* and Winston Churchill at the *Morning Post* became household names in Britain.

To the press this period had demonstrated that wars sold newspapers. However, to the military, the war correspondent had become a nuisance and a security risk in an area it regarded as its own. During the Zulu War of 1879 at the Battle of Ulundi a war correspondent, Archibald Forbes, managed to get his report on the victory telegraphed back to *The Times* before the military authorities had announced it to the world. These war correspondents were stealing the glory of the generals, who would have preferred that the press were not on the battlefield at all.

The military took action to curb the freedoms of the war correspondent on the battlefield in Africa with the introduction of rules of censorship in 1879 at General Buller's request. Lord Kitchener, at this time in the Sudan, did more than most to handicap the role of the war correspondent trying to report his battles.

Kitchener's tactics were to make the twenty-six correspondents with him run exactly the same risks as his soldiers, to limit their telegraphic facilities to 200 words a day, and to give them no help, no briefings, no guidance, and little courtesy. It was not surprising that they hated him, and his disdain for them was behind what was to happen over war news at the outbreak of the First World War.[8]

The introduction of the Press Bureau in August 1914 can be seen as a continuation of the policies Kitchener started in Africa to try to eliminate the need for correspondents in the war zone. However, the communiqués from the Press Bureau lacked any real news, just giving minimal facts relating to the current situation and nothing of the human interest side of war. The prime aim of the Press Bureau was to limit the power of the meddling war correspondent and provide the newspapers with a distraction.

William Beach Thomas, special correspondent with the *Daily Mail*, at this time in France, had already heard rumours to this effect.

A colleague of mine about this time met Mr Winston Churchill, who told him for his information that the war was going to be 'fought in a fog' and the best place for correspondence about the war was London.[9]

Thomas had had no experience as a war correspondent, but had been reporting for the *Daily Mail* since 1907. Born in 1868, William Beach Thomas was the second son of the Revd George Thomas of Huntingdon. Educated at Shrewsbury and Christ Church, Oxford, he was a keen sportsman and had developed a deep love of the countryside. Before turning to journalism in 1899, Thomas had taught at Bradfield and Dulwich. He began as a contributor to the 'By-the-way' column of the *Globe*, and moved on to *Outlook*, where he wrote about the countryside. In 1907 Thomas was interviewed by Northcliffe and joined the *Daily Mail* as a writer about country life. He wrote columns about the *Daily Mail* farm, which was a model smallholding, and his 'Summer Diary' which recorded day-to-day events in the natural world. In the summer of 1912 Thomas had represented the *Daily Mail* at the Stockholm Olympic Games and in the summer of 1914 he found himself an outlaw in France trying to report the hazy events of war.

Having witnessed the fall of Antwerp with the Belgian Field Army, Percival Phillips commented on the barriers and obstacles of reporting close to the British Front.

The 'fog of war' that has settled over this country screens the important movement of the allied armies as effectively as a stone wall built across France from Dunkirk to Ushant. Lord Kitchener's wise precautions, added to General Joffre's determination that his corps commanders shall not be accompanied by war correspondents, makes it impossible for any unauthorised person to pass the barrier they have thrown between the field forces and the outside world.

They have closed towns that appear to ordinary civilians to be far away from the theatre of war. There is a proscribed zone, officially described by the French military authorities, into which no foreigner or native not connected with the operations may enter. Outside that zone, and nearer the English coast, are towns not officially 'out of bounds' which, nevertheless, are unhealthy places for wandering inquirers after information.[10]

British war correspondents visit the Belgian Front. Left to right: Captain La Porte (Belgian Mission), Mr W. Beach Thomas, the *Daily Mail*, Mr P. Robinson, *The Times*. The two men on the right are assumed to be press officers.

The Times correspondent in Paris talked of 'The secrecy of war' on 13 August, by which time there had been no word on the mobilization and whereabouts of the British Expeditionary Force.

> A deep mist hangs over the scenes of war. Not a word comes from the northern area in Belgium, where the armies of four nations are gathering to fight, and reports of outpost engagements communicated last night give little clue to what is happening along the long frontier line from Luxembourg to Switzerland. Two armies lie face to face among the hills, and the only indication that the news affords is that all is well with the French arms.[11]

The Times correspondent later studied the effects of the absence of news on the population of Paris.

> As a matter of fact, it can be safely said that not a single wounded soldier has yet reached Paris, and the big battle has still to be fought. These rumours arise from lack of news. They grow in circulation, because of the hardest thing in the world for a person untrained in accuracy to reproduce, even with a fair approximation to truth, things which he hears. The Government is now opening an information bureau, where, by handing in a soldier's name and regiment on a

card, his relations will be able to learn for certain whether he is safe, wounded or killed.[12]

Philip Gibbs, correspondent for the *Daily Telegraph* and the *Daily Chronicle*, also made his way to Paris in August 1914 and found that on both sides of the Channel, the military authorities were fighting this war behind closed doors.

By one swift stroke of the military censorship journalism was throttled. All its lines of communication were cut, suddenly, as when, in my office, I spoke from Paris to England, and found myself with a half-finished sentence before a telephone which would no longer 'march,' as they say across the channel. Paris and penalties were threatened against any newspaper which should dare to publish a word of military information beyond the official communiqués issued in order to hide the truth.[13]

Since 7 August advance parties of the British Expeditionary Force were on their way to France and the grip of the War Office began to tighten around the press. This agreed censorship is identified in the *Daily Chronicle*'s announcement of how it aimed to report the war.

A newspaper's duty is to give news, but at times of war it has a patriotic duty as well.
  It must give no news which would convey information of advantage to the adversary.
  Throughout this war 'The Daily Chronicle' will refrain from indicating the location and movements of warships and units of the army.
  At the same time 'The Daily Chronicle' has taken complete and energetic measures to supply its readers with full intelligence from every part of the war areas.
  The censorship that we exercise over our news will not affect its value to the ordinary reader of the paper. The special correspondents of 'The Daily Chronicle' are men of world-wide repute, experienced in war, vivid descriptive writers and brilliant news-getters.[14]

From 9 August the British Expeditionary Force had been landing at Le Havre, Rouen and Boulogne in France and this task was completed by 17 August. The new Commander-in-Chief, Sir John French crossed to Le Havre from Southampton on 14 August and was in Amiens by 9 p.m. Although this movement was carried out under a veil of secrecy, the military had no control over the rumours sweeping the country. Vera Brittain in her diary for 11 August noted that British units were already on the continent.

Very little news has come through to-day, probably owing to the censorship of War news. . . . Even to-day it was rumoured that 100,000 British troops are now in Belgium.[15]

However, it was not until 18 August 1914 that *The Times*' headline 'ACROSS THE CHANNEL. BRITISH ARMY IN THE FIELD', announced officially to the Home Front that British forces were now in positions in France.

John Denton Pinkstone French, First Earl of Ypres
(1852–1925), Commander-in-Chief of the British
Expeditionary Force (August 1914–December 1915).
He was appointed Commander-in-Chief of Home
Forces in January 1916.

The following statement was issued last night by the Press Bureau:–

The Expeditionary Force, as detailed for Foreign service, has been safely landed
on French soil. The embarkation, transportation, and disembarkation of men and
stores were alike carried through with the greatest possible precision and
without a single casualty.

Mr F. E. Smith who made this announcement added:–
Lord Kitchener wishes me to add that he and the country are under the greatest
obligation to the Press for the loyalty with which all references to the
movements of the Expeditionary Forces in this country and on their landing
have been suppressed.

   Lord Kitchener is well aware that much anxiety must have been caused to the
English Press by the knowledge that these matters were freely described and
discussed in the Continental Press; and he wishes to assure the Press in this
country that nothing but his conviction of the military importance to this
country of suppressing these movements would have led him to issue
instructions which placed the Press of this country under a temporary
disadvantage.[16]

Following this statement from the Press Bureau most of the mass-circulation
newspapers printed an explanation of their part in this successful operation to move

the BEF to France. The various newspapers told how they had all known about the troop movement, with up to eighty trains a day running to Southampton and the preparations in France for the arrival of the British fighting force, but because of the need for national security they had had to withhold this information until a more appropriate time.

THE LIFTING OF THE VEIL.
The veil is at last withdrawn from one of the most extraordinary feats in modern history – the dispatch of a large force of armed men across the seas in absolute secrecy. What the nation at large knew it knew only from scraps of gossip that filtered through the foreign Press. From its own Press, from its own Government, it learned nothing; and patiently, gladly, it maintained of its own accord the conspiracy of silence.

So long ago as August 8 one of our special correspondents sent us a particular account of the preparations at Boulogne – the quays and harbour buildings cleared, the troop trains in waiting, the French reservists in their red breeches, mowing grass and clearing woods to make great camps between the Kentish-looking woods and fields on one side and the channel on the other.

Not a word of this news did we allow to reach our readers. A few days later and we could have accurately described these camps above the port, crammed with British troops, their enthusiastic reception, by the French people; who yet, characteristically had a little laugh ready for certain peculiarities of the British uniforms; the arrival of General Sir John French on board the scout Sentinel and his reception by the Governor of Boulogne.

Subsequent days brought further details, the story growing little by little into knowledge. News, accredited or otherwise, was constantly trickling through. Yet, save for one or two trifling exceptions in less reputable quarters, not a hint of it found its way into the English newspapers.[17]

The *Daily Mail*'s editorial page commented on the role that the newspapers played at this early stage of the war.

THE BRITISH IN FRANCE.
The British Expeditionary Force is in France. This news officially promulgated to-day, discloses the great secret.

The Press has co-operated in this secrecy. but that is, after all, only to say that the Press has understood its duty to the country and has met in every possible way the wishes of the War Office and Government. Newspapers have proved that they can be potent war auxiliaries by the mere fact of concealing secrets vital to the nation's existence from an enemy whose spies are everywhere and whose secret service funds are lavished with inexhaustible prodigality.[18]

As the *Daily Mail* points out, this early exercise in press restraint should have signified to Kitchener and the War Office that the newspapers of Britain were on their side. This episode shows that the press could be trusted by the Government and

The London Scottish going to the trenches.

military to report the conflict without damaging the national interest, or giving vital information which might be of use to the enemy; they were willing to impose self-censorship on their dispatches.

The official history on the other hand reasoned that any information on war printed in newspapers would surely be of great advantage to the enemy and that restricting the publication of information would be a small price to pay for victory.

> Complete secrecy and the denial of all information to the enemy are of such importance at the opening of hostilities, and it is so difficult to give any information to the newspapers without it reaching the enemy, that absence of news must be regarded as part of the price that the public pay for success in the field.[19]

While the debate raged over how the war should be reported, the correspondents already in Paris were becoming impatient. They had set off before Kitchener had imposed the ban on war correspondents entering the battle zone and were awaiting official recognition so that they could visit the fighting front.

> The officials were very polite and took great trouble to soothe the excited emotions of would-be war correspondents. 'In a few days, gentlemen, if all continues to go well.' They desired our photographs, in duplicate, a medical certificate of health, recommendations as to our mental and moral qualities, formal applications and informal interviews. But meanwhile the war was being fought and we were seeing nothing. . . .[20]

The result of Kitchener's policy was that during this time between August 1914 and May 1915 correspondents in the field of the war zone were treated as outlaws. They could be arrested at any time and by any officer, either French or British who discovered them in the war zone. Kitchener gave orders that any correspondent found out in the field would be immediately arrested, expelled and have his passport cancelled. Under these conditions it was difficult for the war correspondents to get reports and messages to their newspapers. Journalists employed ingenious means to get their stories back to London, such as trusting chance acquaintances on the way to England, bribing cross-Channel steamer employees and even handing their reports in personally and returning to France on the same day.[21]

Tired of waiting in Paris for official accreditation, many correspondents embarked on their own adventures through France and Flanders. One such correspondent trying to avoid arrest was Basil Clarke, reporting for the *Daily Mail*.

> I saw many things for myself in Flanders and France in those early days, and I count it among my achievements that I was never once arrested. The difficulties were numerous. Even to live in the war zone without papers and credentials was hard enough, but to move about and see things, and pick up news and then to get one's written dispatches conveyed home – against all regulations – was a labour greater and more complex than anything I have ever undertaken in journalistic work. I longed sometimes to be arrested and sent home and done with it all.
>
> I evaded the authorities in France and Flanders in 1914–1915 for five months – going to the Front on an average two to three times a week. I had apartments or hotel rooms in three districts, and when things became hot at one place I moved to another of my 'bases'.[22]

The war correspondents worked immensely hard to find war-related stories to send back to Britain. They were not spoon fed by the military or governments and therefore their reports had to be well researched which involved travelling vast distances and talking to the local population who had first-hand accounts of the engulfing war. As they became more reliant on the military between 1916 and 1918, their flare to examine and question what was put before them was less in evidence. This may, however, have had more to do with a war that had stagnated as morale dipped rather than the correspondents becoming military sponges merely there to spread propaganda.

In August 1914 the war correspondents embarked on adventures in a bid to keep the British public informed of what might be happening in France and Belgium. William Beach Thomas commented on this aspect of his life.

> Armed with these purple and voluminous papers I set out on the longest walking tour of my life, and the queerest. It was an autumn of gorgeous weather; and for a fortnight or so I was up at five or six every morning and seldom covered less than twenty miles a day, meeting odd adventures, but seeing nothing direct of the war except shells; and not many of these fell dangerously near. But what they call in the jargon of newspaper editors 'human stories' were unfolded daily.[23]

The negative situation, which Philip Gibbs believed the policies of the War Office and Lord Kitchener caused by not having official correspondents, led to the sense of growing despair and the loss of confidence which was conveyed to the Home Front through the newspapers.

> Owing to the rigid refusal of the War Office, under Lord Kitchener's orders, to give any official credentials to correspondents, the British press, as hungry for news as the British public whose little professional army had disappeared behind a deathlike silence, printed any scrap of description, any glimmer of truth, any wild statement, rumour, fairy tale, or deliberate lie, which reached them from France and Belgium; and it must be admitted that the liars had a great time.[24]

The cracks in this censorship system were already forming as the Allied troops advanced towards the enemy and Belgium. As Beach Thomas explains, because of the lack of any clear definition of the role of the war correspondent already based in France it caused great confusion. As British divisions moved up to Mons on 21 and 22 August and their first engagement with German troops, it became blatantly obvious that the public on the Home Front were totally ignorant about events in France. It was even clearer that the 'bland assurances'[25] from the Press Bureau were in complete contrast to the dispatches they had censored for *The Times*. The public outcry over the famous Amiens dispatch[26] would mean that Kitchener would have to rethink the handling of Western Front censorship.

> The War Office was still without a policy on war correspondents; but some bad habits had grown up without any clear definition. The censors would not publish any article if it indicated that the writer had seen what he wrote of. He must write what he thought was true, not what he knew to be true. New correspondents were not allowed to be sent to France, but no decision was reached to banish the men already in France. Life was made more uncomfortable, that was all; and the result was that a great number came, towards the end of 1914, to be herded together in Calais. It was the one place where life was endurable and regulations lax. Besides, couriers could be found to carry news across the channel, and this was the only method of transporting 'copy'.[27]

NOTES

1. P. Gibbs, *The Souls of War* (Heinemann, 1915), p. 5.
2. Gibbs, *Souls*, p. 6.
3. *The Times*, Monday, 12 March 1962 (London).
4. The *Daily Express*, Monday, 3 August 1914 (London).
5. The *Nation*, 12 September 1914 (London).
6. *The Times*, Wednesday, 5 August 1914 (London).
7. *The Times*, Wednesday, 12 August 1914 (London).
8. P. Knightley, *The First Casualty* (Quartet Books, 1982), p. 54.
9. W.B. Thomas, *A Traveller in News* (Chapman & Hall, 1925), p. 57.
10. The *Daily Express*, Thursday, 27 August 1914 (London).

11. *The Times*, Thursday, 13 August 1914 (London).
12. *The Times*, Thursday, 13 August 1914 (London).
13. Gibbs, *Souls*, pp. 41–2.
14. The *Daily Chronicle*, Friday, 7 August 1914 (London).
15. A. Bishop, *Chronicle of Youth, Vera Brittain's War Diary 1913–1917* (Victor Gollancz, 1981), p. 92.
16. *The Times*, Thursday, 18 August 1914 (London).
17. *The Times*, Thursday, 18 August 1914 (London).
18. The *Daily Mail,* Thursday, 18 August 1914 (London).
19. J.E. Edmonds, *History of the Great War; Military Operations, France and Belgium. December 1915–July 1st 1916* (Shearer, 1986), p. 146.
20. Gibbs, *Souls*, pp. 44–5.
21. Knightley, *First Casualty*, and Gibbs, *Adventures in Journalism.*
22. B. Clarke, *My Round of the War* (Heinemann, 1917), p. 13.
23. Thomas, *Traveller*, p. 59.
24. Gibbs, *Adventures*, p. 217.
25. T. Royle, *War Report* (Grafton Books, 1989), p. 118.
26. *The Sunday Times*, Sunday, 29 August 1914 (London), by Arthur Moore.
27. Thomas, *Traveller in News*, p. 80.

AUGUST TO DECEMBER 1914

As the British Expeditionary Force (BEF) disembarked on to French soil it assembled in an area between Maubeuge and Le Cateau, some 25 miles in length. At the north-eastern end of this formation, the cavalry were in line with the awaiting French Fifth Army. By 20 August the British concentration was complete and as part of the left wing of the Allied offensive the cavalry could be pushed forward into Belgium to engage the enemy. However, as four British divisions advanced on 22 August, reaching the town of Mons, they became exposed in a forward position from the rest of the Allied advance. On 23 August on the northern bank of the canal, just north-east of Mons, the British and German troops basically stumbled into each other. This was to be the first British contact with the enemy.

The area around Mons was not a good position for the British to blunder into the approaching enemy troops, especially with the current danger of being out-flanked. It was an area of waterways, slag-heaps and buildings that could not easily be defended.

> This small area is cut up by wire fences, market gardens, and the usual artificial features which form the outskirts of a provincial town; and it is noteworthy that across this tangle of enclosures no fewer than seven different roads diverge from Mons north-east and north-west to as many bridges. . . . West of Mons the line of the canal is straight, and the actual borders are clear; the ground on both sides of it is cut up by a network of artificial water-courses, chequered by osier-beds, for a breadth of a mile or more. But the opening up of the coal-measures has turned much of the country immediately south of this watery land into the hideous confusion of a mining district. . . . It is, in fact, a close and blind country, such as no army had yet been called upon to fight in against a civilised enemy in a great campaign.[1]

What the 1st and 2nd British divisions found when attacked by the First German Army around Mons was that they were outnumbered by two to one. It was still such a surprise to the local population in the Mons area that life carried on much as normal.

> The morning of Sunday the 23rd broke in mist and rain, which, about 10 A.M., cleared off and gave place to fair weather. Church bells rang, and the inhabitants of the villages near the canal were seen in their best attire going to worship as if the war was utterly distant from them. Trains were running towards Mons crowded with the usual holiday makers.[2]

For most of 23 August the British held their line around Mons with rapid rifle fire which the Germans mistook for machine-gun fire. However by late afternoon many battalions were having to retire to safer ground. With the threatening fall of Namur and the appearance of the German Third Army, French troops to the right of the British were already falling back. This left the British exposed and made their position hazardous with the added danger of being cut off from the French. The action of 23 August cost the British just over 1,600 casualties and had delayed the German advance by one day while inflicting very heavy losses on them.

That night Sir John French and his staff decided to make a general retreat of about 8 miles to conform with his allies. However, alarmed by the fall of Namur, Belgium's last defended fortress, and being outflanked by his allies, French's retreat continued faster and further back. The official history of the First World War describes the state of some of the British troops after the effect of just one day's retirement on the night of 24 August.

Long after nightfall the battalions of the 3rd Division were passing the cross roads in Bavai, the men stumbling along more like robots than living soldiers, unconscious of everything about them, but still moving under the magic impulse of discipline and regimental pride. Marching, they were hardly awake; halted, whether sitting or standing, they were instantly asleep. Yet these men on the eastern flank of the corps had done little fighting and endured little pressure during the day. Worse was it on the western flank, where cavalry and infantry had had hard fighting from dawn till dusk, and many a man had been for over twenty-four hours without sleep or food. And this, it must be borne in mind, was only the beginning of the retreat.[3]

By 25 August the British troops had withdrawn a further 15 miles to the neighbourhood of Le Cateau. During that day the Home Front began to learn from newspaper reports that something was seriously wrong. *The Times* reported:

The battle is joined and has so far gone ill for the Allies. Namur has fallen to the first assault. This, in the words of the official communication issued by the Press Bureau yesterday afternoon, 'necessitates a withdrawal of a portion of the Allied troops from the line of the Sambre to their original defensive position on the French frontier'. The Press Bureau announces this morning that the British troops, which were opposed by two German Army Corps and two cavalry divisions, successfully reached their new position after heavy fighting. The British casualties were not heavy, and the enemy suffered very seriously.'[4]

It must be remembered that the Home Front had no idea of the real nature of events surrounding fighting at Mons and the scale of the retreat. This was the first official communiqué summarizing the position of the BEF that had been released to the newspapers and public. However, the seriousness of the British situation was lost in the Press Bureau's attempt to disguise the reality.

PRESS BUREAU, MONDAY, 2.30 p.m.

The British forces were engaged all day on Sunday and after dark with the enemy in the neighbourhood of Mons, and held their ground.

News has been received that the first line of defence of Namur has been taken. This necessitates the withdrawal of a portion of the Allied troops from the line of the Sambre to their original defensive position on the French Frontier. No information has been received regarding casualties, which will be published as soon as known.

3.45 p.m.

It is announced that Namur has fallen.

TUESDAY, 2 a.m.

The British forces have successfully reached their new positions. Fighting has gone on more or less continuously, but the enemy has not effectively harassed our operation, and the movement has been executed with great skill by the commanders of the 1st and 2nd Army Corps. The casualties cannot be estimated exactly, but are not high. Our forces were opposed by two German Army Corps and two Cavalry Divisions. The enemy suffered very heavily. The position now occupied is well protected.[5]

Vera Brittain's diary for 25 August sheds some light on the impact that this news had on the Home Front. It must have come as a shock to those who had been following the events day by day in the press. First there was no news, then the news from the Front was very vague and now the Home Front were astounded by the turn of events for the BEF in France.

Very grave news from the front this morning, – so much so that all faces look grave, & there are vague rumours in the paper about sudden conclaves at the War Ministry & audiences given by Lord Kitchener in the early morning. The report of the fall of Namur is confirmed; it seems to have been taken without a struggle. . . . All the papers are very pessimistic & no one talks about scare-mongering now; the scare has become only too real, & the warning is lost in the actual.

Two British Army Corps – the 1st & the 2nd – have fought their first battle against the Germans at Mons & have held their ground. No actual casualty lists are yet issued, but the number of them this evening is estimated by Sir John French at 2,000.[6]

What was even more astounding to the Home Front was the dispatch which appeared in *The Sunday Times* on 30 August. Since 25 August the British Army had been in full retreat, managing on 26 August at Le Cateau under General Smith-Dorrien to hold the line an extra day allowing thousands of soldiers to fall back in relative safety. By 30 August and Arthur Moore's Amiens dispatch, the Anglo-French armies had been forced southwards across the River Aisne by German troops. Even the headlines 'BROKEN BRITISH REGIMENTS. BATTLING AGAINST ODDS.

MORE MEN NEEDED'[7] told more than the Press Bureau's statement published on 25 August. One can imagine the debate this caused around many dinning tables in Britain.

> During supper Daddy & Edward read us a very dismal article in the Sunday Times speaking of the tremendous losses in the British Army & the apparent invincibleness of the Germans all round. The situation seems very grave indeed.[8]

What the dispatch highlighted was the inadequate coverage of hard news from the British Front in France for the general public on the Home Front. There appeared to be a complete contrast between the Press Bureau's and the daily newspapers' versions of events, which of course did not show the Government and military leaders in a favourable light. The article, which talks of a 'terrible defeat', caused a storm in Parliament and set alarm bells ringing among the general public who had been awaiting news of great British victories.

> Amiens, August 29.
> I read this afternoon in Amiens this morning's Paris papers. To me, knowing some portion of the truth, it seemed incredible that a great people should be so kept in ignorance of the situation which it has to face. The papers read like children's prattle, gleanings from the war talk of their parents a week ago.
>   Not a word of the fall of Namur (the English papers containing the news are not allowed in Paris, and the Paris Daily Mail was forced to publish a denial of the English Press Bureau's statement which it had published), and considerable talk about new success on the Meuse.
>   This is not well. I would plead with the English censor to let my message pass. I guarantee him as regards the situation of the troops I have nothing to say that is not known and noted already by the German General Staff. There is no reason, either in strategy or tactics, why every word I write should not be published. And to get my information I have broken no promise and no obligation. I have moved far and fast in Northern France between Wednesday morning and the hour of writing. The car has been challenged and stopped perhaps above a hundred times. But the papers that we carried have passed everywhere. On the other hand, it is important that the nation should know and realise certain things. Bitter truths, but we can face them. We have to cut our losses, to take stock of the situation, to set our teeth.
>   First let it be said that our honour is bright. Amongst all the straggling units that I have seen, flotsam and jetsam of the fiercest fight in history, I saw fear in no man's face. It was a retreating and broken army, but it was not an army of hunted men. Nor in all the plain tales of officers, non-commissioned officers, and men did a single story of the white feather reach me. No one could answer for every man, but every British regiment and every battery of which any one had knowledge had done its duty. And never has duty been more terrible.
>   Since Monday morning last the German advance has been one of almost incredible rapidity. As I have already written you, the British Force fought a

terrible fight – which may be called the action of Mons, though it covered a big front – on Sunday.

The German attack was withstood to the utmost limits, and a whole division was flung into the fight at the end of a long march and had not even time to dig trenches. The French supports expected on the immediate right do not seem to have been in touch, though whether or not they were many hours late I cannot say. Further to the right, along the Sambre and in the angle of the Sambre and the Meuse, the French, after days of long and gallant fighting, broke. Namur fell, and General Joffre was forced to order a retreat along the whole line. The Germans, fulfilling one of the best of all precepts in war, never gave the retreating army one single moment's rest.

The pursuit was immediate, relentless, unresting. Aeroplanes, Zeppelins, armoured motors, and cavalry were loosed like an arrow from the bow, and served at once to harass the retiring army columns and to keep the German staff fully informed of the movement of the Allied Forces.

The British force fell back through Bavai on a front between Valenciennes and Maubeuge, then through Le Quesney, where desperate fighting took place, southwards continually. Regiments were grievously injured, and the broken army fought its way desperately with many stands, forced backwards and ever backwards by the sheer unconquerable mass of numbers of an enemy prepared to throw away three or four men for the life of every British soldier. Where it is at present it might not be well to say even if I knew, but I do not know, though I have seen to-day in different neighbourhoods units of it. But there are some things which it is eminently right that I should say. To-night I write at present to the sound of the guns. All the afternoon the guns were going on the Eastern roads. A German aeroplane flew over us, this morning, and was brought crashing down.

An R.E. chauffeur told me that the axle of his car was broken and he had to abandon it. He had no more than left it when it also was blown up. In scattered units with the enemy ever on its heels the Fourth Division, all that was left of 20,000 fine troops, streamed southward.

Our losses are very great. I have seen the broken bits of many regiments. Let me repeat that there is no failure in discipline, no panic, no throwing up of the sponge. Every one's temper is sweet, and nerves do not show. A group of men, it may be a dozen, or less or more, arrives, under the command of whoever is entitled to command it. The men are battered with marching, and ought to be weak with hunger, or, of course, no commissariat could cope with such a case, but they are steady and cheerful, and wherever they arrive make straight for the proper authority, report themselves, and seek news of their regiment.

I saw two men give such reports, after saluting smartly. 'Very badly cut up, Sir,' was the phrase one used of his regiment. The other said, 'Very heavy loss, I'm afraid, sir,' when asked if much was left. Apparently every division was in action. Some have lost nearly all their officers. The regiments were broken to bits, and good discipline and fine spirit kept the fragments together, though they no longer knew what had become of the other parts with which they had once formed a splendid whole.

Certain things about the fighting seem clear. One is the colossal character of the German losses. I confess that when I read daily in official bulletins in Paris of how much greater the German losses were than those of the Allies I was not much impressed. Much contemplation of Eastern warfare, where each side claims to have annihilated the other, has made me over-sceptical in such matters. But three days among the combatants has convinced me of the truth of the story in this case.

The German commanders in the north advance their men as if they had an inexhaustible supply. Of the bravery of the men it is not necessary to speak. They advance in deep sections, so slightly extended as to be almost in close order, with little regard for cover, rushing forward as soon as their own artillery has opened fire behind them on our position. Our artillery mows long lanes down the centres of the sections, so that frequently there is nothing left of it but its outsides. But no sooner is this done than more men double up, rushing over the heaps of dead, and remake the section.

Last week, so great was their superiority in numbers that they could no more be stopped than the waves of the sea. Their shrapnel is markedly bad, though their gunners are excellent at finding the range. On the other hand their machine guns are of the most deadly efficiency, and are very numerous.

Their rifle shooting is described as not first-class, but their numbers bring on the infantry till frequently they and the Allied troops meet finally in bayonet tussles. Superiority of numbers in men, and guns, especially in machine guns, cavalry, and extreme mobility are the elements of their present success.

To sum up, the first great German effort has succeeded. We have to face the fact that the British Expeditionary Force, which bore the great weight of the blow, has suffered terrible losses and required immediate and immense reinforcement. The British Expeditionary Force has won indeed imperishable glory, but it needs men, men, and yet more men.[9]

When the dispatch reached the office of *The Times* in London on 29 August they immediately set about toning down the article, deleting certain paragraphs, before sending it to F.E. Smith at the Press Bureau for censorship. However, the article returned from the Press Bureau with Smith's approval, and him having reinstated the deleted paragraphs and rewritten Moore's conclusion to emphasize the need for fresh reinforcements.

The War Office's reputation had now been dealt a great blow and the outcry prompted the Press Bureau to release an official statement on that Sunday. This sought to set the record straight as to what had happened during the retreat from Mons and also to stress the problems of believing reports from unqualified correspondents in France.

From the Press Bureau, Sunday, 3.40 p.m.
On Monday, 24th, the Germans made vigorous efforts in superior numbers to prevent the safe withdrawal of the British Army and to drive it into the fortress of Maubeuge. This effort was frustrated by the steadiness and skill with which the British retirement was conducted, and, as on the previous day, very heavy

losses, far in excess of anything suffered by us, were inflicted upon the enemy, who, in dense formation and in enormous masses, marched forward again and yet again to storm the British lines.

The British retirement proceeded on the 25th with continuous fighting though not on the scale of the previous two days, and by the night of the 25th the British Army occupied the line Cambrai–Landrecies–Le Cateau. . . .

Sir John French estimates that during the whole of these operations, from the 23rd to the 26th inclusive, his losses amount to 5,000 or 6,000 men. On the other hand the losses suffered by the Germans in their attack across the open, and through their dense formations, are out of all proportion to those which we have suffered.

A later statement says:– (Sunday, 5.30 p.m.)

The Press Bureau has issued an official statement this evening describing the fortunes of the Expeditionary Force during the past few days. This statement, the terms of which have been carefully considered, accurately and fully describe the present situation.

The Bureau has not thought it necessary to forbid the publication of messages sent by correspondents of newspapers dealing with the recent operations, provided that such messages neither give away military information nor disclose the organization or position of troops. These messages, however, should be received with extreme caution. No correspondents are at the Front, and their information, however honestly sent, is therefore derived at second or third hand from persons who are often in no condition to tell coherent stories and who are certain to be without the perspective which is necessary to construct or understand the general situation.

It is hoped that the statement issued to-night will dissipate any apprehensions caused by such reports and restore the necessary perspective to the recent operations.[10]

What the Press Bureau had done was to close the stable door after the horse had bolted. By wanting to withhold and censor the bad news from the Front, yet at the same time stress the need for reinforcements and boost recruitment, the War Office had two opposing aims that it wished to feed to the general public. Instead of the desired effect, the War Office had highlighted to the world the lack of knowledge that the British public and Government had of the early fighting in the war. The Press Bureau had created and brought to the forefront the problems of the uncredited war correspondents who were travelling around France reporting events which the bureau itself had hoped to hide behind a façade of official communiqués. It had been caught withholding unfavourable news from the British public and yet still expected them to fully support the war effort.

To restore the Home Front's faith in official news at a time of public uproar, the Government had to be seen to act. It was not a simple act of blaming the newspapers for publishing untrue and alarmist stories because they had had the blessing of the Press Bureau. On 1 September 1914 the *Daily Mail* reported from the debate on the role of the war correspondent and Press Bureau which arose in the House of Commons.

Despatches respecting the war which appeared in a special issue of The Times on Sunday were the subject of questions in the House of Commons yesterday.

MR. Llewellyn Williams asked whether the Prime Minister was aware The Times yesterday published despatches from two correspondents to the effect that the Army had met with defeat and disaster, that the British regiments had been broken to bits, and the Secretary for War during the day issued a reassuring bulletin contradicting these sensational messages, and that the Press Bureau warned the public against such statements 'because there are no correspondents at the front and information is derived at second and third hand from persons who are often in no condition to tell coherent stories and without the perspective necessary to construct or to understand the general situation,' and whether, having regard to untold pain and anxiety caused by the dissemination of such misleading statements, the Government would not return to the time-honoured practice of this country of allowing Press correspondents to accompany our Army to the front. (Cries of 'No, No.')

MR. Asquith: It is impossible too highly to commend the patriotic reticence of the Press as a whole – (cheers) – from the beginning of the war up to the present moment. The publication to which my hon. friend refers appears to be a very regrettable exception – (cheers) – and I hope it will not recur. I doubt whether my hon. friend's suggestion is the best way under the altered conditions of modern warfare of dealing with the matter. The Government feel after the experience of the last two weeks that the public is entitled to information – prompt and authentic information – of what is happening at the front, and which they hope will be more adequate.[11]

The results of this public clamour for more news exposed by the Amiens dispatch led the War Office, under Kitchener, to provide 'prompt and authentic information' at the Government's request. Kitchener became busy renovating the form of news and information which came from the battle front. Colonel Ernest Swinton, a railway official for the military, was approached by Kitchener on 7 September and appointed to General Headquarters (GHQ) in France. This was with a view to writing articles on the operations and progress of battle of the Army on the Western Front. These reports were first censored in France, before being personally vetted by Kitchener and released to the press under the headline of 'Eyewitness'.[12]

It was a clever way of keeping the war correspondents away from the battle zone and still being in control of the news which was fed to the public and newspapers. It was Swinton himself who saw the appointment of a man who was already part of the military as a concession and a way of stemming the military's critics on the Home Front.

Discontent now became so great at the unnecessary state of ignorance in which the nation was being kept that it was decided to compromise with a half-measure. War correspondents were not to be allowed at the front, but their place was to be taken by some appointed officer.[13]

A few weeks later F.E. Smith resigned from the Press Bureau after it was found that the Mons article had been published at his own request. He was replaced by Sir Stanley Buckmaster on 30 September.

Swinton's inadequate accounts, often very misleading and containing scant truth of the real events on the Western Front did nothing to satisfy the hunger for news from the press and public at large. They were written by a military man and full of military terminology which was of little meaning to anybody outside military circles. There was still no mention of place names or soldiers' battalions, brigades and divisions and they were merely an extension of the official communiqués, again devoid of human interest.

> The system of work was as follows: during the day one of us went out to visit divisional or brigade headquarters on some sector of the front; while the one remaining behind framed a narrative from the Intelligence Summaries which had been received by the previous midnight, from the liaison officers' reports up to that time, and from those of the corps and divisions of the day before. Except on special occasions, the liaison officers usually called between six and seven in the evening, when they had made their official report to the sub-chief of staff. Any time after that, the Intelligence Summaries began to come in. By eight o'clock most of the information due on any day had arrived and the extraction of items and compilation of a news-letter went on up till midnight.[14]

This was the start of a period of conspiracy, of deliberate lies and the suppression of the truth; the foundations of a propaganda process with which we are still familiar today. Swinton freely admits in his book, that some of his articles were used especially for propaganda purposes against the enemy and to keep the Home Front fully supportive of military operations in France.

> The principle which guided me in my work was above all to avoid helping the enemy. This appeared to me even more important than the purveyance of news to our own people. . . . For home consumption – that is for those who were carrying the burden and footing the bill – I essayed to tell as much of the truth as was compatible with safety, to guard against depression and pessimism, and to check unjustified optimism which might lead to a relaxation of effort.[15]

They might of course mislead the Home Front who were the ones fully supporting the war effort, but he was only trying to help the men at the Front.

> On the Aisne we at all times suffered from great preponderance of the Germans in artillery, especially in heavy field howitzers. As, however, we had not got the material means with which to counter this disadvantage, we could only try to mislead the enemy as to the damage he was doing us. In one despatch at this time, in the hope of inducing the Germans to economise, I took some trouble to give an exaggerated account of the manner in which they were wasting expensive ammunition. My articles were still read by Lord Kitchener himself, and I added a private message to him that in this case I had written the exact reverse of the truth. I thought I was justified in misleading our people at home if by so doing I could help the men in the front line.[16]

Under the title of 'Despatch from an Officer at the Front' Swinton produced his first report on 11 September 1914. This basically was a narrative which carried on where the previous official communiqué from the Press Bureau had left off. From here Swinton turned out a semi-weekly yield of narratives until 18 July 1915, when his role became redundant with the introduction of accredited war correspondents to the British Front.

So what became of the journalists searching for the truth and the real face of battle? In the early months of the war the generals at GHQ continued to concoct their eyewitness reports, while the journalists travelled around Belgium and France, dodging the military authorities for fear of arrest and imprisonment, searching for news. Often it seemed to be a matter of luck that the war correspondents in Northern France bumped into people involved in or who had witnessed a major offensive. The Home Front understood that there were major battles going on, but learned little else – it was a case of reading between the lines to find out what had not been said and watching the casualty lists published in national and local newspapers.

From this point until May 1915 the war correspondents operated independently under the regulations imposed by the War Office. It was rare that they actually witnessed the course of battles first hand and therefore they tended to write about the effects of the battle on the wounded and local populations. It was a rather hit and miss approach in which the war correspondents wandered back and forth between the west-coast ports and the British and French armies.

> I had been in the midst of populations in flight, armies in retreat, and tremendous movements of troops hurled forward to new points of strategical importance. Now and again I had come in touch with the British army and had seen something of the men who had fought their way down from Mons to Meaux, but for the most part my experience had been with the French, and it was the spirit of France which I had done my best to interpret to the English people.[17]

By concentrating on the output of the war correspondents we may gain an idea of what news the Home Front actually received. It seems that a widening gap between the reality on the Western Front and the image which was fed to the Home Front emerged.

By 3 September the Anglo-French forces had retreated to the Marne. The British were now across the Marne and blowing up the bridges to try and stop the German advance. They had retreated nearly 150 miles in thirteen days and the Germans at this point were only 25 miles from Paris.

Arthur Moore was not the only war correspondent to come into contact with the British Army retreating from Mons. On 26 August, while in Rouen, Hamilton Fyfe of the *Daily Mail* had witnessed some of the wounded from Mons and first heard of the on-going retreat. By 28 August he had moved up to Dieppe and set about trying to piece together some sort of coherent story from the British and French soldiers who were involved.

> From Our Special Correspondent, Hamilton Fyfe.
> Rouen, Wednesday
> They had all come from the fighting in the neighbourhood of Mons. Here one of General French's army corps was actively engaged; and when this retired, after

holding the enemy back (which was the task assigned to and stubbornly carried out by the British forces on Sunday and Monday last), another army corps moved up into position.

The men composing the divisions which bore the brunt of the attack had to take the field immediately they arrived. In point of fact they only arrived just in time to stem the German onrush. For days they had been travelling and marching. They needed repose. In spite of this they behaved like fresh troops and held their ground magnificently, winning warm praise from General Joffre.

This man belonged to a regiment which was ordered out of Mons on Sunday morning and came under fire at once. They had to drop down and lie where they were all day. When it got dark they did their best to make trenches. 'But I can tell you,' he said, 'while we were out there, with shells coming as regular as a postal delivery, there weren't any heads popping up!'[18]

The first signs of a major engagement observed by Philip Gibbs of the *Daily Chronicle* on his travels round Northern France were at a railway station. Here he first learnt about the difficulties experienced by the British soldiers at Mons.

At a French junction there was a shout of command in English, and I saw a body of men in khaki, with Red Cross armlets, run across a platform to an incoming train from the north, with stretchers and drinking bottles. A party of English soldiers had arrived from a battle at a place called Mons.

With French passengers from another train, I was kept back by soldiers with fixed bayonets, but through the hedge of steel I saw a number of 'Tommies' with bandaged heads and limbs descending from the troop train. Some of them hung limp between their nurses, their faces, so fresh when I had first seen them on the way out, had become grey and muddy, and were streaked with blood. Their khaki uniforms were torn and cut. One poor boy moaned pitiably as they carried him away on a stretcher. They were the first fruits of this unnatural harvesting, lopped and maimed by a cruel reaper. I stared at them with a kind of sickness, more agonized than afterwards when I saw more frightful things. It came as a queer, silly shock to me then to realize that in this secret war for which I was searching men were really being smashed and killed, and that out of the mystery of it, out of the distant terror from which great multitudes were fleeing out of the black shadow creeping across the sunlit hills of France, where the enemy, whom no fugitives had seen, was advancing like a moving tide, there should come these English boys, crippled and broken, from an unknown battle.

I was able to speak to one of them, wounded only in the hand, but there was no time for more than a question or two and an answer which hardly gave me definite knowledge.

'We got it in the neck!' said the sergeant of the R.F.A.

He repeated the words as if they held all truth.

'We got it in the neck!'

'Where?' I asked.

He waved his wounded hand northwards, and said: 'Mons.'

'Do you mean we were beaten? In retreat?'

He shrugged his shoulders.

'We gave 'em what for. Oh, yes, they had to pay right enough. But they were too much for us. Came on like lice . . . swarming . . . Couldn't kill enough . . . Then we got it in the neck . . . Lost a good few men . . . Gord, I've never seen such work! South Africa? No more than child's play to this 'ere game!'

He gave a queer kind of grin, with no mirth in his eyes, and went away with the other wounded men.

Mons? It was the first I had heard of a battle there. And our men were having a hard time. The enemy were too much for us. Was it a retreat? Perhaps a rout?[19]

Later, on 29 August, Gibbs met more British troops near Rouen and from them he was able to gain a description of part of the retreat from Mons. The *Chronicle* reported:

After a series of fantastic little adventures which seemed at the time like a nightmare, with feverish awakenings among crowds of fugitives, in the cattle trucks of troop trains, and on the banks of railway lines, where children who had been carried from their abandoned homes in a great tide of panic picked wild flowers as though the world were at peace, I found myself led by chance into the middle of this real business of war, which until then had been hidden behind the veil of an impenetrable mystery. . . .

I have been into this war zone and have seen during this last five days the men who are holding the lines of defence. I have been among their dead and wounded, and have talked with soldiers marching fresh to the front. I have seen the horrid mess which is cleared up after battle and the grim picture of retreat. But nothing that I have seen or heard from either the British or the French leads me to believe that our allies have been demoralised.

It is impossible to estimate our own losses. Our wounded are being brought back into Havre and Rouen, and undoubtedly there are large numbers of them. But putting them at their highest it is clear to me from all the information I have gained during the last five days, that there has been no overwhelming disaster, and that in the terrible actions fought on the four days from the 23rd to the 27th of August and afterwards in the further retirement from the line of Cambrai and Le Cateau, swinging southwards and eastwards upon St. Quentin, our main forces which were pressed by enormous numbers of the enemy, succeeded in withdrawing in good order without having their lines broken, while inflicting terrific punishment upon the German right.

. . . And it is astounding to see the cheerfulness of our wounded British soldiers at Rouen, where the Red Cross nurses tell admiring stories of their pluck and patience. Yet out of the firing line as well as in the trenches they have had a dreadful time. It is almost true to say that they only rest when they get into the ambulance cart and the field hospital. One of them told me that incessant marching, marching forwards and backwards to new positions, is more awful to bear than the actual fighting under the hideous fire of the

The Wiltshires cheering during the Great Advance.

German guns. They are kept on the move the whole time, except for the briefest halts, when officers and men drop like brown leaves from autumn trees on each side of the road, so utterly exhausted that they are almost senseless, and have to be dragged up out of their short sleep, when once again they tramp on to the trenches to fire a few rounds before the bugle sounds for cease fire and another strategical retirement.

The fighting on the Cambrai–Cateau line seems, from all I have heard, to have been more desperate even than the terrible actions at Mons and Charleroi. It was when the British troops had to swing round to a more southerly line to guard the road to Paris. The enemy attacked in prodigious numbers, and their immense superiority in machine guns did very terrible work among our officers and men. But on all sides from the French officers there is immense praise for the magnificent conduct of our troops, and in spite of all alarmist statements I am convinced from what I have heard that they have retired intact, keeping their line together, without having their divisions broken and cut off. The list of casualties must be very great, but if I can believe the evidence of my own eyes in such towns as Rouen, where the Red Cross hospitals are concentrated, they are not heavy enough to suggest anything like a great and irretrievable disaster.[20]

It was not until 7 September 1914 that Sir John French actually laid to rest questions surrounding the events of Mons with his own personal detailed report. Maybe it was a vain act to finally silence his military critics and partly one to shift the blame on to the French.

The French were still retiring, and I had no support except such as was afforded by the fortress of Maubeuge; and the determined attempts of the enemy to get round my left flank assured me that it was his intention to hem me against that place and surround me. I felt that not a moment must be lost in retiring to another position.

I had every reason to believe that the enemy's forces were somewhat exhausted, and I knew that they had suffered heavy losses. I hoped therefore that his pursuit would not be too vigorous to prevent me effecting my objective.

I deeply deplore the very serious losses which the British forces have suffered in this great battle; but they were inevitable in view of the fact that the British Army – only two days after a concentration by rail – was called upon to withstand a vigorous attack of five German Army Corps.[21]

However, by the time Sir John French's report was published by the Press Bureau on 10 September, the war had moved on and the BEF now found itself fighting on the Marne. The Germans had crossed the Marne on 5 September, which happened to be the same day that French was persuaded by Joffre to stop the British retreat. Now the tide had begun to turn as the BEF advanced in a joint Anglo-French offensive to push the Germans back from the Marne and the outskirts of Paris.

The Marne, a battle which lasted just five days, became important because it marked a point where any hope of a swift German victory in the West was brought to an end. Now the Home Front could forget the failures of Mons and move on to the new British military successes on the Marne, which were to boost morale and restore some of the confidence lost by the generals in charge. On 5 September the BEF were closest to Paris between the rivers Marne and Seine, when orders from Joffre reached Sir John French for a joint military offensive.

However, these arrived too late for French to act on 5 September as the British troops were still marching southwards. With fresh reinforcements now arriving for the BEF, they started their advance a day later than their French allies. While the French troops on either side of the British had experienced fierce fighting, when the BEF advanced they found no enemy in front of them. Their advance continued on 7 and 8 September.

Behind the cavalry screen, the infantry continued its march without serious incident; the arrival of the 'first reinforcements' had tended to raise the spirits of the men, and there was cheering evidence of the enemy's demoralisation. The country near the roads was littered with empty bottles; and the inhabitants reported much drunkenness among the Germans.[22]

This kind of open warfare as seen on the Marne was referred to by the war correspondents in romantic terms for the next four years. Such warfare was not static, the cavalry were out in patrols in front of the infantry searching for signs of the enemy. This was one of the last times this would happen before the spring offensives of 1918.

Liddell Hart believes that the British were successful on the Marne because of two factors which greatly affected the Germans; this had little to do with the actual fighting which in fact was secondary. More important was the decision of General Moltke to abandon the Schlieffen plan which then exposed his right flank to a counter-envelopment and the speed with which his German troops had advanced so far. Because they had advanced so rapidly their supplies failed to keep pace with them, causing fatigue and hunger.[23] By the time, therefore, they reached the Marne the German troops were already shattered. It would appear that the Germans had out-stretched themselves as their communication lines now crossed through Belgium and Northern France and became vulnerable to rear attack. By 9 September the supreme German command had ordered a withdrawal as they felt unable to protect their rear communication lines.

This withdrawal of the German First and Second Armies did not become apparent to the Anglo-French forces until 5.30 p.m. on 9 September, at which time

> . . . it was too late to order a general and combined advance; in fact, both men and horses of both French and British were, after the continuous operations since the 20th August, too worn out for further effort without some rest and re-freshment.[24]

From 9 September the Germans were pushed back over the Marne and by 13 September had retreated over 60 miles to a point across the banks of the River Aisne. Here they stopped exhausted and unable to march further, set up their machine-guns and dug in. They were joined by fresh troops released from the fall of Maubeuge who reinforced them in their trenches, which had now become an important feature of the battlefield.

The Allies, who had been advancing for five days, reached the Aisne, hesitated and stopped in front of the German trenches. Their slowness to advance and follow up the German retreat with a crushing victory ushered in the period of trench warfare we tend today to associate with the First World War.

While the Battle of the Marne was in full swing the outlawed war correspondents were desperately trying to avoid arrest and get their dispatches back to Fleet Street. The Paris correspondent of the *Telegraph* wrote about the difficulties of being a journalist in early September 1914.

> I succeeded in smuggling myself onto one of the stations where trains of wounded were arriving. It is difficult now for a journalist to get anywhere. They are being watched and spied upon with energetic zeal by everyone. It is a wonder that we are even allowed to leave our homes or hotels, and to have our drinks at the cafe like any other inhabitants not under such grave disabilities.
>
> In vain we ask for a permit to go to places fifty or a hundred miles from Paris. We are told at once 'Pas de journalists.' A journalist, therefore, is everywhere tabooed, an outlaw and an outcast in the eyes of the strict public official. We have, therefore, to make the best of it, and it is only through some exceeding act of condescension or toleration that we may venture into a railway station.[25]

If it was almost impossible for a journalist to leave Paris, what hope was there that one might reach the battlefields of the Marne? At this time the inhabitants of Paris were experiencing fear and panic at the closeness of the advancing German Army and the war correspondents witnessed a large public exodus to the countryside. One way to escape from Paris undetected was to blend in with the streams of refugees on the move.

The war correspondents faced a further problem during this period of open warfare. As the enemy was advancing and the correspondents moving round the country, sometimes the two met. If caught, war correspondents were likely to be shot as spies because of their civilian clothes. Arthur Moore, after his Amiens dispatch, was captured by a German cavalry patrol on 2 September 1914; luckily, however, he was subsequently released. Philip Gibbs, on a train at Pontoise faced directly with the rifle barrels and artillery of the enemy positioned on the railway embankment, thought his days as a journalist were over.

> I was sorry my message to the English people might never be read by them. Perhaps after all they would get on very well without it, and my paper would appoint another correspondent to succeed a man swallowed up somewhere inside the German lines. It would be a queer adventure. I conjured up an imaginary conversation in bad German with an officer in a pointed casque. Undoubtedly he would have the best of the argument. There would be a little white wall, perhaps. . . .
>
> After all my message went to Fleet Street and filled a number of columns, read over the coffee cups by a number of English families, who said perhaps: 'I wonder if he really knows anything, or if it is all made up.' Those newspaper men did not get much rest in their quest for truth, not caring much, if the truth may be told, for what the English public chose to think or not to think, but eager to see more of the great drama and to plunge again into its amazing vortex.[26]

As the British crossed the Marne on 6 September the *Daily Telegraph* published the dispatch of war correspondent William Maxwell. He had not been as fortunate as Mr Gibbs and was arrested by a British cavalry officer making his way to Mons.

> Now that the position of the British Army is known to the enemy, there can be no harm in telling the story of how I happened to meet it. I was on my way to Charleroi, where the French were already engaged, when I had the mischance to run into the headquarters of one of our cavalry brigades a few miles to the east of Mons. A youthful Staff Officer, seated by the roadside writing in a notebook, hailed me and immediately recognised me.
>
> 'Awfully sorry, but our orders are strict. I've been a war correspondent myself – in the Balkan war – and sympathise with you.'
>
> In vain I protested that I had already been challenged twice, and that my Laissez passer, signed by the Belgian Minister of War himself, had never been disputed.
>
> 'I shall have to detain you until further orders,' said the Staff Officer.
>
> The hours went by slowly but pleasantly enough, for I was among friends who told me some interesting things about the position and the strength of the enemy, with whom the cavalry scouts were in touch. About an hour before

sunset the Staff Officer, having again consulted the orders with regard to correspondents, decided to send me to divisional headquarters, which were at Givry, some miles to the south-east.

While I waited in the office there a very busy, and harassed young Officer, seeing a stranger, asked who I was, and was told I was a correspondent.

'See that he does not leave the room, and place a sentry over his car,' ordered the Officer.

Half an hour later, while I was having dinner with the General and his staff, the Officer entered the mess, and coming up to me held out his hand.

'It was stupid of me not to ask your name.' he exclaimed. 'We are sending an Officer off with despatches, and, as petrol is scarce, we can save it by using your motor-car.'

I was allowed to return to Mons on the understanding that within a stated time I should withdraw from the area of active operations, and await, at Tournai, the chance that the rules for correspondents in the field would be relaxed.[27]

Some correspondents managed to avoid all these obstacles and actually made it into the battle zone and experienced real warfare for the first time.

Paris, Sept. 7.
I came upon the battle of Meaux with an astonishing suddenness. The car had just shot up the rise that overhangs the little town with the disconcerting rapidity with which the Rolls-Royce takes a hill. And there it was before our eyes in the valley, dense white balloons of smoke from exploding shells, fleecy little convoys of shrapnel bursting in the air, showers of black earth ripped out of the solid ground and sent flying, farmhouses and haystacks flaming; a German aeroplane cruising overhead – a real battle at last.[28]

Called 'the battle of Meaux' by the correspondent, this would have been part of the Battle of the Marne and the dispatch was published on the same day as the British public learnt of a German retreat. *The Times*' headlines for 10 September announced to the world 'BRITISH ACROSS THE MARNE' and 'ENEMY PUSHED BACK 25 MILES'. This information had been received from the French War Office and *The Times* commented

A communiqué issued by the French War Office last night states that the British force has crossed the Marne and that the enemy has retreated 25 miles.

The French official communiqué published in Paris yesterday afternoon was brief but favourable.[29]

It was not, however, until 11 September that *The Times* correspondent managed to reach the rear of the Allied forces between the rivers of the Marne and Aisne. Now he could start to piece together the events, like a jigsaw puzzle. Although he did not directly witness the advance of the Allies, he was able to create a picture of it from talking to the soldiers and refugees who were involved. From 5 miles south of Provins by Montereau the war correspondent reported

Highlanders pipe their way back from the trenches.

I have succeeded, after difficulties so numerous that I have almost lost count of them, in achieving a point about five miles south of Provins, which, as I suppose all the world now knows, was all but gained by the Germans advance at the end of last week. In reaching this point I have travelled practically along the whole line of the Allied Armies – though, of course, to the rear. I have lived, as it were, in the anteroom of battles – for this terrific conflict is no single encounter. I have seen such sights as have afforded me at least a partial knowledge of the tremendous events passing so near to me, I have seen sights too, which for the moment it is impossible to recount. I have talked with all the gallant British lads returning wounded from one or other of the innumerable points of this firing line of hundreds of miles, with Frenchmen, no less brave and bold-hearted, with refugees, whose homes are even now desolate amongst these fields of the dead, lastly with German prisoners – of whom I have encountered, not hundreds but thousands.[30]

Philip Gibbs also reached the battlefields of the Marne, and heard terrible stories of German treatment of local people. It is easy to see how atrocity stories probably began with refugees' tales and were blown out of all proportion by the time they reached the English newspapers.

Again little of the events was actually witnessed, although Gibbs certainly saw the destruction the moving battle had caused.

I remember that I saw the movement of regiments moving up to support the lines of the Allies, and the carrying up of heavy guns for the great battle which had now reached its sixth day, and the passing of Red Cross trains bringing back the wounded from that terrible front between Vic and Noyon, where the trenches were being filled and refilled with dead and wounded, and regiments of tired men struggled forward with heroic endurance to take their place under the fire of those shells which had already put their souls to the test of courage beyond anything that might be demanded, in reason, from the strongest heart.[31]

In mid-September on the Aisne, amid the exhausted German and Allied forces, a deadlock occurred. This was the beginning of siege warfare and the birth of the defensive trench system. For the BEF this posed one major problem, as the official history explained – they had had no training in this type of warfare.

In every respect the Expeditionary Force of 1914 was incomparably the best trained, best organized, and the best equipped British Army which ever went forth to war. Except in the matter of co-operation between aeroplanes and artillery, and the use of machine guns, its training would stand comparison in all respects with that of the Germans. Where it fell short of our enemies was first and foremost in numbers; so that, though not 'contemptible,' it was almost negligible in comparison with continental armies, even of the smaller States. In heavy guns and howitzers, high-explosive shells, trench mortars, hand-grenades, and much of the subsidiary material required for siege and trench warfare, it was almost wholly deficient. Further, no steps had been taken to instruct the army in a knowledge of the probable theatre of war or of the German army, except by the publication of a handbook of the army and annual reports on manoeuvres and military changes.[32]

British artillery being moved into position, 1914.

Before trench warfare completely took hold in France and Belgium both parties raced to 'outflank' each other. This was a race to get ahead of the other by moving around the opponent's open flank; the Allies moving leftwards and the Germans advancing to the right, both hoping to move into open countryside against the rear of the enemy. What stopped these operations was the sea, and from here both sides had no choice but to dig in and adopt a new battle strategy – attrition.

For the war correspondents this change in warfare made their job a bit easier, especially when in late September the BEF moved northwards from the Aisne to Flanders in order to shorten its communication and supply lines with England. Open warfare had meant that the war correspondents had to scour Northern France to locate the main centre of the fighting. With fighting 'contained' in long trench systems it became simpler to watch and understand how battles were progressing. Also, with the BEF now stationed closer to the Channel ports, it was easier to get dispatches back to England. Many war correspondents set up bases in the Channel ports from where they would venture out towards the war zone, such as Philip Gibbs in Dunkirk and William Beach Thomas in Calais.

However, as the First Battle of Ypres shows, with war at a standstill it meant that the British military authorities had better control over who was allowed into the Western Front zone. The war correspondent had less chance of getting near to the Front and witnessing the fighting first hand. The nature of warfare might have changed, but the reporting restrictions had not and the war correspondents were still liable to arrest and deportation.

In London the correspondents listed on the official War Office registry were still waiting, with their horses and servants, to join the British Army. One such correspondent, Henry Nevinson, was becoming impatient.

> I have served as a correspondent for nearly twenty years in many countries and under all sorts of conditions. I think I know all the tricks of the trade, and I have seen many of them practised. But I cannot foresee how any correspondent could give away his country or do the smallest public injury under these regulations, even if he wanted to. Take things as they stand. Twelve of us have been selected to accompany the British Force. It is absolutely impossible to imagine men of this experience and quality giving away our country or making dangerous revelations or mistakes, even if they stood under no regulations at all. They simply would not do it. They would die rather.
>
> We have all engaged servants, bought horses, and weighed our kit. Everything is ready, and yet we are kept chafing here, week after week, while a war for the destiny of the world is being fought within a day's journey, and others of our colleagues are allowed to go dashing about France in motors, almost up to the very front. I do not make light of their splendid courage and resource. I can only envy their opportunities. The vivid pictures they send of panic and destruction, the stories they learn from wounded and refugees, are the only accounts that the British people have been allowed to hear of the reality of the war. But there is other news that we all long to hear, and might hear now without public danger. Secrecy was at first essential, and of the British Force was admirably kept by our editors and other journalists who

knew it well. But absolute secrecy is no longer possible, and when the War Office has itself selected a small body of men whom it is prepared to trust under the very stringent regulations which it has itself drawn up, it seems a pity not to use us just because we are supposed to be good. We are now told that we must wait till the French General Staff sends for the French correspondents. In that case, I fear, we may wait for ever, and our own people and the rest of the world will have to depend for their knowledge of our army's share in the war upon bare official notices of their positions, supplemented by tales of refugees, bewildered or wounded private soldiers, and foreign correspondents, now eagerly encouraged to paint hostile pictures of our soldiers at the invitation of the German Government.[33]

Nevinson was fifty-eight years old and a war correspondent of vast experience having covered conflicts all around the world. He was the second son of a solicitor, had had a strict evangelical upbringing and was educated at Shrewsbury and Christ Church, Oxford. His adventures in journalism began with the *Daily Chronicle* when he reported from the Greek and Turkish War of 1897. From there Nevinson moved to Crete, then to Spain in 1898, and between 1899 and 1902 he was in Natal and Transvaal reporting the events of the Boer War. In 1904 Nevinson was in central Africa, where he exposed the Portuguese slave trade in Angola. He was in Russia between 1905 and 1906, and in India for the *Manchester Guardian*, 1907–8. During the Balkans conflict of 1912, Nevinson was the *Daily Chronicle*'s correspondent with the Bulgarian Army and when war broke out in early August of 1914 he had been in Berlin reporting for the *Daily News*. For a war correspondent with this pedigree it must have been frustrating waiting at the War Office for Kitchener to say the word and let him ply his trade.

While the British forces were relocating to Flanders, the war correspondent George Curnock of the *Daily Mail* found himself in prison, having been arrested as a spy.

Half an hour ago I was released from prison here, after lying two nights and the greater part of two days in the straw with a handful of French peasants, two peasant soldiers and several amicable gendarmes.[34]

However, Curnock was not the only journalist to be locked in gaol. William Beach Thomas and his travelling companion *The Times* correspondent reached Hazebrouck in Northern France and were themselves imprisoned after heated discussions with a British lieutenant.[35] While in Dunkirk in October Gibbs felt that his adventure might be over when he was spotted by some English officers in the quiet sanctuary of a restaurant.

By mid-October the British arrived at Ypres, at exactly the same time as the Germans. Both forces had similar plans to outflank the other, but it was at Ypres that the two clashed. On 20 October 1914 the Germans launched their offensive against Ypres on a much larger scale than the British. It raged all along the line from the Channel to Ypres and as far south as Armentières and this period between October and 22 November became known as the First Battle of Ypres. This was rather more than just one battle, but entailed a number of engagements which again ended in stalemate. What this battle achieved was the destruction of the pre-war concept of the BEF and its regular army. They had suffered more casualties during a month at Ypres than in all the preceding attacks since August. The British Army had been smashed and what was left was a mere framework to which the new Kitchener armies would be added in the spring and summer of 1915.

While the battles raged around Ypres, on the Home Front the debate over censorship and lack of war news had not diminished. On 19 October Sir John French published his dispatch on the situation in France and Belgium for the period from 23 August to 17 September. It told how in the last few days the Allies had retaken Armentières and that the Belgians had successfully engaged the Germans along the River Yser. The military correspondent for *The Times* believed that these dispatches from the Field-Marshal were the only way to gain a full picture of events on the Western Front.

> These dispatches are practically the only authentic reports of operations which are given to the public. They are patently, sincere, wholly devoid of ostentation, and convincing by reason of their modesty and their frankness. They give a most moving picture of the recovery of the Army after its retreat before over-whelming forces, of the tireless struggle against grave difficulties, of the vigour of the pursuit, and of the tenacity of all ranks in the attack upon a defended position of great strength reinforced by heavy guns and occupied with skill. Much of the information which they convey of the composition of the French and German Armies is also more or less new, and consequently the dispatches are illuminating and deserve to be read again and again.[36]

However, by October 1914 the Commander-in-Chief was apprehensive about the policy of excluding war correspondents:

> . . . On the 4th October 1914, Sir John French informed the Secretary of State that accredited journalists of good type, under control, would be less harmful than irregular correspondents.[37]

In London at the War Office Kitchener was also having second thoughts about the severe censorship regulations imposed on news reports from the Front line. As the casualty list continued to rise through the First Battle of Ypres it was important to maintain the interest and support of the Home Front. A way of achieving this was to release more news about the units of troops involved in the battles.

> Lord Kitchener now expressed a wish for more detailed accounts, and for the names of units to be mentioned. It was found, however, that there were so many difficulties in the way of obtaining correct details that the matter was dropped. To give the names of units accurately would have necessitated the corroboration of the officers responsible in order to ensure that justice was done. It would also have called for an amount of checking which would have been impossible to carry out.[38]

The problem highlighted by the events at Ypres was that the Home Front read more news about what was happening on the Belgian and French fighting fronts rather than the BEF's. As the restrictions on war correspondents entering the British Western Front zone were so tight it became easier to report from another Allied sector where officials might turn a blind eye to the war correspondents.

In October 1914 Philip Gibbs was in Dunkirk waiting for an official pass to get him over the Belgian frontier and into the war zone.

My two friends and I were provided with some worthless passes which failed to comply with official regulations. We had no authorized business in Dunkirk, and if our real profession had been known we should have been arrested by the nearest French or British officer, sent down to British headquarters under armed guard and, after very unpleasant experiences as criminals of a dangerous and objectionable type, expelled from France with nasty words on our passports.[39]

By 20 October Gibbs had made it near to the Belgian frontier without an official pass and sent back a morale-boosting report detailing the first hour of the fight for Ypres.

There is excellent progress to-day on the part of the Allied army in Belgium. The enemy has been driven in retreat, heavily shelled from the digue by British naval guns, which found their range marvellously, so that the enemy's artillery had to retire.

A general advance has been made by the allied forces. Many German prisoners were taken, and a large number of Belgian and French prisoners were released from the enemy's hands.

The Germans seem to be losing their morale, and the officers among the prisoners seem very dejected and confess that their armies both in France and Belgium are in retreat. The fighting has been mainly done by the artillery. On all hands there is great confidence, and it is fully expected that during the next week Ostend will be retaken.

PHILIP GIBBS
[This message has been submitted to the Press Bureau, who allow publication but do not accept responsibility for the correctness of the statement.][40]

From there Gibbs, with *Daily Telegraph* correspondent Ashmead-Bartlett, made his way across the Belgian border and into the town of Furnes where they met the staff of an English hospital with a mobile column attached to the Belgian cavalry. Furnes was the Belgian headquarters of King Albert and his staff. Here the two war correspondents stayed for a while working with the convoy of ambulances during the day and writing their dispatches at night.

What appeared in the *Daily Chronicle* were vivid reports of localized heroic deeds and graphic descriptions from the Front. This was something the military authorities at the War Office just could not compete with in their official communiqués, which

Soldiers pushing an ambulance through the mud, August 1916.

were dreary in comparison. With headlines of 'UNDER FIERCE GUN FIRE IN BLAZING TOWN' and 'VIVID STORY OF THE BATTLE OF THE YSER' the human interest side of battle was brought home to the readers of the *Chronicle*.

INTRODUCTION

Within 24 hours of crossing the frontier between France and Belgium I have been under fierce fire in the greatest battle of modern times, which is now being fought on our long battle front extending through both these countries. In Belgium the hottest fighting yesterday (Wednesday, Oct 21) was between Nieuport and Dixmude, reaching to many outlying villages on either side of the River Yser, which are now no more than columns of flames and smoke. It was here that I saw the meaning of war in its most terrible aspects, and plunged into the midst of the city of Dixmude when the bombardment was at its height, and when a raging ball of fire swept its streets.

The story I have to tell is written disconnectedly, perhaps a little incoherently, in two parts, covering two days of experiences, as I have put it down on paper by candlelight and at odd moments. But because the first day of peace was followed by a day under the enemy's shells the transition may not be without interest to the reader, because it shows how in this frightful war only a few fields and a few roads lie between life and death. So I send the narrative as it stands.

PART I

TUESDAY, OCT 20.

By good luck, which began with the chance encounter of an influential friend – I have been able to cross the French frontier and drive into a Belgian town very close to the German front. . . . The staff of an English hospital to which a mobile column is attached for field work in time of battle had come into the town before dusk with a convoy of ambulances and motor-cars.

WEDNESDAY, OCT 21.

The destruction of Dixmude.

It was decided to take three ambulances and two motor-cars. But as Lieutenant de Brogville anticipated a heavy day's work he invited me to accompany the column in a car which I shared with Mr Ashmead-Bartlett, of the 'Daily Telegraph,' who had also volunteered for the expedition. . . .

It was astonishing – as it is always so in war – to find how soldiers quite near to the front are in utter ignorance of the course of a great battle. Many of the officers and men with whom we talked could not tell us where the Allied Forces were, or where the enemy was in position, or whether the heavy fighting during the last day and night had been to the advantage of the Allies or the Germans. They believed, but were not sure, that the enemy had been driven back many kilometres between Nieuport and Dixmude.

At last, after many discussions and many halts we received our orders. We were asked to get into the town of Dixmude, where there were many wounded. . . .

At a turn in the road the battle lay before us, and we were in the zone of fire. Away across the fields was a line of villages, with the town of Dixmude a little to the right of us, perhaps two kilometres away. From each little town smoke was rising in separate columns, which met at the top in a great pall of smoke, as a heavy black cloud cresting above the light on the horizon line. At every moment this blackness was brightened by puffs of electric blue, extraordinarily vivid, as shells burst in the air. Then the colour gradually faded out, and the smoke darkened and became part of the pall. From the mass of houses in each town came jabs of flame, following the explosions which sounded with terrific, thudding shocks.

I think I may say that none of us quite guessed what was in store for us. At least, I did not guess that we had been asked to go into the open mouth of Death. I had only a vague idea that Dixmude would be just a little worse than the place at which we now halted for final instructions as to the geography of the town. . . .

Then we came to Dixmude. It was a fair-sized town, with many beautiful buildings, and fine old houses in the Flemish style – so I was told. When I saw it for the first time it was a place of death and horror. The streets through which we passed were utterly deserted and wrecked from end to end as though by an earthquake. Incessant explosions of shell-fire crashed down upon the walls, which then toppled and fell. A roof came tumbling down with an appalling clatter. Like a house of cards blown down by a puff of wind a little shop suddenly collapsed into a mass of ruins. Here and there, farther into the town, we saw living figures. They ran swiftly for a moment and then disappeared into dark caverns under toppling porticoes. . . .

We stood on some steps looking down into that cellar. It was a dark hole – illumined dimly by a lantern, I think. I caught sight of a little heap of huddled bodies. Two soldiers, still unwounded, dragged three of them out, handed them up, and delivered them to us. The work of getting those three men into the first ambulance seemed to us interminable. It was really no more than fifteen to twenty minutes while they were being arranged.[41]

As the Germans advanced towards Furnes, Gibbs became involved in the retreat of the Belgian Army. He helped to pack up the hospital attached to the Belgian cavalry and drove with it southwards, 25 kilometres to the town of Poperinghe. Here, in a town held by the British, Gibbs risked being arrested to find food and shelter for the ambulance columns.

In this phase of the war, as Gibbs had demonstrated, the war correspondent was more than just an observer of battle. They worked particularly hard for their stories and their descriptions were more realistic than those later produced in the war by accredited correspondents. Further south towards Arras some kind French military officials were aiding William Beach Thomas of the *Daily Mail* and *The Times'* correspondents to witness the destruction inside the war zone. They entered Arras just three days after the fighting had ceased.

By the greatest courtesy and practical assistance of the French General commanding in the district I was enabled to-day to enter the famous town of Arras and see the effects of the barbarous second bombardment delivered against the historic buildings of the town on Wednesday last.[42]

Casualties listed in the newspapers at this point amounted to 1,800 and took up a whole page.[43] Yet very little of the real picture of Ypres and the British fighting front was made available to the Home Front. What details there were did not inspire or contain any more than a broad outline of events with no mention of the soldiers involved. It was as if no human beings were engaged in the fighting and what was described by Swinton provided a clinical view of war.

The following descriptive account, which has been communicated by an eye-witness present with General Headquarters, continues and supplements the narrative published on November 3 of the movements of the British Force and the French Armies in immediate touch with it.

In spite of the great losses which they suffered in their attacks last week, the Germans have continued their offensive towards the west almost continuously during the five days from October 26 to 30. Opposite us it has gradually grown in intensity and extent of application as more men and guns have been brought up and pushed into the fight, and it has developed into the most bitterly contested battle which has been fought in the western theatre of war.

The German artillery has to a large extent been increased by that transferred from round Antwerp. As regards infantry, it is possible that some of the additional troops now appearing on our front have been rendered available by the relaxation of the pressure against our Allies to the North of Ypres caused by desperate and successful resistance made by the latter, by the harassing nature of the artillery fire brought to bear by our ships against the salvo of country along the coast, and by the flooding of an area along the river Yser.

Forces have been massed also from the south, whilst another of the new army corps has definitely made its debut before us. And though the attempts to hack, or rather to blast and hack, a way through us have been made in other directions, they have for the last few days been most seriously concentrated upon the neighbourhood of Ypres.

Whether the motive inspiring the present action of the Germans against that place is an ambition to win through to the port of Calais – as is to be gathered from articles in their newspapers – or whether the operation is due to a desire to drive Allied forces out of the whole of Belgium, in order to complete the conquest of that country with a view to its annexation and to gain prestige with neutrals, is immaterial. What concerns us more closely is that they have been making and are still pressing a desperate attempt to gain the town.

On Monday, the 26th, South of Lys, on our right, the enemy attacked Neuve Chapelle – one of the villages held by us – in the evening, advancing under cover of a wood. They managed to gain possession of a portion of it. North of the Lys, in the centre, bombardment alone was kept up, and some ground was made by us. . . .

On Tuesday, the 27th, the Germans rather focused their principal attention on our right centre and right, and most desperate fighting took place for the possession of Neuve Chapelle. In spite of repeated counter-attacks by our troops the enemy during the day managed to hold on to the northern part of the village, which he had gained the day before.

Towards evening we had gradually regained the greater part of the place by step-by-step fighting when fresh hostile reinforcements were brought up and the entire village was captured by the enemy. They made several assaults against our whole front south of the Lys, but with the exception of their success at Neuve Chapelle won no advantage.[44]

The battles around Ypres again reached stalemate in late November; with winter the campaign season had come to an end. Therefore, the two sides set to work building their Front line trenches, dugouts and communication trenches ready for the spring and further offensives. At the end of 1914 the BEF were left holding a 21-mile stretch of Front from Givenchy northwards to just opposite the village of Wytschaete, which is about 4 miles south of Ypres.

For an army unfamiliar with trench warfare this became a time to develop and implement new technology which might improve the chances of the soldier thrown into a siege situation. All the gadgets and weapons we today associate with trench warfare were at that time still on the drawing board or being tested for the first time. This would have included trench mortars, new types of ammunition and hand grenades and even 'duckboards' to stop soldiers sinking to the bottom of their trenches.

However, while the Western Front may have quietened down to face a cold winter, on the Home Front the question of censorship was still being debated. A letter to *The Times* in November commented on the false perspective of war that the country held. The writer lay the blame for this at the Government's feet and its harsh censorship regulations.

TO THE EDITOR OF THE TIMES

Sir, – Is it not time that the Government took the country into its confidence and told us what, in its opinion, we have got to face? Unless they do, the country is in danger of being misled. Owing perhaps largely to the censorship arrangements, the mass of the people are gaining a false perspective, which is obviously having its effect on recruiting. They read in the official news – as is natural – mainly of the successes and heroism of the Allied troops, and for the rest they are fed for the most part on imaginative and incredible stories of the utter demoralization of their enemies. The determination and vigour with which the Germans are pressing their attacks and the critical nature of the struggle is thus hidden, and the great mass of the public is lulled into the belief that the war is as good as over, and that it is only a question of holding on till the Germans give way.

To anybody who understands the true position this complacent optimism is without foundation. We have got to beat, not hold, the Germans, and the task of driving them out of Belgium alone from line after line of trenches, yard by yard, mile by mile, is bound to be tremendously difficult and costly. We shall do it, it is true, but only if we spare no effort to bring every ounce of the fighting strength of the nation to bear, and means pouring into Belgium men, more men, and even more men, as fast as they can be trained, until a decisive superiority is established and all hope of success to the German arms disappears.[45]

Debate of this kind was not only limited to the letter pages of newspapers. In the House of Commons too press censorship and war correspondence were under discussion following the First Battle of Ypres. It would appear that the Government and military authorities were already contemplating the value of having war correspondents reporting from the British Front in France. Reporting from the House of Commons on press censorship *The Times* noted a reply to a question on war correspondence.

MR. TENNAT said that a list of correspondents representative of the principal agencies and papers desirous of being included had been drawn up by the authorities in collaboration with the agencies and papers in question. There were none at the front now. He was unable at present to give an answer to the question as to when correspondents would be allowed to proceed with their work to visit the fighting line.[46]

This change of heart was in part a response to the lack of British military news from the Front during the fighting around Ypres, but also as a consequence of their French Allies allowing correspondents to tour certain sectors of the Western Front. The Paris correspondent of *The Times* visited the French lines on 20 November with the Government's consent.

Our Paris correspondent, who has been permitted by the courtesy of the Government to visit the French lines, sends a graphic account of the battle of Flanders. This dispatch has the added interest of being the first published in this country by a correspondent who has been allowed officially to visit the fighting line. The British authorities have not yet permitted correspondents to furnish the country with narratives written from the actual scene of the fighting.[47]

Kitchener had outlawed correspondents from entering the battle zone at a time when the Allies on the Western Front had all adopted this policy. Now the British military were alarmed by the developments which gave the Home Front more news of the Allies' fighting than of their own. Correspondents were sending dispatches back from the Belgian and French fronts with their authorities' blessings and yet the British Front still remained in a veil of fog and secrecy – this had to change if the British public were to remain fully supportive of the war effort.

The next six months were to be a testing time for the war correspondents. They were so close to being allowed to the British Western Front and yet so far. Military bureaucracy was not noted for its speed and the correspondents, although now tolerated, were still seen as outlaws. But the machinery had been set in motion and it was only a matter of time before the situation changed.

NOTES

1. J.E. Edmonds, *History of the Great War; Military Operations, France and Belgium, 1914* (Macmillian, 1933), pp. 71–2.
2. Edmonds, *Great War, 1914*, p. 76.
3. Edmonds, *Great War, 1914*, p. 113.
4. *The Times*, Tuesday, 25 August 1914 (London).
5. *The Times*, Tuesday, 25 August 1914 (London).
6. A. Bishop, *Chronicle of Youth, Vera Brittain's War Diary. 1913–1917* (Victor Gollancz, 1981), pp. 95–6.
7. *The Sunday Times*, Sunday, 30 August 1914 (London).
8. Bishop, *Chronicle of Youth,* p. 101.
9. *The Sunday Times*, Sunday, 30 August 1914 (London).
10. *The Times*, Monday, 31 August 1914 (London).
11. The *Daily Mail*, Tuesday, 1 September 1914 (London).
12. C. Haste, *Keep the Home Fires Burning* (Allen Lane, 1977), p. 32.
13. E.D. Swinton, *Eyewitness* (Hodder & Stoughton, 1932), p. 52.
14. Swinton, *Eyewitness*, p. 74.
15. Swinton, *Eyewitness*, p. 53.
16. Swinton, *Eyewitness*, p. 65.
17. P. Gibbs, *The Souls of War* (Heinemann, 1915), p. 157.
18. The *Daily Mail*, Friday, 28 August 1914 (London).
19. Gibbs, *Souls*, pp. 58–9.
20. The *Daily Chronicle*, Monday, 31 August 1914 (London).
21. *The Times*, Thursday, 10 August 1914 (London).
22. Edmonds, *Great War, 1914*, p. 310.
23. B.H. Liddell Hart, *History of the First World War* (Pan Books Ltd, 1972), p. 80.
24. J.E. Edmonds, *History of the Great War; Military Operations, France and Belgium, 1914* (Macmillian, 1933), p. 343.
25. The *Daily Telegraph*, Tuesday, 1 September 1914 (London).
26. Gibbs, *Souls,* pp. 94–5.
27. The *Daily Telegraph*, Sunday, 6 September 1914 (London).
28. *The Times*, Thursday, 10 September 1914 (London).
29. *The Times*, Thursday, 10 September 1914 (London).

30. *The Times*, Monday, 14 September 1914 (London).
31. Gibbs, *Souls*, pp. 127–8.
32. Edmonds, *Great War, 1914*, p. 11.
33. The *Nation*, 12 September 1914 (London).
34. The *Daily Mail*, Wednesday, 23 September 1914 (London).
35. P. Knightley, *The First Casualty* (Quartet Books, 1982), p. 73.
36. *The Times*, Tuesday, 20 October 1914 (London).
37. J.E. Edmonds, *The Official History of the Great War; Military Operations France and Belgium. December 1915–July 1st 1916* (Shearer, 1986), p. 145.
38. Swinton, *Eyewitness*, p. 89.
39. Gibbs, *Souls*, p. 160.
40. The *Daily Chronicle*, Wednesday, 21 October 1914 (London).
41. The *Daily Chronicle*, Monday, 26 October 1914 (London).
42. The *Daily Mail*, Monday, 26 October 1914 (London).
43. The *Daily Mail*, Monday, 26 October 1914 (London).
44. *The Times*, Friday, 6 November 1914 (London).
45. *The Times*, Monday, 9 November 1914 (London).
46. *The Times*, Thursday, 26 November 1914 (London).
47. *The Times*, Tuesday, 1 December 1914 (London).

JANUARY TO MAY 1915

In the last days of 1914 the British War Council began to discuss ways to break the stalemate that had developed on the Western Front. Kitchener and Churchill supported the creation of another war zone in the Dardanelles, to attack Germany via a back door. What was needed to boost morale on the Home Front was a quick victory, and an attack using the so far under-used British Fleet appeared to be the best option. If an operation in the Dardanelles was successful it would be a way of drawing the East European countries into the struggle and of penetrating Austria and the middle of Europe. Communication with Russia would also be enhanced by such an offensive as it would have the potential to open up routes into the Black Sea.

The war was no longer confined to battles in distant countries of the Empire. The general public in Britain were now feeling the effects of war without leaving the British Isles as the Home Front was turned into another legitimate battle zone by Germany. In December the east coast of England was shelled from the North Sea by the German Navy. The targets were Scarborough, Whitby and Hartlepool, and the attacks terrified the public. In January Germany launched the first of many bombing raids on Britain when two Zeppelins crossed the North Sea, and in February a U-boat blockade of Britain was announced in which any shipping entering into an area of water surrounding Britain and Ireland became liable to attack. This did not affect the Home Front straight away, but by 1917, with dwindling food supplies, it became a major issue for the general public.

From the beginning of the year until June 1915 the Home Front had to make major changes and sacrifices in their daily lives. As Taylor explained.

> It marked for Great Britain, and soon other countries, the beginning of a new start of the war. Until this moment, the British people had been treating the war as an extra, a luxury which they could have on top of their ordinary life.[1]

Also changing was the composition of the British Army, which had been shattered after the First Battle of Ypres. During the earlier months of 1915 the first of the new Kitchener battalions made their way out to France. This meant that a large proportion of the Home Front had relatives and friends involved in the fighting at the Front.

At the War Office the regulations regarding the role of the war correspondent were also in a state of transition. At the beginning of February British correspondents were authorized to visit and tour the Belgian[2] and French fronts. Again questions were asked in the House of Commons about the legitimacy of war correspondents in France. This time the Chief Censor from the War Office was asked to explain and clarify the current situation.

THE CENSOR ON HIS DEFENCE

– By our Parliamentary representative.

MR. Joynson-Hicks expressed disapproval of the suppression of news of the capture of Tabriz for a week. The people did not in the least mind knowing the truth if there was bad news. A plea was also put in for fuller news of the achievements of individual regiments.

MR. Sherwell, while admitting there had been improvement in the work of the bureau, complained that it discriminated unfairly between newspapers. 'Recently all the war correspondents were expelled from Dunkirk, and two representatives of English journals were imprisoned by the military authorities in an arbitrary and brutal way simply because they did not clear out early enough. In spite of this order, however, the representatives of one daily paper, on behalf of which discrimination appeared to have been exercised on previous occasions, was allowed to remain in Dunkirk for ten days after the rest had been expelled.[3] I am informed also that the representative of that journal was even in a position to forward Dunkirk news, not indeed owing to direct presence in Dunkirk, but owing to residence in the vicinity of Dunkirk and to facilities which were offered to him by motor transit to enter Dunkirk from time to time.'

'The only thing that could create a panic in this country is for the public to get the idea that they are not being told the whole truth,' said Mr Hume Williams.

Sir Stanley Buckmaster, the Solicitor-General, the Chief Censor: 'He warned the House that if this motion were carried no one would be more pleased than the German Press. For weeks past they had been doing all in their power to convince neutral countries that the British official war news could not be trusted. Were they to have the added satisfaction of reproducing, with all the rich embroidery of which they were capable, the announcement that the House of Commons had said that the action of the Press Bureau had been calculated to cause suspicion?'

MR. Bonar Law

'I wonder if anyone realises what a tremendous event was the battle of Ypres in November last. We had bigger losses there than, I believe, in any battle in which purely British troops were engaged, yet all the accounts we had had were contained in Sir John French's despatches? I think the country might now know more about it.' The Times recently had a very interesting account of the Battle of Soissons, written by someone who had been permitted to go over the battlefield by the French authorities. If permission could be given to journalists to visit other battlefields it would be a great advantage.[4]

One of the first consequences of this was a promise by Mr Asquith to increase the output of Sir John French's personal dispatches. From 17 February the British public were promised bi-weekly progress reports from French at General Headquarters in France. The other major concession took place during the Battle of Neuve Chapelle when four correspondents were invited to visit the British GHQ for a tour.

When in April Sir Ian Hamilton and the Admiralty invited accredited war correspondents to join the Fleet on its journey to the Dardanelles, it became only a matter of time before the same would be done on the Western Front. The *Daily Chronicle* reported

> The Admiralty has set an example to the War Office by not only recognising war correspondents, but by making arrangements for them to accompany the expedition to the Dardanelles.
>
> In view of the special circumstances the number of correspondents able to watch the operations is necessarily very limited. There is one representing the London morning newspapers, one representing Reuters Agency and the Press Association, and one representing the Overseas Press. The London newspapers in combination appointed to represent them Mr E. Ashmead-Bartlett, who is well known as a special correspondent for the 'Daily Telegraph,' and has done excellent work for that journal. Mr L. Lawrence represents Reuters Agency and the Press Association.
>
> Major Peel is in charge of the war correspondents, and will act as Press Censor. An 'Eye-Witness' will accompany the Australian and New Zealand forces, but there will be no 'Eye-Witness' with the British force. There are no correspondents with the French troops.[5]

While an Anglo-French force was on its way to the Dardanelles, Sir John French had plans to recapture Neuve Chapelle, which had fallen to the Germans during the first round of battles near Ypres in November 1915. The main reason for Sir John French's charade was to appease the French General Joffre who believed that a Dardanelles offensive would leave the Western Front sadly neglected. This was to be a sort of display for the benefit of the critics in France who believed that the British were not bearing their fair full share of the war.

French also had to make the decision either to take up more of the Front by relieving the French 9th Corps with his newly trained reinforcements arriving from England or stage an offensive. Joffre wanted to free up his troops north of Ypres so that he could use them in a spring offensive. However, French could not do both as this would leave the British Army very stretched. What French and Joffre agreed to was a compromise: the British troops would relieve only one division of the 9th Corps and would carry out an offensive in isolation.

On 10 March the Battle for Neuve Chapelle was launched at 7.30 a.m. by a 35-minute bombardment by 342 guns on a front of 2,000 yards. The objective was to break through the German trench system at Neuve Chapelle and capture the village of Aubers. As this offensive had been planned by Haig, the cavalry were to wait behind the line in readiness so that if a gap emerged in the line they would ride through and exploit the open countryside. At 8.05 a.m. the barrage moved to focus on the village of Neuve Chapelle itself and the infantry began to cross no man's land. The troops achieved their first objective, and reached the German support line, meeting with little resistance and much surprise. From here they went into the village and after four hours of hand-to-hand fighting it too was captured. The communication system was poor, and unclear messages and the fact that the field

The ruins of Neuve Chapelle following the British bombardment.

telephone line had been smashed by shell fire slowed the battle down. There was a gap of five hours while the troops in Neuve Chapelle waited for Headquarters to give them the go-ahead to advance further. By that time it was too late as the Germans had managed to move fresh forces into the area to repulse further British attacks. A clean break in the German line had been achieved, which only happened on a further two occasions during the whole of the First World War, but it had not been followed up and fully exploited. In the following two days Haig ordered more frontal attacks, but the element of surprise had been lost and this resulted in heavy British losses and very little ground being gained.

Unusually for the Press Bureau, the official communiqué reporting the successful battle appeared in the British newspapers just a day later on 11 March.

BRITISH VICTORY NEAR LA BASSÉE.
BETWEEN LYS AND LA BASSÉE CANAL. – The British Army, supported by our heavy artillery, achieved an important success. It carried the village of Neuve Chapelle (to the east of the road from Estaires to La Bassée), advanced to the north-east of this village (in the direction of Aubers) and to the south-east (in the direction of the Bois de Biez), capturing 1,000 prisoners, including several officers, and some machine-guns. The German losses were very heavy.[6]

Even more shocking was that on 13 March, just three days after the battle had begun, Sir John French's dispatch detailing the fighting at Neuve Chapelle was published in the newspapers. When you consider that French's personal dispatch for Mons appeared in the newspapers on 7 September 1914 and the actual fighting took place on 23 August 1914 the difference is quite astounding.

The Field-Marshal commanding the British Forces in France reports as follows:–

1. Since my last communiqué the situation in our front, between Armentières and La Bassée, has been materially altered by the successful initiative on the part of the troops engaged.
2. Shortly after 8 a.m. on March 10 these troops assaulted and carried the German trenches in the neighbourhood of Neuve Chapelle. The co-operation between the artillery of all natures and the infantry was very good, with the result that the losses incurred were not great in proportion to the result achieved.
3. The mutual support which individual battalions afforded each other during the operations was a marked feature of the attack.
4. Our heavy artillery was very effective. Apart from observed results, prisoners' statements confirm the accuracy of our fire and the damage caused by it.
5. Before noon we had captured the whole village of Neuve Chapelle, and our infantry at once proceeded to confirm and extend the local advantage gained. By dusk the whole labyrinth of trenches on a front of about 4,000 yards was in our hands, and we had established ourselves about 1,200 yards beyond the enemy's advanced trenches. The number of German prisoners captured and brought into headquarters during the day was 750. There are probably more to come in.
6. During March 11 the enemy made repeated efforts to recover the ground he had lost. All his counter-attacks have been repulsed with heavy loss. We continue to make steady progress. Hard fighting is still going on.
7. The local initiative displayed by our troops daily is admirable, and says much for the spirit which animates the Army. The success achieved on the 10th and 11th is a striking example of this spirit.[7]

Two days after Sir John French's dispatch, on 15 March, Colonel Swinton's 'Eyewitness' reports of the events surrounding Neuve Chapelle were issued by the Press Bureau.

At 7.30 a.m. on the 10th the battle began with a bombardment by large numbers of guns and howitzers. Our men in the trenches describe this fire as being the most tremendous both on point of noise and in actual effect they have ever seen or heard. The shrieking of the shells in the air, their explosions and the continuous thunder of the batteries all merged into one great volume of sound. The discharges of the guns were so rapid that they sounded like the fire of a gigantic machine-gun. During the 35 minutes it continued our men could show themselves freely and even walk about, in perfect safety.

Then the signal for the attack was given, and in less than half an hour almost the whole of the elaborate series of German trenches in and about Neuve Chapelle were in our hands. Except at one point there was hardly any resistance, for the trenches, which in places were literally blotted out, were filled with dead and dying partially buried in earth and debris, and the majority of the survivors were in no mood for further fighting.

To the north-east of the village, however, a body of Germans ensconced in some enclosures still continued to hold out for a few hours; three attacks, in spite of the extreme gallantry with which they were conducted, failed to dislodge them; but by about noon the arrival of reinforcements drove the Germans from their last stronghold in the village. This part of the fighting was remarkable for the manner in which every part of the attacking line afforded one another mutual support. . . .

By nightfall we were in possession of all the enemy's trenches on a front of 4,000 yards, representing an advance of more than 1,200 yards from our original trenches at the furthest point. The number of prisoners captured was officially reported to be 750, but there is reason to believe that others were taken who have not yet been sent in.[8]

However, even with all this information being provided by the War Office through the Press Bureau so soon after the events, the Home Front still thought it was being misled by the military. Debates and rumours were spreading around the country with regard to the number of casualties and why the newspapers continued to keep them in the dark. The newspaper casualty lists were getting bigger each day after Neuve Chapelle and, if Vera Brittain's diary for March 20 is any indication, this is how people measured the success of a battle.

There was another terrible long list – 40 officer casualties added to the already large number which have resulted from the awful battle, the dearly-bought victory, of Neuve Chapelle last Thursday & Friday week. The fettered Press kept the world in the dark about it, & it is only through the long casualty lists that we are beginning to realise what it must have been. There are rumours that our losses there amount to 12,000 – & the Germans' to about 20,000. Our dear ones are going out in time to be in the thick of it all.[9]

A letter to the editor of the *Daily Mail*, a week after the battle, really pinpoints why the country still felt in the dark. It explained that, however prompt the information from GHQ in France and the Press Bureau was, in its present military format it conveyed very little to the man in the street. If the truth of the gains had been known at the time of course the military would not have been able to report the battle as a victory. The figures simply did not add up. After three days fighting the British had gained from the Germans land totalling 2,000 yards wide by 1,200 yards deep for 7,000 British and 4,000 Indian casualties.[10] It is no wonder that the military chose to keep the public in the dark.

KEEPING IT DARK.
To the Editor of The Daily Mail
Sir, – Statesmen complain that the working people of the country do not realise the seriousness of the war and that in some cases they are not manufacturing munitions with the steadiness and enthusiasm which are desirable. I suggest that the reason why the working people do not realise the magnitude of the war is that the authorities have set themselves from the very beginning to prevent the people of this country knowing what is going on.

A great battle was fought on Wednesday and Thursday of last week in France. Prompt and brief reports were sent by Sir John French and published on Saturday morning, in which he disclosed that the 3rd and 4th Corps and the Indian troops were engaged. An excellent and spirited description was sent by 'Eye-Witness' and published on Sunday morning. But 'Eye-Witness's' admirable narrative, while it may be interesting to the military historian conveys nothing concrete to the shipbuilder on the Clyde or to the engineer on the Tyne or the men who are making war material at Woolwich. Only this morning have we learned anything of the regiments engaged, although vague reports have circulated as to the extent of the casualties. We were told earlier in the war that the reason why regiments could not be mentioned is that relatives would be rendered anxious for casualty lists. If the German reason is still maintained by the authorities the Germans will get all the information they want from to-day's papers, where a long list of officers killed and wounded is printed. And they will be able to write in between the lines of 'Eye-Witness's' account the names of all the regiments who are in the field. But I should imagine that the Germans knew on Wednesday and Thursday last the names of all the corps they had met in the fight. . . .

This piecemeal method of disclosing information about the war is calculated only to kill enthusiasm and interest and serves no other purpose whatever. It is conceived by those who do not understand the spirit of this nation: they seem to think that losses in war discourage the British people and that the hard facts must be kept from us. That is all wrong. . . .

The British workman is just as patriotic as his comrade in the fighting line and just as ready for sacrifice in the interest of the country.

Tell him what is being done; tell him what has to be done. Trust him. He will not fail you.[11]

It would seem that the general public blamed the lack of news firmly on the Government and the newspapers. So what were the war correspondents of these newspapers doing during the Battle of Neuve Chapelle? Correspondents were still sending their dispatches on the battle from somewhere in Northern France and trying to avoid arrest. However, four lucky British correspondents were at this time being given the full hospitality and tour of British GHQ in France.

At the invitation of the War Office, Philip Gibbs representing the *Daily Telegraph* and *Daily Chronicle*, Valentine Williams for the *Daily Mail* and *Daily Mirror*, Henry Nevinson for *The Times* and the *Daily News and Leader*, and Ernest Townley acting for the *Daily Express* and the *Morning Post* had made their way to the British Western Front with the prospect of experiencing the fighting at first hand.

It seems a strange coincidence that four of the top British correspondents in France were given invitations to join military staff for a week just as the Battle of Neuve Chapelle took place. Although a very cynical observation, it would appear that the military authorities were playing a time-wasting game with these war correspondents and this short period at Neuve Chapelle was a taste of things to come.

Henry Nevinson, with his twenty years' experience of war reporting, was downhearted at not being able to witness any of the fighting around Neuve Chapelle.

An excuse had been made that their presence near the front of such a successful operation might delay reinforcements from reaching the firing line. In his first dispatch from British GHQ Nevinson lamented the changing role of the war correspondent.

But I must say at once that, so far as the actual firing line goes, we should have seen much more if the last two days had not been marked by serious and successful operations in one part of the British front. In the old days that would have been a queer thing for a war correspondent to say. His rule then was to ride as hard as possible to the sound of the guns. But now he moves under orders and goes by motor. It used to be said in irony that no action could begin till he came up. But now his presence is not exactly demanded, though I think the chief fear is lest his car should for a single moment delay the movement of reinforcements along the road.[12]

Gibbs was at General Headquarters when the news came in about Neuve Chapelle. His report conveyed his sense of disappointment at being so close to the battle, but apparently denied any access to it.

Nearly a thousand German prisoners had been taken, and were being brought down from the front by rail. If we liked we might have a talk with these men, and see the character of the enemy which lies hidden in the trenches opposite our lines. It was nearly ten o'clock at night when we motored to the railway junction through which they were passing. . . .

Prisoners being taken during the Great Advance.

I went back to my billet in General Headquarters wishing that I had seen
something of that affair which had netted all these men. It had been a 'day out'
for the British troops, and we had not yet heard of the blunders or the blood that
had spoilt its success. It was hard to have seen nothing so near the front. And
then a promise of seeing something of the operations on the morrow came as a
prospect for the next day. It would be good to see real business again and to
thrill once more to the awful music of the guns.[13]

The results were that in a period when the war correspondents should have been
sending exhilarating and inspiring dispatches of heroic deeds back to the Home
Front, the public had to endure detailed reports of how British Headquarters in
France functioned on a daily basis. It would appear that the military's gamble to
allow correspondents to stay with them during a major offensive had paid off. The
exciting title of Gibbs' dispatch written on 11 March, the second day of fighting
around Neuve Chapelle, was 'HOW THE STRIKING POWER OF THE ARMIES IS
ORGANISED. CONTRASTS OF PEACE & WAR NEAR THE FRONT.'

For three days I have been visiting some of those places in France and Belgium
whose names since the war began, have become familiar as household words. . . .
   During the past six months I have seen something of this war in France and
Belgium. I have been in Flemish towns when they were being shelled to
pieces, and have motored under shell-fire down the long, straight roads of
Belgium. I have trudged with crowds of refugees, and helped to carry
wounded men to field hospitals, and watched the tragedy and the heroism of
this great, grim business of war in two nations unprepared at first for their
ruthless enemy. But this is the first time that I have seen the British Front and
moved about freely among British soldiers and Officers of the Expeditionary
Forces and seen the way in which our own men set about their task. Having
quailed before the eyes of British Staff officers, it is a privilege now to wear a
little tin badge of identification round my neck, to carry a khaki covered
packet of field-dressing in my side pocket and to be provided with War Office
papers providing my right to act as an accredited correspondent for a certain
time-limit.
   In these last three days I have learnt more about machinery of war than I had
gathered during the six preceding months. With extraordinary patience and
kindness Generals and high officers in all branches of the service have
explained to me and a little group of fellow-correspondents the inner workings
of their own part in the organisation of the Army and its bearing upon the
operations in the field. I have been, as it were, into the workshops of war, and
have seen the secret processes by which a Commander in the field is able to
keep his force efficient as a fighting unit and by which all the wastage of war is
repaired.
   Few things have been hidden from us. With splendid candour, trusting our
honour to reveal nothing which might be of use to the enemy, all the officers to
whom we have been introduced have shown us a thousand things which help the
one great purpose of all military organisation – the striking power of an Army in

the field, as it depends upon regularity of food supplies and ammunition, the health and training of troops, mobility of transport, rapid communication with the Headquarters staff, knowledge of the enemy, and moral condition.

'Gentlemen,' said the Staff Officer, who is our guide, philosopher and friend in this visit to the front, 'there has been good work to-day. We have taken Neuve Chapelle, and the operation is proceeding very well.'

We bent over his map, following the line drawn by his finger, listening to details of a splendid bit of work, glad that 500 German prisoners had been taken that day. As he spoke the window rattled, and we heard the boom of another gun. . . . The war was going on, though it had seemed so quiet at the front.[14]

In this dispatch Gibbs wrote that 'few things have been hidden from us' and yet at this point in time he knew nothing of the first British offensive on the Western Front for 1915 taking place outside GHQ.

The *Daily Mail* correspondent Valentine Williams, reporting from the General Headquarters of the British Army in the field on Thursday (11 March), was caught in the same trap.

Since my arrival here on Monday I have had the opportunity of going through the whole organisation of the British Army in the field, which is centred at Headquarters. Of the details of this organisation I shall write later. I am convinced that nothing we may be destined to see in the spectacular line can surpass in sheer impressiveness the miracle of organisation which has gradually built up in the somnolent atmosphere of this quiet corner of France.[15]

Valentine Williams had been with the *Daily Mail* since 1909 reporting from various conflicts around Europe including the Portuguese revolution in 1910, and in 1913 he became their war correspondent in the Balkans. Born in 1883, he was the eldest son of the late G. Douglas Williams who was the Chief Editor of Reuters. It would seem that journalism was an early influence in his life and after being privately educated in Germany he joined the Reuters agency as a sub-editor in 1902.

Rather than witnessing the battle at first hand, Ernest Townley had to imagine the fighting from the sounds that wafted back towards British Headquarters in St Omer. Once again the official reason for not being able to enter the firing zone was a lack of room!

First of all, you may imagine the authorised war correspondent sitting somewhere within easy reach of the trenches, magically endowed with a cloak of invisibility and invulnerability, penning his message as the British troops advance to their latest success – the capture of the village of Neuve Chapelle, some twenty miles or so to the south of Ypres. The bullets are whistling by, the shells are moaning overhead. The battle is hot, and the Germans are giving ground. All around is the fury and the crash of war.

I have been privileged, with a few other authorised correspondents, to hear of this hard fighting while it has been in progress, to hear the guns booming in the distance, and to be within about ten miles of the operations during part of yesterday. My only regret is that I have seen nothing of the fight. The country where it has taken place is so flat that you cannot get a glimpse of the fighting unless you are within easy reach of the German rifle, and there is no room for any but soldiers, within the fire zone. There is, moreover, no available method of approach, for the roads are wanted for the ammunition carts while fighting is in progress.

So, having no cloak of invisibility, the authorised war correspondent was unable to get near this battle. And, having no cloak of invulnerability, he ought, no doubt, to be grateful for not being invited to try. A war correspondent roaming at will along the battle line is a vision of the past, and possibly of the future.

It is not a picture of the moment. My first paragraph, therefore, is only a figment of the imagination, written in no sorry spirit of irony – one's thoughts are far from irony – but simply to try to convey to you at home some notion of how different some of the things near 'the front' are from what you perhaps imagine them to be. For, although at the General Headquarters of the British army in France, and within sound of the big guns, I am writing in a quiet room, and the difficulty I have is to convince myself that war, with all its heroism and endurance, is going on within an hour's motor run of where I sit.[16]

When the war correspondents managed to tour the rear areas of the British fighting line they were able to talk to resting soldiers and German prisoners brought from Neuve Chapelle, and watch an inter-company football match. However, they still had problems moving around – because they were not in Army uniform they aroused suspicion with the local population and on at least one occasion they were almost shot as spies. This highlights the potential problems of accredited war correspondents travelling the British Front in civilian attire.

In a small town in which we pulled up for a while our civilian aspect excited the suspicions of the French police, for an Englishman who is not in Khaki is a strange and almost inexplicable sight to the French folk in this part of the land.

When we had driven on, a telephone message was sent to the next village to stop the cars in which our little party was travelling. We entered the village, turned the corner in the centre, and ran up against a guard of British soldiers stretched across the street. Their rifles were up at their shoulders in a second, and a sharp cry of 'Halt!' rang out.

We stopped, but the rifles remained at the 'ready', and it was an interesting experience to find yourself looking down the business end of a British gun, with a bullet inside it, and a hard-as-nails Tommy glaring along the barrel, his face twitching with excitement at the possibility of having to shoot one of his own countrymen. That we should have been shot to a man if we had attempted to move the cars forward there was no question whatever. The glance of Tommy's eye left no doubt about that.

Happily things were capable of easy and complete explanation, although they took some ten minutes, during which a crowd of women and children gathered round, ready to execrate us perhaps as German spies if the explanations had not been sufficient.[17]

During their tour of the First Army the war correspondents came under the charge of Brigadier-General Charteris, who would later command the accredited correspondents as head of military intelligence. Charteris was amazed at the ignorance of the correspondents and this could explain their extensive tour of the workings of the British GHQ before witnessing any fighting.

The first batch of correspondents had to be treated gingerly. I doubt whether they will really be much wiser after their visit. They arrived, accompanied by three officers from the W.O. who themselves were quite as ignorant of what was actually happening as the correspondents. They were in my charge while in the First Army. I gave them a short explanation of the operations of the past and present, not a word about the future. Then I handed them over to the Administration people, Ordnance, Medical and Supply, and finally sent them on up to the front under charge of one of my own officers. There are many well-known names among the correspondents. They were all most amazingly ignorant, but that was the real justification for their mission as opposed to the official 'Eyewitness'. It is impossible for us here to realize how ignorant the public must be, and in writing copy that the public requires, one must begin with the knowledge of how little they know.[18]

At the end of their week's stay at British GHQ on the Western Front the four correspondents were received by the Commander-in-Chief, Sir John French. This was a fleeting encounter including a quick speech and each correspondent being presented to French. Ernest Townley described the thrill of meeting him.

The folding doors opened, and a short square, sturdy soldier, in plain service uniform, came forward with a firm, decided step. His closely cropped hair was silvery. His grey eyes shone with a steady light. I confess that, adventurous as the life of the newspaper man often is, I felt a thrill when this particular soldier stepped towards me and held out his hand. It was the Field Marshal.[19]

Even a brief meeting with Sir John French could not shake off the despondency of the whole week's adventure for Nevinson. He wanted a more permanent arrangement than a short visit to the British Army in France and a chance to get close to the firing line.

But, unhappily, the brief visit of our small party of correspondents to the 'British Expeditionary Force' is now coming to an end. By permission of the War Office we came at the invitation of General Headquarters, and we have been received throughout not merely with courtesy but with welcome. The officers under whose direction we were placed have worked with ungrudging zeal to make the visit a success, and to show us all that authority allowed. One could desire only two things more – things which, of course, lay beyond the powers of those who organised the various days. One would like, as in the old days of war corresponding, to live with the army rather than pay a call or visit as a guest. The second point is perhaps more difficult to obtain. Owing to various 'operations' in different parts of the line we have never been admitted close to the front. Our officers were obliged even to alter the proposed program which would have shown us something, at all events, of the fighting line and something at least of the enemy. Well, I don't want to play the old war-horse and neigh lamentations over days that do not return; but there was a time when it was the obvious duty and privilege of the correspondent to ride to the sound of the battle, and in those days he was not hurried off at once in the opposite direction so soon as the guns began. Opinions naturally differ about the advantage of entire secrecy or the open publication of an Army's struggles and achievements soon after the 'operations' are over. But one would have thought some compromise between the old way and the new could be devised with a certain amount of profit to our Army and country alike.[20]

The military's experiment in controlling the output of the war correspondents during a major offensive seemed to have been very successful. However, the suppressed truth of Neuve Chapelle still surfaced a month later and caused another public outcry. Sir John French blamed the failure of Neuve Chapelle on lack of shells provided by the Government, the Government then passed the blame on to the munitions workers and the Northcliffe newspapers accused Kitchener. The general public had been lied to and their confidence in the Government, military and newspapers, who had all shown themselves to be unreliable, was shaken.

On 15 April Sir John French's dispatch was issued detailing the main attack on Neuve Chapelle; this was at odds with the earlier one hastily brought out on the third day of battle. He attempted to shift some of the blame by crediting Haig with the conception of the battle and the generals for not moving their reserves up to exploit the initial successes.

The object of the main attack was to be the capture of the village of Neuve Chapelle and the enemy's position at that point, and the establishment of our line as far forward as possible to the east of that place.

The object, nature and scope of the attack, and instructions for the conduct of the operation were communicated by me to Sir Douglas Haig in a secret memorandum dated February 19.

The main topographical feature of this part of the theatre is a marked ridge which runs south-west of Lille to the village of Fournes, whence two spurs run out, one due west to a height known as Haut Pommereau, the other following the line of the main road to Illies. . . .

The Battle opened at 7.30 a.m. on March 10 by a powerful artillery bombardment of the enemy's position at Neuve Chapelle. The artillery bombardment had been well prepared and was most effective, except on the extreme northern portion of the front of attack.

At 8.5 a.m. the 23rd (left) and 25th (right) Brigades of the 8th Division assaulted the German trenches on the north-west side of the village.

At the same hour the Garhwal Brigade of the Meerut Division, which occupied the position to the south of Neuve Chapelle, assaulted the German trenches in its front. . . .

Considerable delay occurred after the capture of the Neuve Chapelle position. The infantry was greatly disorganised by the violent nature of the attack and by its passage through the enemy's trenches and the buildings of the village. It was necessary to get units to some extent together before pushing on. The telephonic communication being cut by the enemy's fire rendered communication between front and rear most difficult. The fact of the left of the 23rd Brigade having been held up had kept back the 8th Division, and had involved a portion of the 25th Brigade in fighting to the north out of its proper direction of advance. All this required adjustment. An orchard held by the enemy north of Neuve Chapelle also threatened the flank of an advance towards the Aubers Ridge.

I am of the opinion that this delay would not have occurred had the clearly expressed orders of the General Officer Commanding First Army been more carefully observed.

The difficulties above enumerated might have been overcome at an earlier period of the day if the General Officer commanding 4th Corps had been able to bring his reserve brigades more speedily into action.

As it was, the further advance did not commence before 3.30 p.m.[21]

What the public had been led to believe was a great victory had now been exposed as a great military blunder. Who could the public trust to bring them real information from the Western Front? A month later on 15 April Vera Brittain noted that the dispatches from Neuve Chapelle were finally published and did not indicate that a victory, which had at first been intimated, had been achieved.

That awful disaster was no victory! It was the result of a terrible blunder. The object was to get into Lille; there was nothing to stop them & the cavalry were ready, only the infantry did not join them because – they were being fired upon by our own guns. . . . It is too terrible – this reckless waste of life, the only thing worth having in the universe. Naturally this horrible truth does not come out in the dispatch – it would undoubtedly stop recruiting if men thought they were to enlist only to be shot down by their own guns.[22]

This was not the only shocking news about the Western Front that the Home Front was to learn of in April 1915. On 22 April the Germans launched an offensive near Langemarck on the Ypres salient, but it was no ordinary attack. What became known as the Second Battle of Ypres saw the debut of a new weapon on the Western Front – poison gas. Sir John French's dispatch of 23 April, under the headline of 'POISON GAS USED BY ENEMY HELPS THEM TO ADVANCE', first alerted the Home Front to the soldier's new danger in the battle zone.

Yesterday evening the enemy developed an attack on the French troops on our left in the neighbourhood of Bixschoote and Langemarck, on the north of the Ypres salient.

This attack was preceded by a heavy bombardment, the enemy at the same time making use of a large number of appliances for the production of

British gunners wearing gas masks.

asphyxiating gas. The quantity produced indicates a long and deliberate preparation for the employment of devices contrary to the terms of the Hague Convention, to which the enemy subscribed.

The false statement made by the Germans a week ago to the effect that we were using such gasses is now explained. It was obviously an effort to diminish neutral criticism in advance.

During the night the French had to retire from the gas zone. Overwhelmed by the fumes, they had fallen back to the canal in the neighbourhood of Boesinghe. Our front remains intact, except on the extreme left, where troops have had to readjust their line in order to conform with the new French line.

Two attacks were delivered during the night on our trenches east of Ypres, and were repulsed. Fighting still continues in the region north of Ypres.[23]

The attack began at 5 p.m. with a bombardment on and around Ypres. At about the same time gas cylinders full of chlorine gas were opened from the German side, and with the favourable wind this death cloud moved towards the Allied trenches. This gas engulfed the trenches of two French divisions who held the left of the Ypres salient and then joined up with the British troops. Panic ensued and Algerian and French troops fled as the gas rolled into the trenches to leave a gap of over 4 miles in the Front line. Those who were not quick enough to realize what was happening suffocated from the effects of chlorine poisoning. Behind the rolling mist of yellow gas the German Army advanced and at 7 p.m. the French guns in this sector went quiet. Ypres was now only 4 miles away and, with the Allied Front in disarray, the Germans were free to walk straight into the town unchallenged. However, after walking forward 2 miles the German troops stopped, probably due to their own fear of this new experimental weapon.[24] The success of the gas had probably taken the German command by surprise, as no fresh reinforcements had been brought up to exploit the attack and the timing of the offensive meant that it was dark before they had a chance to discover its full extent.

Throughout the night of 22 April and during the following day ten battalions of Canadian and British troops strung themselves out across the gaps created by the gas. These were thinly spread and did not form a continual line. However, because the Germans were unprepared and unable to follow up the initial attack the Allied troops had plenty of time to improve their positions by digging and wiring. Primitive instructions on how to combat the effects of gas were issued on 23 April.

> The first instructions sent out were that the troops should hold wetted handkerchiefs or cloth over their mouths, or use respirators made of lint and tape (proposed by Lieut-Colonel N.C. Ferguson, the A.D.M.S. of the 28th Division), damped in any case, but, if possible, dipped in a solution of bicarbonate of soda kept in buckets for the purpose.[25]

The German use of gas had managed without a significant loss to break through the French Front line virtually unchallenged and advance as far as Langemarck and Steensraate bridge.

The official history points out that the tactics used at the Second Battle of Ypres became the model for Haig's future offensives such as Festubert (May 1915) and the Somme (July 1916). By using the artillery bombardment the Germans were trying to add weight to their attack in order to compensate for the fact that they had insufficient numbers of troops involved and only a 'limited objective'.

> The British were driven back by the overwhelming artillery fire, with the assistance from time to time of further discharges of gas, although shell fire throughout was the determining factor. Position after position was gained by the enemy, and the conquest immediately consolidated by trench and wire, the new 'parallel' sometimes being actually the conquered position. Eventually the Germans came to a stop from lack of men and ammunition to continue the process, their resources being required elsewhere – to obtain a great strategic success in Russia, and to hold the Franco-British attacks further south. Such deliberate methods of advance are possible only when the attackers are very superior to the foe in heavy artillery, as they were at Ypres, and as they usually were in the great sieges of history.[26]

The first use of gas, which had been banned under the 1907 Hague Convention, was reported in the newspapers in Britain on 26 April 1915. The *Daily Chronicle* correspondent, who reports somewhere 'North of France' so as not to give his position away to the military authorities, comments on the grim effects of the fumes.

> Having learned that British successes at 'Hill 60' had fired the powder all along the battle line from Ypres to Nieuport, and provoked terrible attacks from the Germans,

I took means to get as near as possible to this 20 mile battlefield, and I am in a position to-day to send you precise details about the fighting of April 22, 23 and 24.

The French soldiers were naturally taken by surprise. Some got away in time, but many, alas! not understanding the new danger, were not so fortunate, and were overcome by the fumes and died poisoned. Among those who escaped nearly all cough and spit blood, the chlorine-attacking the mucous membrane. The dead were turned black at once.

The effect of this poisonous gas was felt over about 6 kilometres of ground in length by 2 kilometres deep. Further than that the gas was too much diluted with air to kill, but suffocated many.

About 15 minutes after letting the gas escape the Germans got out of their trenches. Some of them were sent on in advance, with masks over their heads, to ascertain if the air had become breathable. Having discovered that they could advance, they arrived in large numbers in the area on which the gas had spread itself some minutes before, and took possession of the arms of the dead men. They made no prisoners. Whenever they saw a soldier whom the fumes had not quite killed they snatched away his rifle, and threw it in the Yser, and advised him ironically to lie down 'to die better'.[27]

The *Daily Mail* headline presents a more positive view, 'GAS EFFECTS ONLY TEMPORARY'.

The second frantic German attempt to capture Calais is now in progress. During the whole of this week the enemy has made desperate efforts to pierce the line between Nieuport and Ypres.

(Thursday)
Towards evening a strong north-easterly wind was blowing. The Germans, profiting by this, set fire to a chemical product of sulphur chloride which they had placed in front of their own trenches, causing a thick yellow cloud to be blown towards the trenches of the French and Belgians. . . .

The cloud of smoke advanced like a yellow low wall, overcoming all those who breathed its poisonous fumes. The French were unable to see what they were doing or what was happening.

The Germans then charged, driving the bewildered French back past their own trenches. Those who were enveloped by the fumes were not able to see each other half a yard apart. . . .

At the moment of writing fierce fighting is still in progress in this region, and the Allies seem to have gained the mastery. . . .

I have seen some of the wounded who were overcome by the sulphur fumes, and they are progressing favourably. The effect of the sulphur appears to be only temporary. The after-effects seem to be a bad swelling of the eyes, but the sight is not damaged.[28]

Gas had now become an everyday part of modern warfare and British forces experienced its effect first hand just two days later on 24 April. Localized battles continued into May with fierce fighting until the Allied forces took the initiative with the start of the spring offensive. On the morning of 9 May at 5.30 a.m. British troops began a fight for Aubers Ridge while the French launched their attack in the region of Artois. The British started with an artillery bombardment lasting some 40 minutes and using 637 guns, which announced to the enemy an approaching attack. However, due to the lack of high quality shells, the barrage failed to make the advantage which the troops needed to capture their objectives. The results were the now familiar heavy losses for little gain.

At Festubert on 15 May the British launched their first night attack on the Western Front. Three divisions managed to take 3 miles of trench, advancing nearly half a mile. Yet these results were too late and too small to halt the progress of the political crisis which now loomed over Britain. The generals had so far been papering over their blunders and heavy losses with their total control of information leaving the Western Front. Now the nation wanted justification for battles which had been ordered solely to appease the Home Front.

> To throw good money after bad is foolish. But to throw away men's lives where there is no reasonable chance of advantage, is criminal. In the heat of battle mistakes in the command are inevitable and amply excusable. But the real indictment of leadership arises when attacks that are inherently vain are ordered merely because if they could succeed they would be useful. For such 'manslaughter,' whether it springs from ignorance, a false conception of war or a want of moral courage, commanders should be held accountable to the nation.[29]

The actions of the generals came too late to silence their critics in Britain, as they attempted to shift blame to the Home Front for their poor performance. On 14 May *The Times* military correspondent Charles Repington published his articles based on conversations with the Commander-in-Chief, Sir John French, about the shell shortage. This together with the poor showing in the Dardanelles and the fighting in Flanders ending in stalemate by 19 May yet again rocked the Liberal Government under Asquith. The Government needed to be seen to be giving the public what it wanted – more news from the fighting front – but at the same time concealing the real nature of the war so that support would not disappear before victory was achieved. War correspondents at the Front were about to become part of this plan.

> Asquith the Prime Minister, did not want a public row. He settled on coalition with the Conservatives in order to conceal the facts about both shells and the Dardanelles from the British people, another step towards the position that, if men knew the truth about war, they would not go on fighting.[30]

NOTES

1. A.J.P. Taylor, *The First World War* (Penguin, 1966), p. 86.
2. See the *Daily Mail*, Friday, 5 February 1915 (London), article entitled 'Visit to the Belgian Trenches'.
3. Basil Clarke and Mr Lumby of *The Times* were the last two correspondents to be hunted down in Flanders. See B. Clarke, *My Round of the War* (Heinemann, 1917), p. 13.

4. The *Daily Mail*, Tuesday, 9 February 1915 (London).

5. The *Daily Chronicle*, Saturday, 24 April 1915 (London).

6. The *Daily Chronicle*, Thursday, 11 March 1915 (London).

7. The *Daily Chronicle*, Saturday, 13 March 1915 (London).

8. *The Times*, Monday, 15 March 1915 (London).

9. A. Bishop, *Chronicle of Youth, Vera Brittain's War Diary, 1913–1917* (Victor Gollancz, 1981), p. 162.

10. M. Gilbert, *The First World War* (HarperCollins, 1995), p. 133.

11. The *Daily Mail*, Thursday, 18 March 1915 (London).

12. The *Daily News and Leader*, Saturday, 12 March 1915 (London).

13. P. Gibbs, *The Souls of War* (Heinemann, 1915), pp. 352–3.

14. The *Daily Chronicle*, Saturday, 13 March 1915 (London).

15. The *Daily Mail*, Saturday, 13 March 1915 (London).

16. The *Daily Express*, Saturday, 13 March 1915 (London).

17. The *Daily Express*, Tuesday, 16 March 1915 (London).

18. J. Charteris, *At G.H.Q.* (Cassell, 1931), p. 79.

19. The *Daily Express*, Tuesday, 23 March 1915 (London).

20. The *Daily News and Leader*, Tuesday, 16 March 1915 (London).

21. The *Daily Chronicle*, Thursday, 15 April 1915 (London).

22. Bishop, *Chronicle of Youth*, p. 175.

23. The *Daily Chronicle*, Saturday, 24 April 1915 (London).

24. B.H. Liddell Hart, *History of the First World War* (Pan Books, 1972), p. 187.

25. J.E. Edmonds, *History of the Great War; Military Operations, France and Belgium, 1915* (MacMillian, 1927), p. 195.

26. Edmonds, *Great War, 1915*, p. 210.

27. The *Daily Chronicle*, Monday, 26 April 1915 (London).

28. The *Daily Mail*, Monday, 26 April 1915 (London).

29. Liddell Hart, *History*, p. 192.

30. Taylor, *First World War*, p. 86.

Section Two

OFFICIAL CORRESPONDENCE, JUNE 1915 TO MAY 1917

OFFICIAL
CORRESPONDENCE

Early in 1915 the net grew ever tighter around the war zone, but the yearning for news from the Front grew stronger and not only among the public in Britain. American pressure was put on the French and British governments in a letter from Theodore Roosevelt to the Foreign Office about the deficiency of information provided by them on the progress of battle. It appears that the German propaganda machine was showering information on the American war correspondents and others from neutral countries, while the British and French governments refused to have anything to do with any of these war correspondents. The problem was, therefore, that the American public were being fed on a diet of war news issued wholly by the Germans.[1]

This problem was not limited to the American public alone, as the *Daily Mail* highlighted in an article on the British Government's secrecy over war.

The Germans have this advantage over us, that their public is kept interested in the war. By brilliant war correspondents and constantly changing kinematograph films and photographs, every man, woman, and child knows what the war means and how the nation is fighting. In this country anyone who goes about among the populace finds that few of the masses understand what the war is about. They are told very little of the horrors of war as waged by Germany. They do not understand what defeat would mean to us. They are expected to realise the nature of this mighty struggle – compared with which the war with Napoleon was a mere series of frontier expeditions – from perusal of the amiable optimism of 'Eye-Witness,' whose 'eye-wash,' as it is commonly called at the front, bears about the same relation to the realities as Pepys's prattle did to the thrilling time he lived in.

Secrecy is all very well from the muddler's point of view, as it prevents the public from knowing the facts. But we suggest that if the Government really wants to make the people of this country enthusiastic and to make workmen labour as they do in Germany it should tell us the truth.

It should also use the great news associations and newspapers, and send to the front distinguished writers who will tell us of the splendid deeds of our heroes there.

In all three matters we have much to learn from the Russians and a great deal from the French, who – despite official statements to the contrary – have not only invited between 60 and 70 war correspondents to their Army but are now arranging more.[2]

Since the beginning of the war in August 1914 the newspapers and their proprietors had been engaged in a continual campaign to get their correspondents reporting with the British Army at the fighting fronts. The press had the power to influence the general public and because of this the War Office needed their support. Hardly a week went by without the issue of accredited war correspondents being publicized in the press. There were debates in Parliament, letters and poems from the general public, editorial columns denouncing censorship and graphic dispatches from war correspondents who had avoided capture in France. A poem in the *Daily Express* highlighted the newspaper campaign for greater freedom.

> Oh! I'm the censor of the press
> The 'Express' news I cense, Sir.
> If I don't cense with common sense,
> I'll be the ex-Press Censor![3]

On the Belgian and French fronts accredited correspondents had been following their armies since February 1915. In August 1914 Kitchener explained that war correspondents would only be allowed to accompany the British Army when the French had introduced correspondents to their Front. As this had already taken place it meant that the British public had more information and news coming from war correspondents along the Western Front on the state of the French and Belgian armies than their own.

At home pressure was building up against the Government and War Office to make changes to allow war correspondents to the Front, with the belief that the Defence of the Realm Act could be used to manipulate the press. The Chief Censor during the Boer War, Lord Derby, even spoke out about the Government's policy at a recruiting meeting at Oldham.

> 'There must be some rooted objection to newspaper correspondents,' proceeded Lord Derby, 'as if they were alien enemies. Personally, I can speak with a certain amount of experience, because although it was on a very much smaller scale, I was Press Censor at headquarters in the Boer War. Therefore I know the difficulties under which Press censor suffer; but I think it would be perfectly possible for the Government to allow an accredited correspondent from each of the leading newspapers to be attached in some way to Headquarters.'[4]

In the House of Lords too pleas were made to the Government to reconsider its stand.

> To-day Lord Curzon called for information respecting the march of events in these out lying zones of warfare, and protested against the silence which was being preserved. He said he had received a vast number of letters complaining bitterly of what was thought to be unnecessary secrecy with regard to these secondary operations. When he was in France last week he gathered that the almost universal opinion there was that a quite unnecessary amount of mystery was being observed in this country regarding our military operations. It was causing a feeling of exasperation to grow up against the Government which might weaken their position.[5]

In May 1915, after agreement between the cabinet and the high command at GHQ, five war correspondents representing the British press were allowed to report on the Western Front, but only under close supervision. Rules of censorship were drawn up which included no mention of regiments by name, no mention of places and only the Commander-in-Chief could be quoted directly. The ideal situation for GHQ would have been a war correspondent who would write what he was told was the truth and not ask questions. This is exactly what the military got with Philip Gibbs, Herbert Russell, William Beach Thomas, Perry Robinson and Percival Phillips.

Just as the accredited correspondents had made their way out to GHQ, in Britain an article by Charles à Court Repington, military correspondent for *The Times*, was causing outrage. It demonstrated just how powerful the press could be at raising awareness on the Home Front, but also soured the fragile relationship that had grown between the new correspondents at GHQ and their military masters.

At the outbreak of war Repington had remained in London rather than try and piece together events out in the field. In London he used his military and War Office contacts to acquire information about the fighting situation. Having been educated at Eton and Sandhurst and served in the armed forces, he had much military knowledge and the social contacts to obtain this information. By staying in London he was not subject to the military regulations and censorship controls that the accredited correspondents were with the British Army.

Through his friendship with the Commander-in-Chief of the British Army, Sir John French, Repington was invited to visit the Western Front when most correspondents were banned. Conversations with military staff on his first of many visits in November 1914 gave him a unique perspective on how the British Army was functioning on the Western Front.

> During these visits I went round the British lines several times, saw and talked with most of the chief Army and Corps Commanders, discussed matters with the heads of services, had many conversations with officers and men of all arms and all ranks, and with two successive Chiefs of Staff, Sir Archibald Murray and Sir William Robertson, who were two of my oldest and most valued soldier friends.[6]

On one such private visit to the Western Front during the Battle of Aubers Ridge in May 1915, Repington saw confidential information on the use of shells in battle. This led him on a crusade which was to become known as 'the shell crisis'.

> I was enraged by this loss which was attributed by the troops solely to the failure of the guns, due in its turn to want of shells.
>
> I therefore determined to expose the truth to the public no matter at what cost. I sent off to the Times, on May 12, without consulting any one, a telegram which became famous, and stated, amongst other things, 'that the want of an unlimited supply of high explosive shells was a fatal bar to our success.' These words were my own and were not suggested by Sir John French. The original of my telegram contained much more than saw the light when it was published on

May 14. General Macdonogh censored it, and cut out all allusion to the Rifle Brigade casualties, as well as all my remarks about the want of heavy guns, howitzers, trench mortars, maxims, and rifle grenades.[7]

His article, first published in *The Times*, blamed the British losses in the spring offensives of 1915 on the lack of shells, which the Northcliffe press quickly whipped into a campaign demanding Kitchener's resignation, firmly laying the blame at the Government's feet.

FROM 'THE TIMES' MILITARY CORRESPONDENT.
Northern France, Wednesday.
It is important, for an understanding of the British share in the operations of this week, to realise that we are suffering from certain disadvantages which make striking successes difficult to achieve.

In the mists of winter, at the time of my previous visit to the Army, it was not easy to see the German positions. During the clear days of the past week it has been possible to reconnoitre more closely the German line and to observe what a great advantage the enemy gained before his initial offensive was finally brought to an end in the Battles of October and November last.

From a point north-eastward of Ypres, right down to the south where the British right rests, the Germans hold almost all the undulating but clearly marked heights dominating the positions where we stood at the close of the autumn fighting, and still stand, at Ypres, at St Eloi, around Armentières salient,

A British Maxim gun in action.

along the Aubers Ridge, and farther to the south, on the Vimy Heights. Opposite the French, the Germans hold the high ground, and almost everywhere look down on our positions. . . .

LACK OF HIGH EXPLOSIVES.
The results of our attacks on Sunday last in the districts of Fromelles and Richebourg were disappointing. We found the enemy much more strongly posted than we expected. We had not sufficient high explosive to level his parapets to the ground after the French practice, and when our infantry gallantly stormed the trenches, as they did in both attacks, they found a garrison undismayed, many entanglements still intact, and Maxims on all sides ready to pour in streams of bullets. We could not maintain ourselves in the trenches won, and our reserves were not thrown in because the conditions for success in an assault were not present.

The attacks were well planned and valiantly conducted. The infantry did splendidly, but the conditions were too hard. The want of an unlimited supply of high explosive was a fatal bar to our success.

OUR URGENT NEEDS.
On our side we have easily defeated all attacks on Ypres. The value of German troops in the attack has greatly deteriorated, and we can deal easily with them in the open. But until we are thoroughly equipped for this trench warfare, we attack under grave disadvantages. The men are in high spirits, taking their cue from the ever-confident and resolute attitude of the Commander-in-Chief.

If we can break through this hard outer crust of the German defences we believe that we can scatter the German armies, whose offensive causes us no concern at all. But to break this hard crust we need more high explosive, more heavy howitzers, and more men. This special form of warfare has no precedent in history.

It is certain that we can smash the German crust if we have the means. So the means we must have, and as quickly as possible.[8]

To the British public this highlighted the fact that the Government was out of touch with the real military situation in France. This factor influenced many people in the spring of 1915 and contributed to the collapse of the wartime truce between the Conservatives and Liberals, which resulted in the formation of Asquith's coalition government. Out of the debris of the shell crisis, the Ministry of Munitions was created with Lloyd George at the helm. For Repington the future was not so rosy. He was banned from France and not able to visit the Western Front until March 1916.

Douglas Haig banned Repington from the First Army headquarters and laid the blame for the whole shell crisis on the presence of British war correspondents at the Front. In Haig's opinion Repington had supplied sensitive information to the enemy and therefore compromised the security of the British Army. For Haig this affair only increased his distrust of the press and accredited war correspondents at the Front. This attitude was to last well into 1916, even when he was Commander-in-Chief.

After heavy artillery fire on British positions mentioned in Repington's articles, Haig made the following entry in his diary for 18 May 1915:

> I at once wrote to C.G.S. and recommended that no newspaper correspondent be allowed to come so close to the front during active operations.[9]

The shell shortage demonstrated the potential power of the newspaper industry, which A.J.P. Taylor believed was at its most influential at this point during the First World War.[10] The military could no longer keep the likes of Northcliffe, Beaverbrook and the Fleet Street editors ignorant of the situation in France.

> The very absence of press freedom, in fact, created the situation which the Government had been so anxious to avoid – the presence of journalists like Repington going to the front in 'an entirely private capacity'. As far as the press was concerned, the best outcome of the Repington affair was that the Government at last acted upon the newspaper industry's demands for more information about the progress of the war.[11]

What the military and Government learnt was that it was just as important to keep the newspaper proprietors involved in the war effort as it was the war correspondents. By including newspaper proprietors such as Northcliffe in military led campaigns there was less chance of them becoming engaged in crusades which were against the High Command's interest. This period became one of learning for the press, the military and the Government which resulted in the foundations of a trusting relationship, evident after May 1917. It was the beginning of what Sanders and Taylor described as absorbing the power of the press.

> By absorbing whenever possible the power of the press into the service of government, by making some of its members an integral part of the defence of the realm, and by the provision of honours and appointments to certain leading editors and proprietors thereby giving them a vested interest in the survival of the system, the British Government was thus able to exploit the enormous potential of the press for the duration of the war.
>   In short, the British press became the servant of official propaganda more out of willing acquiescence than as a result of Government coercion.[12]

The first British accredited correspondents to join the British Army in the field at GHQ for an indefinite period were John Buchan,[13] Philip Gibbs, Percival Phillips, Herbert Russell and Valentine Williams.[14] This group changed from time to time when correspondents were ill or away lecturing and writing books. Other correspondents who passed through the press camp at GHQ included Basil Clarke, H.M. Tomlinson, Hamilton Fyfe, Filson Young, Percival Gibbson, George Dewar, Prevost Battersby, Frederick Palmer and Henry Nevinson.
   John Buchan replaced Henry Nevinson for *The Times* and *Daily News and Leader* in May 1915. Nevinson was now the accredited correspondent for the *Manchester Guardian* in the Dardanelles. Buchan was an unusual choice as he had no previous

Mr Herbert Russell of Reuters agency being presented to the King, Abbeville, 9 June 1917.

experience of war correspondence and had made his name as an author. Born in 1875, the eldest child of a minister of the Free Church of Scotland, he was educated at Hutcheson's Boy's Grammar School and Glasgow University. He was awarded a scholarship to Oxford and became President of the Union in 1898 and also began his career as an author. Between 1901 and 1903 Buchan worked in South Africa with the task of the resettlement of the country after the Boer War. In 1907 he became the literary adviser to T.A. Nelson, publishers, where he first turned to writing history. At the outbreak of the First World War John Buchan was thirty-nine, seriously ill and bedridden. At this time he started his *History of the Great War*, which was published by Nelson and by the end of the war amounted to twenty-four volumes. He also began his novel *The Thirty-Nine Steps*. In 1915 Buchan had recovered sufficiently to join the staff of *The Times* and make his way to France as an accredited war correspondent at British GHQ.

A new face on the Western Front was Herbert Russell, the Reuters' correspondent who had been reporting from the Gallipoli campaign before moving to GHQ in May 1915. He was the eldest son of the novelist W. Clark Russell, born in 1869. Educated at the Royal Grammar School, Newcastle upon Tyne, Russell started his career in journalism with the *Newcastle Chronicle* before joining the *Daily Express* when it was launched by Sir Arthur Pearson.

For those newspapers which could not afford to support a correspondent on the Western Front or had not had their correspondent selected there was the option to take the Reuters' output from Herbert Russell. After being published in their own newspapers, most of the articles written by the accredited correspondents were recycled a few days later and used in newspapers all around the Empire and world. Local and provincial newspapers in Britain tended to rely on this method as they did not have the resources and finances for correspondents on every Allied Front. This diet of recycled reports was supplemented by news from local soldiers home on leave, letters from soldiers at the Front and news and pictures from local families with men fighting in France.

All the accredited correspondents were billeted in a small house in the village of Tatinghem which was near General Headquarters at St Omer. When the five correspondents first arrived they were received by the Commander-in-Chief, Sir John French, who made a speech welcoming them to the British Army and set out the facilities which would be freely available to them.

> He was pleased to welcome us within his Army, and trusted to our honour and loyalty. He made an allusion to the power of the Press, and promised us facilities for seeing and writing, within the bounds of censorship.[15]

The war correspondents now had the chance to pursue the truth of the events on the Western Front. It was also an opportunity for them to make amends and move away from the poor image their profession had been given by the Government and military authorities between August 1914 and May 1915. The introduction of journalists to the Western Front could have helped the Home Front in their search for the truth. What was created, however, was a group of correspondents who conformed to the great conspiracy, the deliberate lies and the suppression of the truth.

By a stroke of genius on the military's part they were able to keep the war correspondents compliant on the false pretext that they had access to any part of the Front and could write whatever they wished, as long as it did not infringe the rules of censorship. Most importantly the war correspondents were given an officer's uniform and the right to wear a green armband, the mark of the intelligence services answerable to Brigadier-General Charteris and Press Officer Colonel Hutton Wilson. They had become another part of the Army, a tool in the propaganda machinery. Accordingly they were not able to speak freely and to seek the truth because of the conflict of interest which existed between giving the Home Front a true idea of the war and the need to remain loyal to their military masters.

Philip Gibbs, in a conversation with one of his Army censors, discovered that the Press Officer's orders from the Chief of Intelligence were to waste the time of the war correspondents brought to GHQ.[16]

When William Beach Thomas arrived on the Western Front to replace Valentine Williams at the end of 1915 he too confirmed the story that some of the press officers had orders to waste the correspondents' time.

> Just before I reached Tileque the chief of them [Press Officers] was told in precise terms to 'waste the time of the correspondents'. The War Office had given way to pressure, but still clung to the idea of escaping any publicity not officially provided.[17]

The official history tended to support the view that correspondents were needed to add legitimacy to what was actually a policy of suppression.

> The new Commander-in-Chief [Haig] was averse to the press representatives being 'spoon-fed' and held the view that when, for military reasons, it was necessary to withhold information from the public, it could only be done with the co-operation of the correspondents.[18]

This conflicting loyalty was expressed by Lyn Macdonald and leads one to the conclusion that when the press and the military authorities joined forces the first casualty was truth. The reporting of the truth of the war had ceased to be the main objective of the war correspondents.

> It was a brilliant move. From now on, the war correspondents, attired in the King's uniform, were, to all intents and purposes, Officers of the Army, conscious of their debt to it and conscious too of their duty to keep up morale and to reinforce that 'continuing loyalty' of the people at home.[19]

The daily routine of the war correspondent, with official censor in tow at all times, tended to be one of piecing together stories of the valour and achievement of the British Army – watching preliminary bombardments, trying to get as close as was safe to the fighting front and then interviewing anybody behind the lines, from wounded soldiers to German prisoners. On 14 July 1916 Perry Robinson explained how the war correspondent structured his day.

> The plan of the war correspondent is, on such an occasion, to push up with your motor-car as far as the regulations or the enemy will let you go. Then you leave the car in some place where it is least likely to get in the way of our traffic or the enemy's shells, and go on foot. We went by the way where the wounded were dribbling back to the first dressing station. It is always a dreadful sight, and grows none the less dreadful by familiarity; the lightly wounded coming walking down, their wounds in head or limb hastily done up in a handkerchief or with the bandage of an emergency dressing by themselves or by a comrade, those more seriously hurt but still able to limp or walk being helped by another with an arm round the waist; some carried pick-a-back; saddest of all, those who can only come on stretchers, some unconscious, some able to move an arm or to look up and smile – they will always smile – but a terrible sight all of them.[20]

Every morning after breakfast the accredited war correspondents were briefed by the Press Officer on any overnight developments and actions which had taken place. From this information the fighting line was divided up into sections and the correspondents drew lots for which areas they would cover that day. At the start of a new offensive they would leave for their allotted zones before dawn with their Press Officers in tow to witness the preliminary bombardment and tour the rear areas talking to the wounded, prisoners of war and walk over newly captured land. This was a time when the correspondents gained a personal view of war in the traffic going to and from the Front lines. By mid-afternoon the correspondents would move further back to the Divisional and Corps Headquarters in their sections to gain the latest battle information and reports. It was a way of adding detail and information on the larger scale of battle to the personal experiences they had already witnessed in the morning. At approximately 4:30 p.m. all the war correspondents would meet up back at GHQ and over a cup of tea outline their narratives from their respective fronts. Once all the information from the correspondents had been pooled, each retired to their rooms to compose dispatches on their typewriters before dinner at 8:30 p.m.

Once reports had been written they were submitted to the waiting censors with their blue pencils, then sent on to the signals at GHQ where they were telephoned back to the War Office, London who distributed them to the various newspapers around the country and Empire. After the report left GHQ the War Office in London had no right to censor the material in any way and the newspapers had to print reports in full without alterations.[21]

> We identified ourselves absolutely with the armies in the field, and we wiped out of our minds all thought of personal 'scoops', and all temptation to write one word which would make the task of officers and men more difficult or dangerous. There was no need of censorship of our dispatches. We were our own censors.[22]

The correspondents had become sponges of the Army, absorbing their version of events and then turning it into patriotic valour and achievement fodder for the masses on the Home Front. The truth disappeared under the façade that censorship regulations were in force to prevent the enemy from gaining access to information which might be of use to them. But who was the real enemy to the warring generals and accredited correspondents, the Germans or the public and politicians in Britain who had the power to bring an end to the war through other means?

However, as Gibbs admitted, the correspondents did not really need regulations as they were their own censors and therefore the Army's control of information cannot be considered the only reason why the Home Front was ignorant of the fighting. William Beach Thomas promoted the same idea concerning censorship in his book *A Traveller in News*.[23]

At first glance it would appear that the suppression of the reality of war by the military was to save the reputations of the generals and commanders, whose goal was total victory over the German Army, or at least a major foothold in Flanders from which they could guard against further German attack on the British Isles. Yet undercutting this is the self-censorship of the war correspondent for the benefit of the Home Front, which they did not want to unduly alarm.

> The real aims [of the military] were, first, to provide colourful stories of heroism and glory calculated to sustain enthusiasm for the war and ensure a supply of recruits for the front, and second, to cover any mistakes the high command might make, preserve it from criticism in its conduct of war, and safeguard the reputations of its generals.[24]

Douglas Haig, First Earl of Bermersyde (1861–1928), Lieutenant-General commanding First Army Corps (August 1914–December 1915). He replaced Sir John French as Commander-in-Chief of the British and Empire Forces on 19 December 1915.

This view that P. Knightley put forward was not a complete picture of the relationship between the military and the press. It is incorrect to believe that the British press was being controlled by the Government or military and, as Colin Lovelace identified, the press during the First World War was too powerful an institution to be stifled.[25] The press was willing to circulate official propaganda because it was working towards the same goals or, as Sanders and Taylor pinpointed, 'because of a coincidence of views'.[26]

It appears that the relationship between Haig and the press was in a constant state of flux. It began as one of distrust at the start of war, but developed into cooperation during the Battle of the Somme as propaganda became more important in influencing and manipulating politicians and the Home Front. From Haig's writing at the Battle of Atbara in 1898 one can discern his dislike of the war correspondents and he would doubtless have preferred them to have stayed in London where they were easier to control.

> The class of war correspondent is very low indeed, . . . The work performed by all newspaper correspondents is most degrading; they can't tell the whole truth even if they want to do so. The British public likes to read sensational news and the best war correspondent is he who can tell the most thrilling lies.[27]

Haig seemed cautious and suspicious about using the war correspondents to his advantage as they tended to meddle in the important affairs of the war, which might destroy the support given by the Home Front. Haig's views of the war correspondents were recorded in his diary for 13 June 1915. Having lunch with Percival Landon, special correspondent at the *Daily Telegraph*, and Brinsley Fitzgerald, French's Private Secretary, the topic of conversation turned to the Repington affair.

> The former [Fitzgerald] was anxious that I should relax my orders that 'no correspondents should be allowed to go beyond the Lawes River towards the front.' He admitted that I had good reasons for objecting to the presence of correspondents after Repington's article in The Times about our gun positions near La Couture. And he said the intrigues which the Northcliffe Press were engaged in were astounding. Now five correspondents had been authorised to represent the English Press and they were to be staying at St. Omer. Of the five, Northcliffe had managed to have practical control over three. I said all this showed additional reasons why my rule should not be relaxed, but I said that if a correspondent wished for any good reason to go forward beyond the line named, I would have each case considered on its own merits, and if the reasons were adequate, a 'pass' would be granted. He thought this would be quite satisfactory.[28]

Later, at the end of 1915 when William Beach Thomas joined the correspondents at GHQ and interviewed Haig, it would appear that the Repington episode was still a matter of contention.

> The first time that I had an interview with him he brought up the incident of The Times military correspondent. Colonel Repington came over by special invitation to spend a day or two at the front, and had written a dispatch which, it was alleged, caused a battery to be shelled. It was as good as proved that the shelling and the dispatch had no connection whatever; but the incident was deeply impressed on the military mind. When General Haig resuscitated the incident I could not help retorting: 'But he was a soldier!' I thought then and I think now, that a civilian, a trained journalist, accustomed to reporting is much less likely to give away any secrets than a writer technically skilled in warfare. He is not interested in the technique but is deeply interested in the more human and general aspect.[29]

Philip Gibbs' first impressions of Haig were that he scorned the presence of journalists at the Front.

> For a time we believed that our doom was sealed, knowing his strong prejudice against us, and in the first interview we had with him, he did not conceal his contempt for our job.[30]

It would appear that paranoia was the driving force behind the military's policies with regard to news and censorship at this time. The war correspondents had been sent to GHQ to report in a more humane way than the official military line. At all costs they were not to be trusted.

They suggested that our private letters should be tested for writing in invisible ink between the lines. They were afraid that, either deliberately for some journalistic advantage, or in sheer ignorance as 'outsiders,' we might hand information to the enemy about important secrets. Belonging to the old caste of Army mind, they believed the war the special prerogative of professional soldiers, of which politicians and people should have no knowledge. Therefore as civilians in khaki we were hardly better than spies.[31]

This may have been the case in June 1915. However, the relationship between correspondents and the military was a rapidly changing one, mirrored in part by the developing trench warfare tactics to which the generals were having to adjust. For them it was a time of experimentation with new forms of warfare, new weapons technology with creeping barrages and artillery plans, new infantry formations and attacking strategies which needed time to perfect. As the generals became more confident about their battle tactics, so they became more open with the press and war correspondents. The tactics employed at Loos in September 1915 were to be the model for the British generals' offensive battles until late 1917. For the war correspondents too, Loos was to become the standard formula for the reporting of battles.

Already by June the official reporter and new correspondents were working together. Swinton, the author of 'Eyewitness', was invited to dine with the accredited correspondents.

It was a case of the professionals entertaining the amateur 'black leg', who had been essaying their work. After the criticism which had been directed at me during the past eight months, it was a pleasant surprise to find myself amongst a set of such friendly and hospitable hosts.[32]

Six weeks later Swinton's 'Eyewitness' descriptions from the Front ceased, no longer required as the output from the accredited correspondents fulfilled the military's requirements. By the autumn of 1915 neutral and foreign correspondent bureaus on the British Western Front were being developed and by the time of the Somme in 1916 the military correspondent Repington had interviewed Haig; such was the pace of change between May 1915 and May 1917.

NOTES

1. P. Knightley, *The First Casualty* (Quartet Books, 1982), p. 79.
2. The *Daily Mail*, Monday, 19 April 1915 (London).
3. The *Daily Express*, Saturday, 13 March 1915 (London).
4. The *Daily Mail*, Friday, 23 April 1915 (London).
5. The *Daily Mail*, Wednesday, 21 April 1915 (London).
6. C. Repington, *The First World War, 1914–1918. Personal Experiences, Volume I* (Constable & Company, 1920), p. 27.
7. Repington, *First World War*, p. 36.
8. The *Daily Mail*, Saturday, 15 May 1915.
9. R. Blake (ed.), *The Private Papers of Douglas Haig, 1914–1918* (Eyre & Spottiswoode, 1952), p. 93.

10. A.J.P. Taylor, *English History, 1914–1945* (Oxford University Press, 1992), p. 26.
11. T. Royle, *War Report* (Grafton Books, 1989), p. 133.
12. M. Sanders and P.M. Taylor, *British Propaganda During the First World War* (Macmillan Press, 1982), p. 31.
13. Replaced by Perry H. Robinson in April 1916.
14. Replaced by William Beach Thomas in December 1915.
15. P. Gibbs, *Realities of War* (Heinemann, 1920), p. 22.
16. Gibbs, *Realities*, p. 11.
17. W.B. Thomas, *A Traveller in News* (Chapman & Hall, 1925), p. 105.
18. J.E. Edmonds, *The Official History of the Great War; Military Operations, France and Belgium. December 1915–1st July 1916* (Shearer Publications, 1986), p. 147
19. L. Macdonald, *Somme* (Papermac, 1984), p. 80
20. H.P. Robinson, *The Turning Point; The Battle of the Somme* (William Heinemann, 1917), pp. 59–60.
21. Gibbs, *Realities*, p. 19; B. Clarke, *My Round of the War* (Heinemann, 1917), p. 174.
22. P. Gibbs, *Adventures in Journalism* (Heinemann, 1923), p. 231.
23. Thomas, *Traveller*, p. 106.
24. Knightley, *First Casualty*, p. 81.
25. C. Lovelace, *British Press Censorship During the First World War*; Boyce, Carran and Wingate, *Newspaper History: from the 17th Century to the Present Day* (Constable & Company, 1978), p. 307.
26. Sanders et al., *British Propaganda*, p. 30.
27. G.J. Groot, *Douglas Haig 1861–1928* (Unwin Hyman Limited, 1988), p. 63.
28. Blake, *Private Papers*, p. 95.
29. Thomas, *Traveller*, p. 105.
30. Gibbs, *Adventures*, p. 232.
31. Gibbs, *Realities*, p. 10.
32. E.D. Swinton, *Eyewitness* (Hodder & Stoughton, 1932), p. 123.

LOOS, SEPTEMBER 1915

The Battle of Loos in late September 1915 was the first major offensive to be fought under the new rules allowing accredited war correspondents to visit the fighting front. This was the period in which war correspondents became household celebrities, their dispatches filled full pages of the newspapers and their names became part of the headline news itself.

The plan for the Loos offensive was successively postponed from early August to the final date of 25 September 1915. It had been initiated by Joffre's threat that without the full cooperation of the British he might be dislodged and the French politicians would resolve a separate peace. Kitchener, therefore, had ordered Sir John French to follow Joffre's directive and carry out the Loos plan.

At the time Haig voiced the opinion that the chosen area of battle was one where a rapid advance would be impossible; it necessitated attacking across coalfields and through a 'wilderness of miners' cottages'.[1] As Alan Clark pointed out, the Loos' pylons which stood at the pitheads outside Loos village gave the Germans perfect observation of the whole Front and consequently of the preparations for battle.[2]

The Battle of Loos was to be the first time the British Army used gas on a wide scale across a battlefield. It was used to try and compensate for the lack of high-explosive shells available at the time and the deficiency of heavy guns in the pre-attack bombardment. Haig wrote to Sir William Robertson about the importance of gas to the success of the attack.

In my opinion, under no circumstances, should our forthcoming attack be launched without the aid of gas.[3]

He believed that the assault should be postponed until conditions became more favourable if the wind was not blowing from a direction between north-west and south-west, yet this was overruled by GHQ. It would seem that much now hinged on the success of the gas to help in the breakthrough of the enemy lines. Plans were drawn up for the use of gas which might penetrate up to a distance of 2 miles, which would enable the troops to rush the Germans' second-line defences. However, on the appointed day what little wind there was blew in the wrong direction, the gas therefore having a negligible effect, except that it hung around the British Front line and poisoned its own men.

The first day's battle began on 25 September at 6 a.m. with six British divisions climbing out of their trenches and walking towards the German Front line through no man's land. The military tactics for the first time underlined the need to gain as much enemy land as possible rather than calculated strategical objectives, probably in response to the lack of shells and artillery resources. The official history emphasized this change in battle strategy.

An army chaplain tending British graves.

Instead of a series of deliberate advances from position to position, every effort was to be made to press forward and gain as much ground as possible in the first rush.[4]

The Battle of Loos witnessed a dramatic change in the tactics of the generals in charge. This altered the way in which the common soldier's life was valued in any offensive. From this time operations were justified, particularly the number of casualties, on the basis that they were a way of weakening the enemy through attrition rather than a planned quick breakthrough.[5]

For the first time too war correspondents with their censors were out early that morning taking up positions on the high ground as close as possible to the fighting. However, the first news of the ongoing battle for Loos to reach the Home Front was from Sir John French's headquarters in a dispatch called 'BRITISH OFFICIAL REPORTS'.

Sir John French reports as follows:–
General Headquarters, Sept. 26, 9.50 a.m.
Yesterday morning we attacked the enemy south of La Bassée Canal to the east of Grenay and Vermelles.

We captured his trenches on a front of over five miles, penetrating his line in some places to a distance of 4,000 yards.

We captured the western outskirts of Hulluch, the village of Loos and the mining works round it, and Hill 70.

Other attacks were made north of the La Bassée Canal which drew strong reserves of the enemy towards these points of the line, where hard fighting took place throughout the day with varying success. At nightfall the troops north of the Canal occupied their position of the morning.

We made another attack near Hooge on either side of the Menin Road. The attack north of the road succeeded in occupying the Bellewaarde Farm and Ridge, but this was subsequently retaken by the enemy.

The attack south of the road gained about 600 yards of the enemy's trench, and we have consolidated the ground won.

Reports of captures up to the present include about 1,700 prisoners and eight guns, besides several machine guns, the number of which are not yet known.

The report in Friday's German communiqué that we attempted to make an attack on the previous day south of La Bassée Canal which broke down under hostile artillery fire is false. No attack was attempted.[6]

What the official report lacked in human interest the war correspondents at the Front made up for in their dispatches which were the main topic in all the newspapers on 29 September 1915. Each paper boasted of the special angle it now had on the war: 'FULL ACCOUNT OF THE BRITISH ADVANCE, BY OUR SPECIAL CORRESPONDENT AT HEADQUARTERS IN THE FIELD',[7] 'FIRST STORY OF THE GREAT BATTLE',[8] or 'VIVID STORY OF THE GREAT BATTLES OF THE SLAG HEAPS'.[9] No longer was a battle described in long-winded military terminology, but the war correspondents were giving the readers on the Home Front an insight into the fighting of the common soldiers in the trenches. The *Daily Chronicle* correspondent Philip Gibbs reported from British Headquarters on 26 September, the day after the start of the Loos offensive.

The attack which has begun a battle along 500 miles of front started, as far as the British lines were concerned, before the dawn broke yesterday. For several days previously the usual artillery bombardment had increased in intensity on both sides.

Here in Flanders, the enemy, as though suspecting movements of the troops behind our lines, expended a great quantity of shells, especially opposite the Ypres salient, so that the destroyed city had its ruins churned up again by high explosives.

Then on Friday there was a lull before the storm which was about to break with greater violence. It seemed as though these millions of men on both sides of the line were waiting in tense expectation of fate. . . . Then suddenly the bombardment began. All the batteries from the Yser to the Somme seemed to fire together as though at some signal in the heavens in one great salvo. The earth and the air shook with it in a great trembling which never ceased for a single minute during many hours. . . .

But it was of good augury. Never before in this war have our guns spoken in such loud clamour. This was the work of all those thousands of men in the factories at home who have been toiling through the months at furnace and forge. They had sent us guns, and there seemed to be shells enough to blast the enemy out of his trenches. Our chance had come for a real attack.

It began. East of Vermelles, south of La Bassée Canal, and in the plain of Lens, our men were out of their trenches before daylight and at deadly grips with the enemy.

A ruined street in Loos.

They were advancing steadily over ground which was no longer barred to them impregnably by the enemy's trenches, upon which they had peered through sandbags and loopholes for many months. Those trenches had been smashed and crumpled by our artillery fire, and only in the dug-outs were men still living, dazed by the intensity of the bombardment and stupefied into their inevitable surrender.

It is too soon yet to give any details of this heroic advance to the outskirts of Hulluch and through the village of Loos to the neighbouring minefields and the slopes of Hill 70.

No man saw the attack unless he took part in it, and then only his own immediate environment. The battalions disappeared into a fog of smoke from shells and bombs of every kind. They fought behind a veil from which came only the noise of battle and later the first stream of wounded.

The divisions engaged in this struggle yesterday fought with the spirit of men who knew their Empire's life depends upon them, and gave their own lives with noble generosity. Among them were battalions of the New Army, 'Kitchener's men', who charged with a valour beyond words of praise, and with a passionate courage, which swept away all resistance – a terrible resistance – until their object was attained and their sacrifice consummated.[10]

Valentine Williams of the *Daily Mail*, reporting on the same day as Gibbs, witnessed similar action.

The tension of the past few weeks was broken yesterday by the thunder of the guns which rolled almost incessantly throughout the day right along the Allies' front from the North Sea to the Vosges. . . .

The region about Loos where we have made an advance of several thousand yards over a front of five miles is typical mining country, its flatness broken only by numerous slag-heaps, tall, black, pointed hills, pit-heads and squalid villages generally surrounded by clumps of trees. From Grenay the land rises to Loos, a large village which is easily distinguishable even at the longest distance by a very striking landmark in the shape of a bridge-like pit-head christened by our soldiers 'The Tower Bridge'. From Loos the ground descends and rises again to where Lens, the mining city, lies on the slope of a ridge surrounded by industrial suburbs and pit-heads.

It is too soon to write in any detail about the operations, as fighting is still in progress. The attack at Loos completely surprised the Germans, according to the prisoners taken there, with many of whom I spoke this afternoon. They describe our bombardment as 'unspeakable,' and say that the first thing they knew about the assault was the appearance of lines of British troops streaming away over their trenches to the right and, the next moment, the inrush of a horde of khaki-clad figures upon their trenches from three sides. They declare that their ammunition ran out and their rifles, for reasons which they profess to ignore, became useless, so that they were obliged to surrender.

A long green strip of waste ground beside a railway station completely occupied by German prisoners – such was the heartening prospect that met my eyes this afternoon at the railhead from which the prisoners in the present fighting are expedited to the coast for transhipment to England. I reached the railhead about half-past two and found some 750 Germans standing and sitting about in the sunshine. A motley group of French women and children stared open-mouthed at the unusual spectacle from behind the sturdy figures of the British escort with fixed bayonets. Close at hand the horses of the troops of cavalry who had brought the prisoners down from the front were tethered. In the centre of the picture was a staff officer looking rather worried at the prospect of dealing with the dense crowd of prisoners, who seemed to fill every inch of the field. Some 500 more prisoners were already in a long train standing on the adjacent siding.

The prisoners stood and sat there just as they had been at Loos and in the neighbourhood yesterday, their uniforms of grey-greens with red piping all smeared with mud. There were a score or so of wounded among them, men with faces hugely swollen beneath bandages thick with clotted blood, men with their heads bound up and their hair matted with blood, men with arms in slings, the swelling caused by the ligature bulging from under their shirt sleeve.[11]

The two articles highlighted the fact that the war correspondents had not actually experienced as much of the battle as perhaps they would have wished. From their vantage point, a black slag-heap beyond Noeux-les-Mines, the battlefields of Loos were hidden behind the smoke and dust of war. It seems a strange choice of vantage point for the correspondents; was it chosen with their safety in mind or because the military wanted to limit their access to the battle? This decision naturally influenced the correspondents' dispatches because they only had the noise of the artillery and the returning wounded and prisoners on which to base these early reports. Often, in order to enhance their dispatches, the correspondents would give a detailed account of the local environment through which the troops might be advancing and state that as the fighting was ongoing it was premature to write of results.

John Buchan, correspondent at *The Times* and the *Daily News and Leader*, reported the Battle of Loos in a typical manner.

> When it is possible to tell the full story of Saturday's doings the British people will find that they have good cause for pride in the new armies they have raised since last September. Old Regular battalions and Territorials played their part in the advance, but the central movement on Loos was entrusted to one of the new divisions.[12]

In all the reports from the accredited correspondents there was no mention of the first British attempt to use poisonous gas in this offensive battle. A general remark on the secrecy of High Command during the Battle of Loos by Philip Gibbs might suggest that the war correspondents were unaware of the use of gas.

> It was the habit of our High Command to conceal its objectives and minimize their importance if their hopes were unfulfilled.[13]

However, even if the war correspondents had known that gas was being used by the British Army it is unlikely that this information would have been passed by the censors for their dispatches. The Allies had an image to uphold on the Home Front and with neutral countries, and the use of gas, if known to the world, might have damaged the British cause.

Readers on the Home Front at the time did indeed learn from the correspondents that some of the new Kitchener battalions had been involved in the battle. However, in order to find out which battalions these were the reader would have had to become something of an investigator by examining the casualty lists that were to follow and scouring provincial newspapers for letters from soldiers at the Front.

The outcome of the first day of fighting around Loos, after some initial British success, was deadlock as the British troops met the undestroyed wire of the newly prepared German second line. Yet reading the war correspondents' confident descriptions of the events they hardly justify the results obtained. Only the dispatch from John Buchan gave a hint of the problems with a warning to the public to be patient.

> In a war so vast as this, where everything is in large type, and anxiety is spread over days and weeks instead of hours, it is difficult to keep the barometer of public opinion steady. Consequently, one may repeat, even at the risk of being a bore, that the ordinary man at home will do well for his own comfort to remind himself constantly of the great and dominating facts of the situation, to refuse to be dismayed by delays and checks, and to remember that the most successful campaigns Britain has ever fought have been full of depressing and even apparently hopeless moments.[14]

Studying the war correspondents' dispatches on the first day of the Battle of Loos the question arises whether their lack of detail of the actual battle is due to military censorship or the fact that they themselves did not know the results of fighting. Of course the latter is a more probable explanation – the war correspondents knew only as much as the military generals themselves while fighting was in progress. The results and conclusions drawn on the success of the Battle of Loos would take days and weeks to filter back to GHQ and be fully realized, by which time they were old news to the Home Front.

On the right flank during the first day troops broke through the German Front line and so Haig called for the reserves (21st and 24th Divisions). French, who had been jealous of Haig, had kept these new Kitchener reserves far in the rear behind the First Army. The journey of the two divisions up to the Front on 25 September 1915 was described by the Official history.

It was like trying to push the Lord Mayor's procession through the streets of London, without clearing the route and holding up the traffic.[15]

It took three days for the two divisions to march into position in the Front line trenches. The reason for this was that movement to the Front line could only be carried out between 6 p.m. and 5 a.m. for fear of being spotted by enemy observation aeroplanes. During the day the troops rested in billets and late on 25 September they were still over 40 miles away from the firing line. They were in no condition to face immediate action – they had had no food, had marched several miles, and were exhausted. The march to the battlefields of Loos by the 64th Brigade was described by the Brigadier-General in command as having been

. . . carried out over heavy plough in necessarily irksome formation by compass-bearing. The absence of all transport necessitated the man-handling of machine-guns with their ammunition, also 1,000 bombs per Battalion, and 50 additional rounds per man. After two nights and days under arms on the march, it is not too much to say that the men arrived on the battlefield in an exhausted state. Nevertheless there was never a word of complaint, and the elan with which the advances were made was nothing short of astonishing.[16]

The official communiqué issued from General Headquarters reporting the fighting of 26 September mentioned nothing of the problems the new Kitchener battalions had been experiencing in moving up to the battle or their progress during the second day of Loos.

General Headquarters, 10.30 pm, 26th September.
There has been severe fighting to-day on the ground won by us yesterday, the enemy making determined counter-attacks east and north-east of Loos.

The result of this fighting is that except just north of Loos we hold all the ground gained yesterday including the whole of Loos itself.

This evening we retook the quarries north-west of Hulluch which were won and lost yesterday. We have in this fighting drawn in the enemy's reserves, thus enabling the French on our right to make further progress.

The number of prisoners collected after yesterday's fighting now amounts to 2,600. Nine guns have been taken, and a considerable number of machine guns.

Our aeroplanes to-day bombed and derailed a train near Loffres, east of Douai, and another which was full of troops at Rosult, near Stamand. Valenciennes Station was also bombarded.[17]

Philip Gibbs also failed to mention the problems which faced the new Kitchener battalions in his dispatch. However, the blame for not being able to write about the results of the day's fighting rests firmly with French and there is a suggestion in this dispatch that the Commander-in-Chief indeed had something to hide. The dispatch ends strangely with Gibbs not portraying the continued battle as an outright success and even giving the impression that it was hard to tell whether the Allies had lost or gained. This was left for French to sort out and answer at a later date.

To-day – Sunday, the 26th – while the fighting was in progress, there was brilliant sunshine and a cloudless blue sky, good for artillery observation.

Through all the day there was no cessation to the awful cannonade. Of the results nothing can yet be said until the Commander-in-Chief lifts the veil which hides them all. . . .

British General Headquarters, Monday, Sept 27.
The great battle which began before dawn on Saturday last still continues along the whole front, and where the British are advancing is intensely concentrated along the line between La Bassée and Lens, with the French on our right working upwards from the captured town of Souchez. . . .

Hour after hour the cannonading continued, and to sit like an ant on the edge of the field of fire was an experience which no man could forget.

But the human side of it was invisible. None of those generals or staff officers who were gathered at different parts of the line upon the rising ground could see through the veil to where masses of brave men were fighting and falling and struggling forward in the dreadful business out there.

Battalions and Brigades went into the smoke and fog, and their progress was only known when little voices whispered to men lying out in far fields at the end of telephone wire, to which they listened with strained ears. From all parts of the field of the battle the whispers came, and were passed on to headquarters, where other men were listening. This brigade was doing well. That brigade was hard pressed. The Germans were counter-attacking at this or that point. From behind the mist came the news of life and death, revealing things which no onlooker could see, things which cannot yet be told.

To-day our men were fighting a continual action with varying successes at different points, with losses and gains which cannot be summarised or sorted out until the Commander-in-Chief has them all in his hands and gives us the net result in those sentences of his which we read as message of our fate.[18]

Valentine Williams of the *Daily Mail*, like Gibbs, did not mention the results of the day's fighting, choosing instead to make a feature of the weather to fill newspaper column space. With dispatches such as these it may be more important to consider what is not said. Each time weather descriptions are more prominent than the fighting of the day, maybe there is strong reason to believe that the battle was not going in the Allies favour and was, therefore, not discussed. The only other possible reason for this might be that the correspondent had been nowhere near the battlefield that day.

Sunday, Sept. 26, 8pm.
Heavy fighting is in progress about Hulluch and Hill 70. The Germans are counter-attacking in force. The guns have been thundering continuously since noonday. The grey weather in which dawn broke yesterday and which in the course of the day turned to rain has passed away. To-day saw the resumption of the Indian-summer with a westerly breeze and hours of warm and delightful sunshine. . . .

The Army is full of confidence. It is buoyed up with the sudden change from stagnation of the winter to the present state of activity.[19]

Percival Phillips actually mentioned that battalions of the new Kitchener army were involved in the second day of the Loos offensive. However, the Home Front reader received little information about what happened to the new soldiers climbing over the trench top into no man's land. The article was vague and the Home Front was unlikely to understand what a 'heavy price' essentially related to in terms of numbers of men.

The New Army proved itself a worthy successor to the Army of tradition. As fine exploits will be recorded of the wresting of this strip of mining country from the invaders as those performed at Ypres and Festubert and other historic spots within the unbroken British line.

Battalions of the New Army gained their first experience of heavy fighting while capturing a position as strong as many stormed by the veterans of a year ago. The price was heavy, but they paid it without faltering. We may be proud of them.[20]

How the raw recruits managed to walk across no man's land as calmly as they did is not known because the war correspondents' passing remarks did not convey how harrowing this must have been. Alan Clark in his book *The Donkeys* set the scene.

As the British infantry advanced they started to come across little pockets of dead and dying from the detachments of the 2nd Brigade that had pressed too far the previous day. Some of these, delirious, stood up and screamed at them to turn back, or to fetch stretcher-bearers, or to duck down and join them in an adjacent crater. But the discipline of the two Divisions never wavered.[21]

The two divisions entered the Battle of Loos on 26 September with an attacking strength of just under 10,000 men. Within three-and-a-half hours of battle their casualties mounted to 385 officers and 7,861 men;[22] the Germans had such

Cheerful 'tommies' wearing German helmets.

insignificant casualties that they were not recorded at all. This adds another dimension to Percival Phillips' phrase, 'heavy price'.

From the German Front line, through the fog across no man's land, could be seen lines of advancing troops in wave formation, walking towards them. With their machine-guns in position they gunned down the newly trained British troops where they stood in no man's land, the German soldiers hardly believing what they were witnessing. They nicknamed this scene 'Leichenfeld Von Loos' ('field of corpses').[23]

Although barely mentioned by the war correspondents in their dispatches, the protection and misuse of these two new Kitchener divisions was to become a sore point in the relations between French and Haig. In November 1915 both were to very publicly blame each other for the failure of the Loos offensive to achieve its full potential. The official history of the Battle of Loos examines the effort of these new recruits and explains the failure of the 21st and 24th Divisions to reach and take the German's second line. This suggests the failure was mainly as a result of the inexperience of the new recruits, who lacked battle discipline.

The 21st and 24th Divisions failed because the direction of large bodies of troops is an art which cannot be acquired in a year of hard training. Rank and file, if of good will, can be taught the elements of their duties – to march, shoot and obey – in a few months. Soldiers may thus be created in a short time, but not Officers; still less Divisions, which, composed of all arms, require not only that individuals and units should be fully trained, but also a knowledge of staff work and team work which takes much experience and long practice to acquire.[24]

What would have been disturbing to the Home Front had the information been available is the way in which these newly formed divisions were regarded by the warring generals. The divisions were sent into battle without first being given any time to acclimatize to the alien environment. In the end maybe they had just become victims in a power game between Sir John French and Sir Douglas Haig, who were more interested in their pursuit of personal glory.

> The 21st and 24th Divisions were imperfectly trained, had never been in the line, far less in battle, and did not know the ground; but given the opportunity which had been offered, with the German infantry on the run and guns limbering up and going, they were probably adequate to take a certain advantage of it.[25]

The official history neglected to explain the generals' rivalry and their roles in the failure of reserves to gain the German's second line. Haig accused French of keeping the reserves too far from the Front and refusing to hand them over early enough on 25 September to exploit the earlier successes. In turn French insisted that these divisions had been placed in Haig's possession in plenty of time to take advantage of the German collapse, but criticized Haig and his First Army for not making arrangements to ensure clear access for the reserves to reach the Front.

On its way to the Front on 25 September the 64th Brigade (part of 21st Division) were held up for over an hour by a train accident and orders issued at 10.30 a.m. that day did not reach the brigade until midday, and were not completed till 4 p.m. The troops suffered as the battalions had to move off to the Front without having any hot food because their vehicles had been delayed by congestion. They did not reach their allotted attack position until 7 a.m. on 26 September. By this time there was no way these troops could have taken the German's second line, as fresh German soldiers had been deployed, their defences had been rebuilt and strengthened with more barbed wire and the British divisions' artillery was not yet in position to aid the progress of the infantry.

The official history implied 'in retrospect' that the raw recruits of these divisions were seen as participating in an experiment to deploy new battle attack ideas. Fresh troops, untarnished by the fighting, might bring new vigour to the battle plan, having not picked up the habits of soldiers who had been in the war many months. This was an inferred opinion expressed by the Commander-in-Chief of the day. For the generals it would seem that their new volunteer army had little value except as an experiment to test untried ideas on the battlefield. The official history explained that

> Indeed the Commander-in-Chief selected the 21st and 24th Divisions, because he shared the opinion expressed at the time by some officers who had been in the Ypres salient, that Divisions long engaged in trench warfare, had got out of the way of attacking and manoeuvring in the open, and therefore it was preferable to employ untried ones.[26]

The Commander-in-Chief had selected troops who had never been in the Front line trenches, let alone gone over the top to storm the German defences. They had never

Field Marshal Sir Douglas Haig at the victory
march of the Allied troops, London, 19 July 1919.

faced enemy fire and had themselves only been in possession of rifles since the end
of May 1915. It would seem the 21st and 24th Divisions, which had landed in France
less than two weeks before on 9 and 10 September, were to be the British generals'
new weapons against the enemy in the Battle of Loos.

The British High Command's tragic blundering at Loos did not go unnoticed, even
though not reported in the London press, and soon after the battle, in December,
Sir John French was replaced as Commander-in-Chief. However, this decision had
little to do with the power of the press, but owed much to the underhand dealings of
Haig and William Robertson, whose access to the Prime Minister and the King
influenced their view of the battle as a failure.

French in his dispatches from the Battle of Loos in turn blamed Haig for its failure
and destroyed any papers which could have implied otherwise. Eventually Haig got
French removed and himself selected as the new Commander-in-Chief. What is
paradoxical about this situation is that after Haig had called for French's removal, he
then continued to use the same tactics employed at Loos on a much grander scale
during the Battle of the Somme.

P.H. Liddle attributed a change in the psychological make-up of battle for the
common private soldier to the events at Loos, and yet this had little effect on the
Home Front.

For those who experienced it and survived, Loos expunged the last of any
lingering vestiges of innocence about the nature of battle experience in
France.[27]

The Home Front did not understand just how costly the sacrifice was on the Western Front and this fact would not penetrate their consciousness until after the war had ended.

As for the accredited war correspondents they too lost any naïvety regarding their role at the Front. It was during the Battle of Loos that Philip Gibbs observed the true role of censorship in the propaganda process.

> Again it seemed to us [war correspondents] that the guiding idea behind the censorship was, not to conceal the truth from the enemy, but from the nation, in defence of the British high command and its tragic blundering.[28]

John Buchan wrote of the Battle of Loos,

> I fear we have paid a big price for success.[29]

Messinger in his book on British propaganda in the First World War commented on Buchan's dispatches during the Loos campaign. Messinger suggests that all war correspondents wrote in this way and held the view that the war might soon be over. This diminished with the failure of a breakthrough at Loos.

> His reports were full of detail and tried to bring home to civilian readers some of the less pleasant facts, such as the roads crowded with soldiers and supplies and the destruction of property. But Buchan did not focus on the most painful parts of the experience of soldiers at the front, apparently because he shared the optimism of so many observers at the time that the war would soon be over.[30]

Winter drawing near signalled the end of the campaigning season on the Western Front and the prospect of more heavy fighting in 1916. In October Buchan left the press camp to take up a position in the Army as a lieutenant in the Intelligence Corps where he prepared accounts of battle for the generals and commanders of the British Army. Valentine Williams also left in December as he had been given a commission in the Irish Guards. They were to be replaced by Perry Robinson and William Beach Thomas in time to report on the 'big push' over the Somme. Yet there were already signs that the military were beginning to trust and use the war correspondents to their own advantage within sensitive branches of the Army.

The work of accredited correspondents at the Front during the Battle for Loos had done little to improve the Home Front's knowledge of events and may in fact have increased the gap between their understanding and reality. In the autumn of 1915 Repington was still perplexed by the lack of knowledge that the Home Front had about the war in progress.

> The ignorance of the people concerning war, owing to the censorship, is unbelievable. Lunching at the Hautboy, on my way to my mother's, near Ockham, the other day, the proprietor – a good-class intelligent man – told me that the Serbians were going to beat the Germans; that there was nothing in

front of our Army in France; and that we were going to be in Constantinople in ten days' time. These are the kind of beliefs into which the country has been chloroformed by the censorship.[31]

Both Repington and Gibbs drew the conclusion that censorship regulations imposed upon them by the military were the reason for this unrealistic view. However, in 1916 and 1917, when the military regulations were somewhat relaxed, there was no sign of a corresponding narrowing of the gap between the reality of the soldier's life and the knowledge of the person on the Home Front. One reason for this is contained in John Terraine's assumption that it was the historian who specifically needed to identify phases of the First World War as battles.

It is necessary for historians, in order to trace the outline of this monstrous, perpetual-motion conflict, to identify particular phases of it as 'battles'. . . . But these are titles only; they represent swelling tides in an ocean that was never still. For the soldiers, the difference between a 'battle' and an 'interval' was one only of degree of misery and danger.[32]

The historians were not alone in this practice. This method of identifying battles was also used at the time by the war correspondents in their dispatches and newspapers. Battles such as Loos were headline news and sensationalized by the press, but once the battles had died down so did the news and information from the Western Front. It was as if nothing of interest to the Home Front was happening in France. While in France during quiet periods the soldiers carried out their routines day after day in the trenches; to the Home Front it was as if the war had temporarily ceased. Column space in newspapers fluctuated from a full page spread at the height of battle on the Western Front, to less than a line a week during the winter months. News from other fronts around Europe would then take precedence over the Western Front in an attempt to feed the general public's craving for war news.

The Home Front, therefore, had no idea of the routine of war, and the fighting soldiers were alienated by the war correspondents' dispatches because to them the war was one long battle against being killed. What the correspondents failed to mention in their reports for fear of appearing too mundane indeed contributed greatly to the Home Front's lack of understanding of the reality of war.

After the offensive around Loos the British Army settled down in a defensive position for the winter months. The excitement of the 'over the top' experience had gone, and the soldier had a daily routine and a weekly pattern. There were three parts to the day in the trench cycle for a battalion. After an average of a week resting behind the lines a battalion would move up to the trenches for a stint of anything from three days to a week in the firing line. This was followed by a similar period in the support trenches before returning to the reserve position.

The daily routine for the private soldier in the trenches also followed a three-tier system, which started with 'stand to' just before dawn. This was thought to be the time when the trenches were most likely to be attacked by the enemy and the soldiers would be at the ready on the firestep of the trench to repel any aggressors. During daylight hours the trenches were a quiet place; it was time to catch up on sleep, or clean one's rifle as another soldier kept watch on the firestep. Activity in the trenches was kept to a minimum for fear of being seen by the German observation posts (and the snipers out in no man's land); they could detect movement and the German artillery would focus attention on the area in question.

At night the trenches became a hive of activity. Weary troops at the Front could be relieved by a fresh battalion, the rebuilding of shell-shattered trenches undertaken, working and observation parties sent into no man's land and vital supplies of rations and munitions moved up to the Front line. These routines went on from day to day, week to week with divisions moving around the different sectors of the British Western Front.

The three-tier system also filtered through into Haig's plan for battle. First the artillery would weaken the enemy's defences, the infantry would then advance to take these trenches and lastly the cavalry would push the gains opened up by the infantry through into the enemy's rear.

Some attempts were made by the press to try and bring the experiences of the Western Front to Britain. The *Daily Mail* turned a London park into a Western Front trench mock up through which the general public could walk and there were other such exhibitions held around the country.

Stalemates were not the stuff of daring deeds and the Government needed a war of movement and victories if they were to continue fighting. Most of all they required public support to keep the war machinery turning and consequently propaganda processes were employed to enhance the battle gains and the general portrayal of the war. This propaganda obscured the whole picture of the war, portraying it as a 'Boys' Own' type of story, narrated by the war correspondents and through films such as *Britain Prepared*[33] with its underlying message of a war of movement.

After the breakdown of the Loos offensive in September 1915, the very public feud over tactics between the Commander-in-Chief and his general resulted in Haig replacing Sir John French. Now Haig was free to use the same tactics as French but on a larger scale. At the start of 1916 morale on the Home Front and on the Western Front was at an all-time low. Haig needed a breakthrough to boost the flagging spirits of a country still in principle fully behind the war, patriotic and pressing for military victory.

After an Allied conference on strategical decisions for the coming year at Joffre's Chantilly headquarters the idea of a joint offensive between France and Britain on the Western Front was conceived. The Battle of the Somme was not planned with any strategical foresight or even considered a prize worth winning. It was chosen as the place where the British and French lines joined on the Western Front. Here the two Allies could fight side by side on a grand joint offensive to push the Germans back to Berlin.

The beginning of a new year saw the war correspondents attached to GHQ move to a château near Tileque and the arrival of William Beach Thomas from the *Daily Mail*. A favourite and friend of Northcliffe, he would be with the British Army for most of the next four years.

In February 1916 the Germans launched an offensive against the French on the Western Front. France was now in danger of collapse from the German pressure at Verdun. Britain therefore had two choices, to fight and relieve the French, or attempt to make peace with Germany.

This pressure on the British to relieve the French Army on another part of the Western Front necessitated the Battle of the Somme being brought forward by Haig from August to July 1916. However, by June the German offensive at Verdun had ground to a halt and reached stalemate. A.J.P. Taylor believed that because it ceased a month before the Somme attack it had little bearing on the July offensive.[34]

June of that year saw the Germans send out a peace emissary to the French Government to discuss the possibility of terms. Maybe peace was possible in theory, but in practice, given the strength of public opinion, it was not. In this climate of public opinion, in which a war was still very popular, a compromise peace would have been regarded as no better than a defeat. It was probable that most of the politicians and the ordinary man on the street had no knowledge of the German peace offers and neither did they suspect that the Battle of the Somme would be so grossly mismanaged. The start of the July offensive saw the end of the German suggestions of peace. Britain had invested so much that it was fully committed to France, and therefore the only return for this investment was a total victory over the German Army.[35]

The Battle of the Somme in July 1916 is seen as the turning point in the war for the Allies. Yet it was also the most tragic day of the war for Britain as regards casualties. It is estimated that on 1 July 1916 alone there were nearly 60,000 casualties sustained by the Allies against the deep German defences. Reports of the major offensive were awaited with almost universal optimism from the Home Front.

NOTES

1. A.J.P. Taylor, *The First World War* (Penguin Books, 1966), p. 97.
2. A. Clark, *The Donkeys* (Pimlico, 1991), p. 140.
3. J.E. Edmonds, *History of the Great War; Military Operations, France and Belgium, 1915* (Macmillan, 1928), p. 157.
4. Edmonds, *Great War, 1915*, p. 154.
5. See T. Travers, *The Killing Ground. The British Army, the Western Front & the Emergence of Modern Warfare, 1900–1918* (Routledge, 1993), p. 43, for the concept of 'structured and predictable battle'.
6. The *Daily Chronicle*, Monday, 27 September 1915 (London).
7. The *Daily Mail*, Wednesday, 29 September 1915 (London).
8. The *Daily Chronicle*, Wednesday, 29 September 1915 (London).
9. The *Daily Express*, Wednesday, 29 September 1915 (London).
10. The *Daily Chronicle*, Wednesday, 29 September 1915 (London).
11. The *Daily Mail*, Wednesday, 29 September 1915 (London).
12. The *Daily News and Leader*, Thursday, 30 September 1915 (London).
13. P. Gibbs, *Realities of War* (Heinemann, 1920), p. 125.
14. The *Daily News and Leader*, Thursday, 30 September 1915 (London).
15. Edmonds, *Great War, 1915*, p. 278.
16. R.C. Bond, *The King's Own Yorkshire Light Infantry in the Great War 1914–1918* (volume III, Percy, Lund, Humphries and Co., 1928), p. 796.
17. The *Daily Chronicle*, Monday, 27 September 1915 (London).
18. The *Daily Chronicle*, Wednesday, 29 September 1915 (London).
19. The *Daily Mail*, Wednesday, 29 September 1915 (London).
20. The *Daily Express*, Thursday, 30 September 1915 (London).
21. Clark, *Donkeys*, p. 172.
22. J. Laffin, *British Butchers and Bunglers of World War One* (Alan Sutton Publishing, 1988), p. 35.

23. Clark, *Donkeys*, p. 173.
24. Edmonds, *Great War, 1915*, p. 345.
25. Edmonds, *Great War, 1915*, p. 398.
26. Edmonds, *Great War, 1915*, p. 398.
27. P.H. Liddle, *The Soldier's War, 1914–1918* (Blandford Press, 1988), p. 55.
28. P. Gibbs, *Adventures in Journalism* (Heinemann, 1923), p. 232.
29. J.A. Smith, *John Buchan, A Biography* (Rupert Hart-Davis, 1965), p. 196.
30. G.S. Messinger, *British Propaganda and the State in the First World War* (Manchester University Press, 1992), p. 88.
31. C. Repington, *The First World War, 1914–1918. Personal Experiences, Volume I* (Constable & Company, 1920), p. 57.
32. J. Terraine, *The First World War, 1914–1918* (Leo Cooper, 1983), p. 63.
33. C. Urban, *Britain Prepared* (Urban/Vickers 1914).
34. Taylor, *First World War*.
35. M. Middlebrook, *The First Day of the Somme* (Penguin Books, 1971), pp. 272–92.

THE SOMME, 1 JULY 1916

Harry Perry Robinson joined the accredited correspondents with the British press camp at GHQ in France during April 1916. He replaced John Buchan of *The Times* who had joined the Army as a lieutenant in the Intelligence Corps. Writing for the *Daily News and Leader* and *The Times*, Robinson was at fifty-six the eldest accredited correspondent on the Western Front. He was born in 1859 the son of a cleric and was educated at Westminster School and at Christ Church, Oxford. In 1883 Robinson moved to the United States and began a career in journalism; he edited and owned the *Railway Age* between 1883 and 1900.

On his return to Britain, between 1901 and 1914 Robinson had been *The Times* special correspondent visiting many parts of the world and at the same time writing books. His publications in this period included two novels, books on natural history and a study on America in the twentieth century. At the time of the outbreak of war in August 1914, Robinson was married for the second time and had one son. During the first months of the war he found himself reporting the developments in Belgium before moving across to the fighting front in Serbia in 1915.

Even when reporting from the Front Robinson still managed to pursue his passion for nature. During one quiet period he and a fellow correspondent hunted for specimens of the Purple Emperor butterfly. To assist him in this Robinson had had sent from London some female Emperors which were then placed in a cage within the press château's garden to attract male Emperor specimens. His love of nature was often to find a place in his war dispatches.

It was about the time that Robinson joined the press camp that the accredited correspondents first encountered Sir Douglas Haig in his new role as Commander-in-Chief. This audience took place in a château near to Montreuil where GHQ was then situated and gave the correspondents the chance to put their grievances directly to Haig. Accompanied by General Charteris for support, Haig listened to the problems the war correspondents' had experienced while with the British Army. Topics included the liberty to mention units and the names of troops engaged, to give the honour to the troops and increased recognition of the soldiers, and relaxation of the rules of censorship. Philip Gibbs believed that Haig's ignorance of the war correspondents' purpose or requirements highlighted his blindness to the new psychology of nations in war and their important role within it.

'I think I understand fairly well what you gentlemen want,' he said. 'You want to get hold of little stories of heroism, and so forth, to write them up in a bright way to make good reading for Mary Ann in the kitchen, and the man in the street.'[1]

The King (centre right) talking to Mr Perry Robinson (centre left) of *The Times*, Thiepval, 12 July 1917.

At the end of the gathering Haig promised to make a note of the war correspondents' grievances and where possible relax the rules of censorship. Many of the points raised would indeed be resolved in later phases of the war, as it always took months for changes to filter through the military system.

Yet this meeting was a major turning point in the relationship between the military and press who were for the first time discussing face to face the problems of censorship. Just a year before in May 1915, Haig as Commander of the First Army would have preferred accredited correspondents to be banned from the front lines. Now the correspondents were being invited to Haig's château and asked to comment on their role within the military. This was the start of a period of complete trust between the military and press, a phase which was to be firmly established in 1917.

Robinson made his way to Amiens in the spring of 1916 and a house in the Rue Amiral Courbet owned by Mme de la Rochefoucault. This was to be the British correspondent's base during the Battles of the Somme. Leaving Britain Robinson could sense the Home Front's excitement at the impending offensive. However, he did not share this feeling upon reaching France.

When I left England for the British Front early in April, 1916, there was much talk of the 'great push' which was about to begin. All London whispered of it. I heard men in the railway carriages talk of it as a matter of fact; and on the train which took us to the boat for Boulogne the air was full of tales of it. When I arrived at the front, I found no talk of it at all. . . . In England the belief in the great spring offensive found its justification in the famous saying attributed to Lord Kitchener in the preceding autumn. 'When', it was reported that he had been asked, 'is the war going to end?' 'I don't know when it will end,' he was alleged to have replied, 'but it will begin next April.' And the British people had only a hazy idea of what the organisation of a great Army meant, which is natural, as there had been nothing in British history to teach them.[2]

The Home Front optimism was not shared by the British GHQ because of the uncertain French situation on the Verdun Front. Here pressure on the French Army's trenches had made them reassess their contribution to the 'Big Push' in favour of a reduction of the fighting front and troops. Discussions between Haig and Rawlinson documented in the official history show how plans had now been settled in favour of wearing out the enemy rather than attempting to win a decisive victory. In fact it would seem they were contemplating how this offensive would effect their success a year later.

On the 29th May, Sir Douglas Haig told General Rawlinson, also referring to the matter in a letter to the C.I.G.S., that, in the circumstance of the reduction of French assistance, the first object to be aimed at was the wearing out of the enemy, and that he was to keep in view the necessity for getting troops into favourable positions for the spring campaign in 1917, so as to make sure of success next year.[3]

This was not the news to inspire the troops to action or to gain and keep the support of the Home Front, who wanted an early and victorious end to the war.

Propaganda meant that the realistic view of the battle could not be allowed to reach the private soldier or the common man on the Home Front. Therefore, the propaganda machine which had created 'a war to end all wars' was now in full production on the 'Big Push' which would see the beginning of the end of the war. The British generals also needed to persuade their Allies (mainly the French) that they were still fully committed to a major offensive in 1916.

What is noticeable about the battle and its preparation is the lack of control the generals had after the offensive had begun. This is probably why so much time and forethought went into the preparation and planning for every eventuality during the battle. When a battle was under way all the generals could do was to wait in their GHQ, many miles behind the Front line for hopefully good news about captured objectives and the state of the day's play so that they could plan the next morning's action. By 16 June 1916 Haig speculated as to how the battle should proceed after the first objective had been captured.

Should the enemy's resistance break down, the advance was to be 'pressed eastwards far enough to enable our cavalry to push through into the open country beyond the enemy's prepared lines of defence. Our object then will be to turn northwards, taking the enemy's in flank and reverse, the bulk of the cavalry operating on the outer flank of this movement, whilst suitable detachments (of all arms) should be detailed to cover the movement from any offensive of the enemy from the east. For the latter purpose, the line Bapaume–high ground east of Mary–high ground west of Croisille-Moanchy Le Freux is of tactical importance.'[4]

This communication void between military Headquarters and the troops at the Front during a battle may go some way to explaining the huge casualties experienced on the first day of the Somme. With little control, once an offensive began it was almost impossible to stop proceedings because of the time taken for orders issued from General Headquarters to reach the Front line. This had already been witnessed during the Battle of Loos as the 21st and 24th Divisions moved up to the firing line and on a later phase of the Somme fighting for Flers-Courcelette. It is possible to examine just how long communications and orders actually took to complete. The official history commented on the Somme that

> An important consideration was the time allowed that the fighting troops had to prepare for an attack; it had been estimated that at least six hours are required for the passage of orders from Corps to company commanders. . . .[5]

This was why the generals planned and prepared rigid battle maps which attempted to incorporate every eventuality; as soon as an offensive was under way they had lost control of the situation and could then do very little to alter their course of action.

As more troops moved into the Somme sector for the 'Big Push' it gave the new Kitchener battalion time away from the trenches to prepare for battle. This was a time for battalions to practise manoeuvres and training in mock trenches behind the Front line. At night vital supplies had to be carried up to the front lines and ammunition dumps had to be maintained so that the artillery could sustain their five-day bombardment against the German trenches. For the soldiers in reserve during June this meant dangerous journeys up to the front lines in working parties carrying gas cylinders and bombs. At any moment a shell could drop while the men were transporting their explosive supplies through the rain-flooded trenches. However, it was important that everything was in place for zero hour, and it was not as dangerous as being part of a raiding party out late at night in no man's land, observing how the bombardment was progressing against the enemy's defences. These patrols would crawl out of the trenches and move around in the waste land, checking that no man's land had been cleared of barbed wire and the German defences destroyed.

With more battalions moving towards the Somme in the months leading up to the offensive at the end of June the soldiers had more spare time on their hands waiting for zero hour. There was time for a few inter-battalion boxing competitions and the odd concert, and to watch the exciting bombardment while contemplating the success of the future battle.

The artillery was to play a major role in this preparation as the bombardment was to be the longest of its kind and was intended to wipe out any German resistance, allowing the infantry to walk through the German trenches without so much as a fight. To the war correspondents this bombardment and its fire power was very impressive, as they watched guns amass on this 16 mile front in the weeks before the 'Big Push'. When the bombardment was in full swing the soldiers and generals wondered how anything could survive it. The noise of the guns could be heard back on the south coast of England and with this intensity of fire power the German Army must have expected an attack before too long on this once very quiet sector of the Western Front. Even the war correspondents such as Perry Robinson had never experienced anything like the intensity of this bombardment.

> Never since the war had entered on its stationary phase in the existing positions had there been anything approaching in scope and intensity the shelling and miscellaneous fighting which raged along a hundred miles of front. It was only the overture; but it was stupendous and terrifying, even though what one saw or heard was only a small section of the dreadful whole.[6]

However impressive this show of fire power was, reports from the raids into no man's land brought back a different picture. The artillery were using the 18 pounders as shrapnel shells in the task of cutting the barbed wire which stretched across no man's land. The shell would explode above the ground showering it with steel balls, in theory cutting the wire. However, in practice the shell exploded too soon to cause damage to the wire or too late and exploded harmlessly into the ground.

The British generals had not calculated the number of dud shells that failed to explode during the bombardment, which has been estimated at up to a third of all shells fired. This had been caused by the shell crisis of 1915; in the furore to produce more shells on the Home Front the mass production had led to a reduction in quality.

Reports from no man's land on the numbers of unexploded shells and uncut wire were discounted by the generals and because the German artillery had not fired back in great number it was thought to have been destroyed. Instead of firing back, with the resulting risk of having their artillery pinpointed and blown up before the start of the offensive, the German Army played a waiting game in their deep dugouts, waiting for the bombardment to cease so that they could reply.

The one thing that the British generals had not planned for and could not plan for during the offensive was the weather. As the bombardment started up for its planned five days of intensive fire, the weather changed for the worse. Violent thunderstorms and heavy summer storms started on 24 June, the same day as the bombardment of the enemy trenches began. More heavy downpours occurred on 26 and 27 June and the trenches were in a terrible state, as a private soldier remarked while on a working party 'got wet through and sludged up to the eyes'.[7] It was still raining on the morning of 28 June as battalions moved forwards towards the Front line from their divisional bases. The trenches and roads needed time to dry out and there were fears that the battlefield could be flooded and prevent easy access across no man's land.

Among the war correspondents there was a sense that the British Army was not ready for an assault on the scale of the 'Big Push'. The preparation may have been a grand show of force, but it still failed to extinguish the fear and foreboding of the correspondents and soldiers alike.

Soldiers moving a big gun along a muddy hillside on the Western Front.

To us, looking on, the preparations were a matter of immense interest. It is hardly necessary to say that nowadays war correspondents are taken into the confidence of the Higher Command only to an extremely limited extent; but with the combined observation and inference a group of trained correspondents commonly arrive at a good deal more information than is intentionally given to them. I have less shame in confessing that we all had, I believe, profound misgivings, because those misgivings were, to the best of my knowledge, shared by every man in the Army. I doubt if there was a man in France, outside of that extremely small circle which knew everything, who believed that we were as yet in any way fit for the great offensive or able, if we began, to carry it through to any really large end. There could, perhaps, be no higher praise for those who were in supreme command than is contained in that statement. To every one else the splendour of our Armies, the magnitude of our organisation and resources, the perfection with which our plans had been prepared and were carried out, came as a revelation and an amazement.[8]

At 11 a.m. on 28 June 1916 the planned offensive which was to have been in full swing twenty-one hours hence was postponed by forty-eight hours to 1 July 1916. This was a great blow to all the soldiers who were already moving up to the front lines, as it meant to them the anxious uncertainty of waiting for the 'Big Push' to begin, if at all. The main reason for this deferment was the unusually wet weather. However, it gave the British artillery two extra days to really destroy the German defences and concentrate on the job of clearing uncut wire in no man's land. Consequently, 28 and 29 June were renamed 'Y1' and 'Y2', with 1 July being 'Z'.[9]

On the evening of 30 June 1916 the war correspondents had an unexpected visitor to their house in Amiens – General Charteris, the Chief Officer of the Intelligence section with information on the impending offensive. William Beach Thomas recalls this late night meeting.

General Charteris, the Chief Intelligence Officer, came to us at night in Amiens, and having carefully closed the door and inspected the room almost stagily, announced the Great Endeavour and suggested an appropriate spot beside the road into Albert for watching the battle.[10]

The preparation by the military for the Battle of the Somme included for the first time cooperation with the war correspondents. It was not an everyday occurrence for General Charteris to visit the press camp with details of the best vantage points from which to witness a battle. Charteris had also arranged for the correspondents to use official wires during the first day, so that their dispatches could be sent straight back to Fleet Street to make the morning papers. This contrasts completely with the arrangement at Loos when dispatches reached the London newspapers four days later. In his book on life at GHQ, Charteris describes the arrangements that were made for the correspondents for the opening battle of the Somme.

The correspondents are divided into three parties, each with one officer attached. They will be given full facilities for seeing whatever can be seen. The officers with them have authority to interview Staff Officers to get detailed information. The G.S.O. in charge of Press as a whole will come here everyday to get the latest information available, which the Press correspondents can embody in their articles. In addition to their articles, they will be allowed to send over the official wires in time for the morning papers a joint cable which they themselves will prepare.[11]

With the inside information from General Charteris, early on 1 July the accredited correspondents made their way to a vantage point which overlooked Fricourt on the battlefield close to the Albert–Bapaume road. The attack was set to start at 7.30 a.m., there were clear skies and a temperature of 72°F. However, at zero hour the correspondents could see little of the action for the smoke and dust thrown up by the battle. Philip Gibbs recounted the morning leading up to the start of the offensive.

A staff officer had whispered a secret to us at midnight in a little room, when the door was shut and the window closed. Even then they were words which could be only whispered, and to men of trust. 'The attack will be made this morning at 7.30.'
So all had gone well, and there was to be no hitch. The preliminary bombardments had done their work with the enemy's wire and earthworks. All the organisation for the attack had been done, and the men were ready in their assembly trenches waiting for the words which would hold all their fate. . . .
It was 7.30. This moment for the attack had come. Clouds of smoke had been liberated to form a screen for the infantry, and hid the whole line. The only men

I could see were those in reserve, winding along a road by some trees which led up to the attacking points. They had their backs turned, as they marched very slowly and steadily forward.

I could not tell who they were, though I had passed some of them on a road a day or two before. But, whoever they were, English, Irish, or Welsh, I watched them until most had disappeared from sight behind a clump of trees. In a little while they would be fighting, and would need all their courage.

At a minute after 7.30 there came through the rolling smoke-clouds a rushing sound. It was the noise of rifle fire and machine-guns. The men were out of their trenches, and the attack had begun. The enemy was barraging our lines.[12]

The *Daily Express* correspondent Percival Phillips during much of the Somme battles was in Britain recovering from what his paper described as 'a serious illness incurred during the execution of his duties with our army in the field'.[13] His temporary replacement John Irvine, in his dispatch for 1 July, described the landscape as they waited for the first positive news from the battlefield below.

The great day of battle broke in sunshine and mist. Not a cloud obscured the sky as the sun appeared above the horizon – in the direction where the German trenches lay. But, anon, a purple haze crept up, which grew in intensity as the morning advanced, and the view of distant objects was veiled in obscurity. . . .

From a ridge a little to the west of Albert, overlooking the town and commanding a wide view of the beautiful undulating country, I witnessed the last phase of the bombardment which preceded the advance. It was six o'clock (summer time) when we arrived there. The guns had been roaring furiously all through the night. Now they had, so to, speak, gathered themselves together for one grand final effort before our British lions should be let loose on their prey. . . .

A perceptible slackening of our fire soon after seven was the first indication given to us that our gallant soldiers were about to leap from their trenches and advance against the enemy. Non-combatants, of course, were not permitted to witness this spectacle, but I am informed that the vigour and eagerness of the first assault were worthy of the best traditions of the British Army. I have myself heard within the past few days men declare that they were getting fed up with life in the trenches, and would welcome a fight at close quarters. . . .

We had not to wait long for news, and it was wholly satisfactory and encouraging. The message received at ten o' clock ran something like this: 'On a front of twenty miles north and south of the Somme we and our French allies have advanced and taken the German first line of trenches. We are attacking vigorously Fricourt, La Boiselle, and Mametz. German prisoners are surrendering freely, and a good many already fallen into our hands.'[14]

Beach Thomas, standing on the hill overlooking the battlefield, was becoming frustrated at not being able to interpret what was going on.

Such a view of battle gives no hint of the fortune of the day; and men in high places were as ignorant as we. No true news was known by anyone for hours.

One division could not tell its neighbour division where the men were or how far the trenches were won. Flashes of hope, half-lights of expectation, hints of calamity only penetrated the smoke and dust and bullets that smothered the trenches. . . . The tension was unendurable. The telephones, the carrier pigeons, the guesses of direct observers, the records of the runners, the glimpses of the air-men, all combined could scarcely penetrate the fog of war. The wounded who struggled back from German trenches themselves knew little.[15]

Strangest of all the reports of the moments before the start of the offensive was Perry Robinson's account of the intense bombardment. He was on the same ridge as the other correspondents, trying to measure the rate of the dropping shells with his teeth!

There were places which were like mouths of furnaces, where there burned a permanent glow flecked and illumined with never-ending streams of white sparks. One ordinarily measures the weight of a bombardment by the number of shells that burst in minute. In this case, counting was hopeless. Fixing my eyes on one spot I tried to wink my eyes as fast as the lightning flickered, and the shells beat me badly. I then tried chattering my teeth; and I think in that way I approximately held my own. Testing it afterwards in the light, where I could see a watch face, I found that I could click my teeth some five or six times in a second.[16]

The first day's battle was reported in excitable and optimistic tones, but in a very vague nature. The first reports of the start of the offensive were sent by official wire from the correspondents at about 9.30 a.m.

British Offensive, – At about 7.30 o'clock this morning a vigorous attack was launched by the British Army. The front extends over some 20 miles north of the Somme. The assault was preceded by a terrific bombardment, lasting about an hour and a half. It is too early to as yet give anything but the barest particulars, as the fighting is developing in intensity, but the British troops have already occupied the German front line. Many prisoners have already fallen into our hands, and as far as can be ascertained our casualties have not been heavy.[17]

William Beach Thomas, writing for the *Daily Mail*, believed that

The very attitudes of the dead, fallen eagerly forwards, have the look of expectant hope. You would say they died with the light of victory in their eyes.[18]

Philip Gibbs also reported the battle.

The attack which was launched to-day against the German lines on a 20-mile front began satisfactorily. It is not yet a victory, for victory comes at the end of a battle, and this is only a beginning. But our troops, fighting with very splendid valour, have swept across the enemy's front trenches along a great part of the line of attack, and have captured villages and strongholds which the Germans have long held against us. They are fighting their way forward not easily but doggedly. Many hundreds of the enemy are prisoners in our hands. His dead lie thick in the tracks of our regiments.

And so, after the first day of battle, we may say with thankfulness: All goes well. It is a good day for England and France. It is a day of promise in this war, in which the blood of brave men is poured out upon the sodden fields of Europe.[19]

In a later message from Gibbs at 7.15 p.m. on the evening of 1 July it is clear that the sweeping advance across the Somme had slowed down somewhat as the enemy fought back.

The progress of the battle has been marked by steadily increasing intensity throughout the day, the fighting north of the river Ancre (a branch of the Somme which crosses our line, four miles north of Albert), being particularly severe. The enemy in several of the villages has made a strenuous resistance to our attacks, but the gallantry of our troops has resulted in a gradual working round of various strong points. Fricourt (three miles east of Albert) is now nearly surrounded.[20]

The Observer's reflection on the day's events commented that

A grandeur of being beyond all that our country has known before is purchased for those who live by those who die. For Britain, these days are only at the beginning of what may come. The new Armies, fighting with a valour and fibre never surpassed by any people, have our best hopes.[21]

The Reuters war correspondent, Herbert Russell, sent his first telegram to his office in London at 9.30 a.m., reporting optimistically on the start of battle.

It is too early as yet to give anything but the barest particulars as the fighting is developing in intensity but British troops have already occupied the German front line. Many prisoners have already fallen into our hands and as far as can be ascertained our casualties have not been heavy.[22]

A further telegram sent by Herbert Russell at 1.15 p.m. gives more information about the battle.

'Good progress into enemy territory.' British troops were said to have fought 'most gallantly', and to have taken many prisoners. 'So far the day is going well for Great Britain and France.'[23]

It was not until the second day of battle that the news started to filter through, with more emphasis being placed upon the ferocity of the fighting. Telegrams sent to Reuters during 2 July suggested that all was not well.

'The progress of the battle has been marked by steadily increasing intensity throughout the day.' . . . A telegram at noon on the second day was noteworthy for what it did not say. The hoped-for great breakthrough had not taken place. 'The situation on the British front appears not to have changed since yesterday evening . . . The troops are in excellent spirits.'[24]

With regard to information on casualties for the first day of the Somme, many of the generals at GHQ had little idea of how the battle was progressing. The communication network along the 16 mile battle front had broken down into rumours and conflicting status reports of advancing troops. Haig's first mention of casualties in his diary is on 2 July and the number is seen as normal wastage.

The A.G. reported to-day that the total casualties are estimated at over 40,000 to date. This cannot be considered severe in view of the numbers engaged, and the length of the front attacked.[25]

During the first day of the Battle of the Somme casualties among the British Army amounted to 57,470 men. Martin Middlebrook compared his estimate of the casualty figures with the losses encountered in complete wars.

The British Army's loss on that day exceeds its battle casualties in the Crimean war, the Boer war and the Korean war combined.[26]

However, at the time these types of figures were never mentioned in any war correspondent's dispatches. By the time the true picture of events reached the war correspondents (greatly diluted by GHQ) news of the first day's 'splendid' fighting had already been dispatched and published in the British newspapers. If accurate information on the sheer enormity of the disaster and the full extent of the losses took several days to reach generals at GHQ in France, what hope did the war correspondents have of reporting the truth to ordinary people in England? Maybe the only way to discover the reality of the battle and verify some idea of the casualty figures was not to read official reports and correspondent's dispatches, but to turn to the 'Rolls of Honour' published in newspapers such as *The Times*.[27]

The preparations for war correspondents during the first day of the Somme may have backfired on the military with regard to the use of the official wire to speed up the dispatches back to England. Correspondents had been encouraged by the Army's Intelligence section to send reports hurriedly put together to England before corroborated information was available. When the reality of the Somme started to filter through to the Home Front the output of the war correspondents would be embarrassing to both journalists and military command. It would also affect the morale of the Home Front as a mighty conquest proclaimed on the first day would, over time, turn out to be rather less of a triumph than at first reported. Martin Bell, a present-day war correspondent, calls this effect 'premature exhilaration' and suggests that it could be as damaging to Home Front morale as a total defeat itself.[28]

However, just as the First World War saw the military adopt a new style of warfare, so the handling of information had to go through a learning process. Both the military and press learnt a valuable, but embarrassing lesson from the first day of the Somme. For William Beach Thomas, writing after the war, it became a shameful event in his distinguished career.

> A great part of the information supplied to us by the Intelligence was utterly wrong and misleading. We sent off in common, on their authority, a short cable message to say that all went well for England and France. Neither we nor the Intelligence knew how complete and costly in life was the defeat from Gommecourt to Albert. . . . The dispatches were largely untrue so far as they dealt with concrete results; but I think they must stand as in some measure an historic event. . . . For myself, on the next day and yet more on the day after that, I was thoroughly and deeply ashamed of what I had written, for the very good reason that it was untrue, so far as I had transgressed the limits of description. Almost all the official information was wrong. The vulgarity of enormous headlines and the enormity of one's own name did not lessen the shame.[29]

For the Army's Intelligence section it was an experience in the balancing act of information over censorship, which was not to be repeated. During the Somme the press camp was enlarged to included Allied and foreign accredited correspondents on a permanent footing, which involved the training of new press officers. Neville Lytton, one such trainee who would later chaperon the accredited foreign correspondents on the British Western Front, had to understand the complicated censorship policy.

> My immediate C.O. was now Colonel Hutton Wilson, who ran that branch of G.H.Q. known as ID; for a week I stayed with the British Press at Amiens trying to learn the job of press censorship. It is not quite so easy as it might appear, for it has to be done at terrific pace against time, and the problem of how much information you are giving to the enemy is not fixed, but varies every single day. At that time press censorship was in its infancy and the censors were absurdly over-cautious; later on we got a much better liaison with the operation staff of all units and our methods became more elastic.[30]

As more information on the state of battle reached the Home Front during the early days of July within the British Army there was an apparent power struggle developing against Haig for the prize of Commander-in-Chief. This challenge was led from England by the Chief of the Imperial General Staff, Sir William Robertson. Although the success of 14 July relieved some of the pressure on Haig, there was still heavy criticism about the high casualties from prominent people on the Home Front.

It was because of this challenge to his position as head of the British Army that Haig enlisted the support of Lord Northcliffe to influence the Home Front. Alfred Harmsworth (Lord Northcliffe) was a journalist and newspaper proprietor, born in 1865. His rise in the newspaper publishing world made him primarily responsible for establishing popular journalism and the most powerful man in Fleet Street,

Lord Northcliffe and Mr Winston Churchill outside the Foreign Office, Paris, 29 November 1917.

controlling *The Times*, *Daily Mail*, *Evening News* and *Daily Mirror* at the beginning of the war. Since the war had begun in 1914 Northcliffe had campaigned for Kitchener's appointment to the War Office, against press censorship, for a Ministry of Munitions and then against Kitchener during the shell crisis and for compulsory national service.

At Haig's invitation Northcliffe toured the armies in France during late July before visiting the Italian Front. Labelling himself a special correspondent, Northcliffe's dispatches were first printed in his newspapers before being republished in a book called *At the War*.[31] These dispatches were always very sympathetic to the Haig cause and did much to counteract Haig's critics on the Home Front. Northcliffe said of Haig after his visit to the Western Front,

> Sir Douglas does not waste words. It is not because he is silent or unsympathetic – it is because he uses words as he uses soldiers, sparingly, but always with method.[32]

In his diary Haig talked about his dealings with Northcliffe during Northcliffe's social visit to the Western Front in late July 1916. It certainly adds weight to the theories that this relationship was exploited as a way to silence Haig's critics through Northcliffe and to influence public opinion. Haig's diary records his meeting with Northcliffe and Haig's influence within their relationship.

And N, was, he said, much pleased with his visit, and asked me to . . . send him a line should anything appear in *The Times* which was not altogether to my liking.[33]

Haig later believed that Lloyd George's visit to GHQ France in September 1916 was with the sole intention of finding material which he could use against Haig's Western Front strategy. Shortly afterwards leading articles in the Northcliffe press appeared which were extremely critical of Lloyd George. Haig himself said of Lloyd George

Breakfast with newspaper men, and posing for the cinema shows, pleased him more than anything else. No doubt with the ulterior object of catching votes.[34]

It appears that Haig's relationship with the press and its proprietors was enhanced by their support for him during this period. A letter from Haig to Lady Haig in November 1916 reveals just how much the relationship with the press had developed and how he was now more relaxed around them.

I leave all the questions connected with the Press to 'John' [Charteris] who has a section in his office which deals with them. I only receive some of the principal ones, like Northcliffe and Robinson of *The Times*, Strachey of the *Spectator*, the *Saturday Review* and Such.

But I tell them all that they can go anywhere, and see whoever and whatever they like – there are no secrets. They also can write what they like, but I beg them to remember that we all have the same object, viz, beat the Germans – so they must not give anything away which can be of use to the enemy. I must say that the correspondents have played splendidly. We have never once had to complain of them since I took command.

When I come over I'll try and get Lord Northcliffe to come and lunch with us one day as he has been such a help latterly to the Army and myself.[35]

There had been such a change in the relationship between the Commander-in-Chief and the press since May of 1915 that even Charles Repington was invited to tour the Front and interview Haig. According to Repington his 8 July meeting with Haig was strained to say the least.

He said that he welcomed criticisms, but when I mentioned the criticisms which I had heard of his misuse of artillery on July 1, he did not appear to relish it, and denied its truth. As he was not prepared to talk of things of real interest, I said very little, and left him to do the talking. I also had a strong feeling that the tactics of July 1 had been bad. I don't know which of us was the most glad to be rid of the other.[36]

While the two were never going to become best friends, they were at least meeting in the same room. It is a measure of just how relaxed Haig and the military command were becoming toward the press.

The dispatches of accredited war correspondents for July 1916 detail the same objectives and sector of the Front as the account of my great uncle, Private Woodhead of the 10th Battalion, King's Own Yorkshire Light Infantry (KOYLI).[37] Under the rules of censorship and the Defence of the Realm Act, war correspondents were unable to reveal the names of regiments and the places where they were stationed. To get around this the correspondents would give hints to the Home Front readers as to the troop's origin. Therefore, names such as 'Yorkshire Boys', 'Manchesters' and 'North Country Lads' were given as clues to the Home Front as to the identity of battalions. Most of the Kitchener battalions had been formed from volunteers of local populations and therefore these clues narrowed down the choice of units fighting in a battle. Provincial newspapers could then be consulted as a further source for the activity of a regional battalion, where the Home Front could study the casualty lists, letters and photographs of local soldiers in an attempt to understand a unit's involvement in battle.

By piecing this together with what information is available today from Private Woodhead's diary, the war correspondents' dispatches, the 10th Battalion's war diary of the KOYLI and the 64th Brigade instructions for objectives on the first day in July,[38] it would seem that they all correspond with each other. It is possible, therefore, to draw comparisons between these three types of account and try and identify what is propaganda, the myth of our present-day image of the First World War and the reality of battle.

15955 Private Benjamin Woodhead (1895–1916) of the 10th Battalion, King's Own Yorkshire Light Infantry. He was killed in action, 17 September 1916.

On 6 July 1916 the war correspondents were touring the rear areas of the British Front interviewing troops that had been involved in the first day's fighting on the Somme. The war correspondents were trying to flesh out the events of 1 July with stories and tales from the soldiers who had experienced the fighting first hand. Perry Robinson and John Irvine had been taken by their press officer to talk to the soldiers who were fighting around the Montauban section and Philip Gibbs and William Beach Thomas were with the troops who had fought near Fricourt.

It is important to remember in these articles that war correspondents had been taken to meet soldiers who had been involved in successful operations on 1 July. There is little information from the areas north of Albert up to Serre where the troops had not achieved objectives and, therefore, one can assume that the correspondents were supervised very carefully by their press officers with regard to which troops would be interviewed.

On 6 July both Philip Gibbs and William Beach Thomas had been taken to the divisional billets of the 21st Division at a place called La Chaussée where they talked with the Yorkshire boys of the King's Own Yorkshire Light Infantry. Here Philip Gibbs put together their stories of 1 July.

HEROIC INCIDENTS IN THE ADVANCE.

Philip Gibbs, July 6.
The officer who came round the village with me had a lonely look. After battle, such a battle as this, it is difficult to keep the sadness out of one's eye. So many good fellows have gone. . . . But they were proud of their men. They found a joy in that.

The men had done gloriously. They had won their ground and held it, through frightful fire, 'The men were topping.'

There were a lot of Yorkshire men among them who fought at Fricourt, and it was those I saw to-day. They were the heroes, with other North Country lads, of one of the most splendid achievements of British arms ever written down in history.

Some of them were still shaken. When they spoke to me their words faltered now and then, and a queer look came into their eyes. But, on the whole they were astoundingly calm, and had not lost their sense of humour.

In the first advance over No Man's Land, which was 150 yards across to the enemy's front line trench, some of these men could remember nothing.

It was just a dreadful blank. 'I was just mad at the time,' said one of them. 'The first thing I know is that I found myself scrambling over the German parapets with a bomb in my hand. The dead were lying all around me.'

But a sergeant there remembered all. He kept his wits about him, strangely clear at such a time. He saw that his men were being swept with machine-gun fire, so that they all lay down to escape its deadly scythe.

But he saw also that the bullets were first washing the ground so that the prostrate men were being struck in great numbers. He stood up straight and called upon the others to stand, thinking it would be better to be hit in the feet than in the head. Then he walked on and came without a scratch to the German front line.

Here and in the lines behind there was a wreckage of earth from our bombardment, but several of the dug-outs had been untouched and in them during our gunfire men were sitting, 30 feet down, with machine-guns ready, and long periscopes, through which they could see our lines and first wave of advancing men.

Before the word reached them, those German machine gunners had rushed upstairs and behind the cover of their wrecked trenches fired bursts of bullets at our men.

Each gun team had with them a rifleman who had a crack shot, and who obeyed his army orders to pick off English officers. So they sniped our young lieutenants with cool and cruel deliberation. Two of them who were dressed as privates escaped for this reason. Many of the others fell.

'With so many officers gone,' said one of the Yorkshire lads, 'it was every man for himself, and we carried on as best we could.'

They carried on as far as the second and third lines, in a desperate fight with German soldiers who appeared out of the tumbled earth and flung bombs with a grim refusal of surrender.

'Well, if you're asking for it,' said one of our men – and he hurled himself upon a great German and ran his bayonet through the man's body.

There was not much killing at that spot. When most of our men were within ten yards many of the Germans who had been flinging bombs lifted up their hands and cried 'Mercy!' to those whom they had tried to blow to bits.

It was rather late to ask for mercy, but it was given to them. There was a search into the dug-outs – do you understand that all this was done under great shell fire? – and many Germans were found in hiding there.

'I surrender,' said a German officer, putting his head out of a hole in the earth, ' and I have a wounded man with me.' 'All right,' said a Yorkshire sergeant, 'fetch him up, and no monkey tricks.'

But out of the hole came not one man, but forty, in a long file that seemed never to end, all of whom said 'Kamerad!' to the sergeant, who answered, 'Good day to you! – and how many more?'

They were a nuisance to him then. He wanted to get on and this was a waste of time. But he sent back 42 prisoners with three lightly wounded fellows of his company – he could not spare more – and then advanced with his men beyond the German third line.

Bunches of men were straggling forward over the shell-broken ground towards the German line at Crucifix trench, to the left of Fricourt. They knew that this trench was important, that their lives were well given if they could capture it. And these Yorkshire boys from the hills and dales thought nothing of their lives so that they could take it.

They unslung their bombs, looked to the right and left, where German heavies were falling, cursed the chatter of machine-guns from Fricourt village, and said,

'Come on, lads!' to the men about them. Not one man faltered or turned back, or lingered with the doubt that he had gone far enough.

They stumbled forward over the shell craters, over dead bodies, over indescribable things. Crucifix trench was reached. It was full of Germans who were hurling bombs from it, from that trench and the sunken road near by.

The Yorkshire boys went through a barrage of bombs, hurled their own, worried through the broken parapets and over masses of tumbled earth, and fought single fights with big Germans, like terrier dogs hunting rats and worrying them. Parties bombed their way down the sunken road.

Those who fell, struck by Germans bombs. shouted 'Get on to 'em, lads' to others who came up. In bits of earthworks German heads looked up, white German faces, bearded, and covered with clay like dead men risen. They put up trembling hands and cried their words of comradeship to those enemy boys.

'Well, that's all right,' said a Yorkshire captain. 'We've got the Crucifix. And meanwhile our guns are giving us the devil.' Our gunners did not know that Crucifix Trench was taken. Some of our shells were dropping very close.

'It's time for a red light,' said the Yorkshire captain. He had a bullet in his ribs, and was suffering terribly, but he still commanded his men. A red rocket went up, high through the smoke over all the corners of the battlefield. Somewhere it was seen by watchful eyes, in some O.P. or by some flying fellow. Our guns lifted. The shells went forward, crashing into Shelter Wood beyond.

'Good old gunners!' said a sergeant. 'By God, they're playing the same game to-day!'

But other men had seen the red rocket above Crucifix Trench. It stood in the sky like a red eye looking down upon the battlefield. The German gunners knew that the British were in Crucifix Trench. They lowered their guns a point or two, shortening their range, and German shells came crumping the earth, on either side, registering the ground.

'And where do we go next, captain?' asked a Yorkshire boy. It seemed he felt restless where he was. The captain thought Shelter Wood might be a good place to see. He chose ten men to see it with him, and they were very willing.

With a bullet in his ribs – it hurt him horribly – he climbed out of Crucifix Trench, and crawled forward, with his ten men to the wood beyond. It was full of Germans. At the south-west corner of it was a redoubt, with machine-guns and a bomb-store. The Germans bombers were already flinging their grenades across to the Crucifix.

The wounded captain said that ten men were not enough to take Shelter Wood – it would need a thousand men, perhaps, so he crawled back with the others.

They stayed all night in Crucifix Trench, and it was a dreadful night. At ten o'clock the enemy opened an intense bombardment of heavies and shrapnel, and maintained it full pitch until two o'clock next morning. There were 900 men up there and in the neighbourhood. When morning came there were not so many, but the others were eager to get out and get on.

The Yorkshire spirit was unbeaten. The grit of the North Country was still there in the morning after the first assault.

Queer adventures overtook men who played a lone hand in this darkness and confusion of battle. One man I met to-day – true Yorkshire, with steel in his eyes and a burr in his speech – it was stranger to hear the saxon words he used – rushed with some of his friends into Birch Tree Wood, which was not captured until two days later.

There were many Germans there, but not visible. Suddenly the Yorkshire lad found himself quite alone, his comrades having escaped from a death-trap, for the wood was being shelled – as I saw myself that day – with an intense fire from our guns.

The lonely boy, who was a machine-gunner without his gun, thought that things were 'pretty thick,' as, indeed, they were, but he described the risks of death were less if he stayed still than if he moved.

Presently, as he crouched low, he saw a German coming. He was crawling along on his hands and knees, and blood was oozing from him. As he crawled, a young Yorkshire soldier, also badly wounded, passed him at a little distance in the wood.

The German stared at him. Then he raised himself, though still on his knees, and fired at the boy with his revolver, so that he fell dead. The German went on his hands again to go on with his crawling, but another shot ripped through the tree, and he crawled no more.

It was fired by the man who had been left alone – the young man I saw to-day. 'I killed the brute,' he said, 'and I'm glad of it.'

Our shells were bursting very fiercely over the wood, slashing off branches and ploughing up the earth. The lonely boy searched about for a dug-out and found one. When he went down into it he saw three dead Germans there, and he sat with them for more than eight hours while our bombardment lasted.

There was another lad I met who was also a machine-gunner, and alone in the battle zone. He was alone when fourteen of his comrades had been knocked out. But single-handed he carried and served his gun, from one place to another, all thorough the day, and part of the next day, sniping odd parties of Germans with bursts of bullets.

Another sturdy fellow I met came face to face with a German, who called out to him in perfect English.

'Don't shoot. I was brought up in England and played footer for Bradford City. . . . By Jove! I know your face, old man. Weren't you at the Victoria Hotel, Sheffield?'

It was a queer meeting on a battlefield. One of the grimmest things I have heard was told me by another Yorkshire boy. A German surrendered, and then suddenly, as this lad approached to make him prisoner, pulled the detonator of a bomb and raised it to throw.

'I put my bayonet right close to him so suddenly that he was terrified, and forgot to fling his bomb. Then a queer kind of look came into his eyes. He remembered that the blooming bomb was going off. It went off, and blew him to bits.'

That is war. And the men who have told me these things are young men who do not like the things they have seen. But, because it is war, they go through to the last goal with a courage that does not equal.

The men of this division next day took Shelter Wood and Fricourt, and captured many prisoners.[39]

Beach Thomas' dispatch on Fricourt contained the same stories about Crucifix Trench and Birch Tree Wood as Gibbs' but his was more of a narrative of the main events than individual soldiers' tales and stories.

Fricourt village, the strongest place in the line, was left to the enemy, unattacked. On the other side of it an amazing fight was fought. This German promontory of Fricourt, flanking the right of the advance, was full of undestroyed machine-guns (I found the very emplacements two days later), and before the end of the day it was given rather wider berth than was at first intended. But in the face of every menace, up the great bare regular hill in front of them the troops, most of them English, struggled so persistently that at the end of the day they reached the landmark at the top, sent up a signal that they were in Crucifix Trench, under the conspicuous Calvary and line of trees that fringe the slope.

The difficulties were of every sort. A message had reached them that the division on the left had won all along the line, but the news was premature. The advance was an advance only of small groups who could not make good the ground till later. So this division was running a double gauntlet between walls of enemies. Machine-guns fired from the right flank and left flank, sweeping all lateral roads clean. Our officers were picked off by snipers, who stood beside each enemy's machine-gunner. Crucifix Trench, which had been knocked to pieces by our enemy guns, gave poor shelter and was bombarded heavily from ten to twelve on Saturday night by the enemy. But our miners, including the Durham Light Infantry, fought a great fight, and the men did more than hold firm. They made sallies and pushed out little efforts everywhere, especially in the small woods.

I saw a score of these efforts from the opposite hill during the next two days. This new army division – who for no fault of their own had partially failed in a previous battle – began an advance which lasted without intermission for three days and three nights. They fought up the hill and over the crest, always advancing but never gaining the length of a cricket pitch without close and bitter opposition.

The next day you could tell by the bodies lying on the field just where the machine-guns had mown a swathe, and what troops – at that point all were English county troops – had 'faced the music' nevertheless. They had crossed a sunken road, exactly as a driven rabbit would cross a ride, with expert shots on either side. Some were left in the road, but some got over.

The advance never ceased, in spite of all, till the full objective was attained, the end reached, the aim won after seventy hours. And it was all intelligent fighting, never blind. Once when they were checked, lighter trench mortars, which did admirable work throughout, were hurried forward, the artillery were informed, and a flanking piece of trench cleared by bombs. Then the advance went on as before. Scores of individual feats of daring were recorded.

A machine-gunner (who had made one of the small party feeling their way into Birch Tree Wood towards the right) found himself in the sequel all alone, forced to hide for the whole night in a shell hole, while the wood was being blown to pieces. I had seen that very bombardment from the opposite hill by our artillery. Incidentally he killed one German officer who had painfully raised himself on his haunches to shoot one of our wounded.

In front of Crucifix Trench, to the left, the enemy made repeated bombing attacks from a redoubt. In reply, a wounded officer and a handful of men even made an effort to take this hornets' nest themselves. It was not finally captured until the third night, but in it there surrendered 700 prisoners; 400 more were taken in Crucifix Trench. Two other woods, where German machine-guns had successfully hidden, were occupied earlier.

In the end, after two days of bulldog fighting scarcely surpassed in the war, the division joined hands with troops advancing through and behind Fricourt. The German line, the strongest fortifications ever elaborated on the field, was broken, and a mile and more of land behind it carried and made strong.[40]

The correspondent for the *Daily Express*, John Irvine, who had been with the troops who fought at Montauban that day still managed to write about the troops around Fricourt as well. This is because of the pool system which operated between the British war correspondents on the Western Front. Personal scoops were not allowed and the war correspondents divided the fighting line up between them and then pooled information at the end of each day because it was the only way to cover such a vast front.

John Irvine's information on the troops fighting around Fricourt, mentions that they had fought at Loos. The 21st Division, including Private Woodhead's battalion, had been some of the first of the new Kitchener Army to fight at Loos and this, along with the named objectives, is a major clue to the soldiers' identities.

Some further details also have reached me to-day concerning the hot work of the Yorkshires (who fought at Loos). Their immediate objective was the Crucifix Trench – a formidable stronghold of the enemy. The moment they quitted their sheltered positions a deluge of bullets was rained on them. The casualties were heavy, but the survivors, cheering and shouting, reached the Crucifix, and after a desperate hand-to-hand combat, in which they were able to 'get in' with the bayonet, they drove the enemy before them, killing and capturing considerable numbers.

Many of their officers fell in the assault. One officer with a bullet in his ribs displayed conspicuous courage. The Germans now were counter-attacking, but this gallant Yorkshireman, regardless of his wound, led a small party of volunteers into an adjacent copse known as Shelter Wood. In the south-west corner of the wood they ran up against a redoubt which was full of Germans, and were forced to take whatever cover they could find. Signals were made to inform our artillery, who were shelling the copse, that some of our men were there. The Germans noted the signals and directed a terrific fire on the wood and the Crucifix Trench. Our men stood it all without flinching, though by this time, as a sergeant remarked to me, 'it was a case of every man for himself; but we stuck it.'[41]

Private Woodhead's diary of events around 1 July were a personal account written at the time. It was not subject to any Army censorship, although it had been made an offence to keep personal diaries, for fear they might be captured by the enemy. His account begins on 28 June, which would have been the original start date, if the weather had not intervened.

Everything postponed for 48 hours, still living in suspense. June 29th just like any ordinary day nothing unusual happened. Bombardment a little stronger if anything. June 30th we are leaving here for trenches and attack at 7.30 a.m. Reach Aberdeen Ave[42] at 7 p.m. and have to wait until 11 p.m. before we can move up into front line. Get up at last and (Saturday morning) trenches absolutely full of troops, and I never heard such a bombardment in all my life. Our chaps pull up all the barbed wire for a clear passage,[43] all the chaps singing as they worked. Daylight, July 1st and every gun we possessed was firing its very hardest. French mortars, Stokes guns, 18 pounders, Oh! what a din. Well half an hour to go and everybody happy. At last, the first wave[44] over just as three mines[45] go up and I thought the world was coming to an end. Our lads singing and straight over to their object[46] they went and cling to it until late Saturday night and then relieved to go in Germans' first line as support. Was taking a message to Headquarters and a big shell blew me out of the trench, I knew nothing until the afternoon and it covered me with green stuff. Well all the night we were shelled in Brueifiar trench (very heavily). July 2nd, the 62nd Brigade make an attack and succeed in taking Shelter Wood.[47] Our Brigade[48] captured about 1,000 prisoners. On working and rations parties all that day and night. July 3rd, we had a bit of a rest to start with and then dug a fire step all round the captured trenches. At 8 p.m. we were relieved and marched to Derrancourt[49] sidings and got some grub. Left there 6 a.m. and cycled to a place called La Chaussée. Been here two days now and it is lovely to be away from the guns a little while. July 6th we had an inspection by Division General[50] and he thanked us for our gallant conduct.[51]

It had taken Private Woodhead's battalion hours to get through the jam-packed trenches full of troops to their allotted position on the Fricourt to La Boisselle road next to Sausage Valley. A reason for this delay is found in the war diary of the 64th Brigade.

The delay was caused by the condition of the working party of the 14th Northumberland Fusiliers (pioneers) allotted for the work with the Brigade. This party had been ordered to be in position by 11.15 p.m. but many of its men and the officer in command were drunk, and blocked PIONEER AVENUE. The party finally got to its place about 1.15 a.m. The whole Brigade was in position about 3 a.m.[52]

It would take less time to get to their objective for the day of Crucifix Trench. For the 64th Brigade the 9th and 10th Battalions KOYLIs would lead the attack with the 1st East Yorks and 15th Durham Light Infantry in close support.

If Private Woodhead's description of the last hours of the bombardment is anything to go by, then the Germans must have known it was almost time for the start of the British offensive and what would have made the Germans doubly sure were the exploding mines at 7.28 a.m. However, by a stroke of luck the battalion moved out into no man's land before the bombardment lifted at 7.30 a.m., and the first wave was already on its way as the three mines exploded, as observed by Private Woodhead, which was 7.28 a.m. This is important because it gave the battalion an advantage, which many battalions did not have by waiting until the allotted 7.30 a.m.

> The attack of the Brigade was led by the 9th and 10th K.O.Y.L.I. During the final five minutes of intense bombardment, the leading companies left the Russian sap and succeed in crawling forward into No Man's Land.[53]

When the bombardment finally lifted, the Germans leapt from their deep dugouts straight to their machine-gun posts to find many British battalions were just climbing out of the trenches, into full view. As the KOYLIs had already crawled across no man's land by this time, the heavy machine-gun fire which was met caused less damage and could be dealt with at close range.

> As soon as the bombardment ceased, the lines of both battalions rose and went forward, and in spite of heavy losses, they pressed on, never wavering, the lines in the rear coming up and filling the gaps. The German wire had been well cut, and the Yorkshiremen, although met by a shower of stick-bombs, rushed in and overran the position.[54]

By 8.00 a.m., only half an hour from the start of the 'Big Push' the 64th Brigade had covered a mile of ground and reached the Sunken Road. Some parties had made it to Crucifix Trench, the brigade's first objective.

> 8.15 a.m. All four Battalions and the attached working party pressed on and reached the first objective – CRUCIFIX TRENCH – ROUND WOOD – close behind the artillery barrage.[55]

At 2.30 p.m. an attempt was made by the 10th Battalion KOYLIs and the 15th DLI to take Shelter Wood from the position of Crucifix Trench, which failed.[56] The official history recorded the cost of the day's fighting.

> The capture of the two lines of trenches had been carried out within ten minutes from the start, but at great cost, more than half of the two leading battalions, including most of their officers, having fallen.[57]

From this point until 3 July, when they were relieved, they spent their time consolidating the position achieved. The casualties to the 9th and 10th Battalions

KOYLIs and sheer exhaustion prevented any further advances on 1 July. Heavy losses had been incurred from the machine-gun fire in no man's land: during the first hour almost half of the soldiers and most of the officers had been killed or wounded.

Private Woodhead was one of the lucky ones this time and he cheated death only by being knocked unconscious by a shell while running back across no man's land with a message for Headquarters. Lying unconscious probably saved his life in no man's land as he was not exposed to the machine-gun fire which showered the waste land, cutting down so many soldiers where they stood. The war diary of the 21st Division reports that

> The 9th K.O.Y.L.I on the right and the 10th K.O.Y.L.I. on the left also suffered severe casualties from M.G. fire when crossing 'No Man's Land'.[58]

Brig-Gen Headlam commanding the 64th Infantry Brigade described this scene in more detail in his account of 1 July.

> 7.25 a.m. The front lines of the 9th and 10th K.O.Y.L.I. began to leave the trenches with view of getting well into 'NO-MAN'S-LAND' before the artillery barrage lifted from the German front line. The succeeding lines followed in quick succession. Almost immediately after our men began to show in the open the German Machine Guns got to work, not withstanding the barrage. As soon as this lifted many Germans also lined their parapets, and opened fire. The majority of the casualties in the Brigade occurred during the passage of 'NO-MAN'S-LAND'. The men, however, never hesitated, and went straight on in gallant fashion. They dealt promptly with the Germans on the parapets and once the main German network of trenches was passed, we suffered no damage from hostile rifle or M.G. fire from our immediate rear.[59]

Further advances were impossible because the officers who might have led their troops onwards lay dead or wounded on the battlefield. One major reason for the huge number of deaths in no man's land was directly related to the weight each soldier had to carry. The average soldier's pack weighed about 66 lb,[60] and this, coupled with the shell-torn wasteland terrain that they had to cross, made quick and speedy movement of the troops to their objectives impossible in the face of the German machine-gun fire. They simply became bogged down by the weight of equipment which included trenching tools, groundsheets, two gas helmets, sandbags, water bottles, mess tins, extra rations and ammunition.

In their dispatches concerning the fighting at Fricourt, the war correspondents mention all three objectives of the 10th Battalion, KOYLI which were 'Crucifix Trench, Shelter Wood, and Birch Tree Wood'.[61]

On the day in question, 6 July 1916, the 10th Battalion, KOYLI had returned to divisional billets behind the Front line for inspection at a place called 'La Chaussée'.[62] Philip Gibbs commented on this inspection.

> I went today again among the men who fought at Fricourt. Some of them had come back behind the lines, and outside their billets the divisional band was

playing, but not to much of an audience, for of those who fought at Fricourt in the first assault there are not large numbers left.[63]

In these two sentences casualties are only referred to vaguely. A fairer picture of the real casualty figures is contained in Private Woodhead's account for the first day, which seems to correspond with the battalion's records and the divisional reports of casualty figures.

On 6 July Private Woodhead was at a 21st Divisional parade and inspection by Divisional General, Major-General D.G.M. Campbell; this would account for Philip Gibbs' mention of the divisional band playing. Private Woodhead recalled

Having nice weather and have about 250 left out of about 1,000. In our section we have 20 out of 53.[64]

This provides more information about the casualties mentioned by Philip Gibbs. The war diary of the 10th Battalion supplements Private Woodhead's figures.

Officers; wounded 16; killed 9;
Other ranks; wounded 292; killed 50; missing 135.[65]

A battalion's fighting strength was about 750 out of 1,000 men at any one time, and therefore Private Woodhead's figure of 250 men left compares favourably with the battalion's records. These accounts make it possible to understand more of the language of the war correspondents concerning the number of casualties. Philip Gibbs went on to describe the picture of the battalion's casualties, but just how many on the Home Front could understand what these numbers actually meant?

After the battle, such a battle as this, it is difficult to keep the sadness out of one's eyes. So many good fellows have gone. . . . But they were proud of their men. They found joy in that. The men had done gloriously.[66]

It should be appreciated that there have been changes in the English language – new words have replaced old ones and meanings have altered. There are differences between the essentially romantic feudal language of the 'high' diction which died with the First World War and present-day rhetoric. This can be seen in certain phrases used, such as 'to perish' ('to die'), 'the fallen' ('the dead on the battlefield') and 'the red wine of youth' ('the blood of young men').[67] With hindsight, if this is correct, the style of language used by the war correspondents in the context of the First World War might have at least warned the Home Front of high casualty rates considering the tight censorship laws in operation.

It is possible that the style of language used during the First World War has contributed to the present-day misunderstanding of battle. The war correspondents' use of language tended to make the battle appear romantic, recalling medieval notions of combat, and may explain the changes in language which later took place.

It was a bayonet duel as two medieval knights might have fought in the old days with heavy swords.[68]

The focus on the sensational aspect of battle has been enhanced by out-of-context footage from such films as *The Battle of the Somme*, 1916.[69] The over-the-top scene lasts for less than a minute in a film of 1 hour 17 minutes and yet today is recalled as the main image of the Battle of the Somme.

Propaganda information needed to be exciting if it were to keep the public interested in the news from the Western Front. Stalemates and trench warfare did not provide the images of success and victory which the Home Front craved in return for their support. Propaganda was, therefore, used to exaggerate and appeal to the patriotism of the public in order to encourage support for war. Consequently, the propaganda image of the First World War has naturally become part of the present-day perception of battle.

The war correspondents' dispatches and the film *The Battle of the Somme*[70] made war exciting to the reader or viewer and in doing so part of the reality of battle was lost. From Private Woodhead's entries in his diary it would appear that war was far from the exhilarating 'over the top' into no man's land experience portrayed in the media. During his year of service before his death Private Woodhead had only been ordered four times to

Fix bayonets, load up rifles, Advance.[71]

Far from the exciting descriptions of hand-to-hand combat, the soldier in the trench was more likely to be killed by the constant shell fire between the lines. The average routine of a private soldier consisted of seven days in the trenches, another seven days in support and then time spent in billets behind the lines. Private Woodhead found that much of his time was taken up in working parties, digging firesteps, clearing barbed wire or carrying supplies up to the Front. The rest of the time was spent moving around the different sectors of the Western Front on tours of duty or relaxing at the cinema, enjoying a game of football between battalions or boxing competitions or even the odd concert.[72]

It was in such quiet times that the war correspondents would adopt the direct propaganda approach in the form of straight appeals to the Home Front. What else was there to write about, as it was hard to make the routine of everyday war sensational and exciting? The answer was to exploit the important role of the Home Front in keeping the soldiers fighting on the Western Front. A dispatch of 24 July 1916 by Philip Gibbs first thanked the Home Front for its achievements, but then made a direct plea to the labour force involved in the production of guns and ammunition to continue its work.

The work of our artillery is a wonderful achievement, and all the success we have gained during this great battle has been largely due to the science . . . and labour of all those thousands of men at home who have sweated in soul and body to make the guns and ammunition.[73]

Later in the same dispatch Philip Gibbs ended with some words of warning.

The munition workers at home must not relax their efforts if we are to continue our success. It is by their labour that the lives of our men can be saved. All the time it is a battle of guns.[74]

Another tactic was to report the German side of battle, on how they thought, worked and lived across no man's land. These were put together from interviews with German prisoners, touring captured dugouts and the interpretations of letters and documents left behind by the German Army.[75]

Private Woodhead's diary is not, however, free from all propaganda, in keeping with the film material and the dispatches of the war correspondents. Private Woodhead was also influenced by some propaganda themes and reiterates them in his writing. Nevertheless, it is important and interesting to take into consideration the propaganda ideals he was unable to accept and reproduce. He had firm views on how to recruit the boys at home, after his arrival on the Western Front.

Oct 26th 1915. On the road here are plenty of graves. They are the silent testimonies and would make the chaps at home *join* if they could see them.[76]

Other types of propaganda which can also be identified in Private Woodhead's diary are those that have been passed on to him in the form of exaggeration and lies heard. In the preparation for the Battle of the Somme the number of guns coming up to the Front was commented on.

On our front there is 97 guns to every square mile, with 4,000 rounds of ammunition.[77]

However, although this information was passed down to the soldiers it was simply not true. The figure was more likely to be 467 heavy guns for the whole 16 mile British Front, which works out at only 30 guns per square mile.[78]

What Private Woodhead does not choose to reinforce is the style of language used in the dispatches of the war correspondents. He expressed no desire to fight hand-to-hand with the enemy, which contradicts Philip Gibbs' notions of the romantic medieval style of battle.

Here at least, in spite of the machine-gun, men looked into each other's eyes and were killed advancing in the sight of their enemies . . . for a couple of hours it was more like old-fashioned fighting.[79]

To Private Woodhead war was not just another cricket match or a game, as the war correspondents would have the reader believe, but it was real. For all the soldiers the war was a localized experience, individual soldiers fighting for their bit of wood, trench or ditch in which the world outside mattered little. Theirs was a fight for survival on a day-to-day basis, not part of a phase or battle or war game on which the war correspondents reported. Martin Bell comments on the outlook of a soldier in war, 'The war may begin as a fight for his country, but it ends as a fight for his life'.[80]

While the war correspondents combed the billets and back areas of the British Front for heroic stories, localized fighting continued and the generals prepared for the next phase of the push forward. By 14 July 1916 the British troops would again be on the offensive for Bazentin Ridge. The difference in this second offensive on the Somme was that there was to be no long drawn out preliminary bombardment to wear out the enemy, just an energetic, but brutal, five minutes to start at 3.45 a.m.

The dawn attack was a success and, starting from the northern edge of Mametz Wood, the soldiers advanced in an easterly direction capturing the woods which safeguarded both the villages of Bazentin Le Petit and Bazentin Le Grand. However, the speed of the success of 14 July must have taken the generals by surprise as they were ill prepared to play the advantage and use the cavalry. Reports from the Front on that morning declared High Wood[81] to be empty of Germans. The cavalry finally reached the Front at 5 p.m. and did not advance until 7 p.m., by which time the Germans were back in High Wood and little was achieved.[82]

The good news from the Front reached Fleet Street the following day with the *Daily Chronicle* declaring in its headline that the 'GERMANS SURRENDER FREELY'. Its correspondent Philip Gibbs managed to dispatch a brief report on the day's results and successes.

PRESS CAMP, 2.30 p.m., Friday.
Later reports tend to confirm the first accounts of the success of the British attack this morning. The Germans' second line was carried with small losses, prisoners surrendering freely.

One regimental commander and staff, three artillery officers, and about 150 infantry officers and men had reached one camp alone up to 9 o'clock this morning.

In addition to the villages already captured, Bazentin Le Petit (about three-quarters of a mile N.W. of Bazentin Le Grand) has been taken by storm. Fighting is also proceeding around Ovillers (half-mile N. of La Boisselle), practically the whole of the village being in our hands.

Several German counter-attacks against the positions just won have been successfully repulsed, and our troops are now consolidating their gains.

The troops are in high spirits over their successes.[83]

The first full dispatches detailing the fighting for Bazentin Ridge were published in the newspapers on 17 July, proclaiming success in breaking the German second line of defence. In Beach Thomas' dispatch there was little description of the fighting, but he gave a valuable insight into how the correspondent spent his time collecting the information for the final piece. The officer in the motor car with Beach Thomas was likely to have been one of the 'on the spot' censors and correspondent guides, whose job was to try and waste the time of the journalists. Neville Lytton, a press officer in the making for the new foreign press camp, found this difficult, particularly the censorship imposed.

Censorship is a thing which should be done every day or not at all; it is only constant habit that can give people the requisite judgment to admit as much of the truth as possible without letting pass any indiscretions. Therefore I think it would have been better to let me censor the articles right away; if I had censored them badly it would have been so easy to say that a subordinate officer had blundered and had, in consequence, lost his job.[84]

With his press officer in tow, Beach Thomas spent the morning of 14 July at a vantage point for the start of the offensive, then in the afternoon he wandered close behind the Front line talking to the wounded and prisoners coming off the battlefield.

The pith and point of to-day's great battle is that British troops stormed and broke the second German line. For the first time in the western war the second attack of a series, when all hope of surprise was over, equalled and repeated the vantage of the first. . . .
    Everywhere I went later in the day I saw prisoners: and officers in a motor-car, accompanied by one of our staff officers; wounded in wagons, and ambulance cars along with our wounded; cagefuls of prisoners gobbling with avidity the biscuits and bully beef – of this they spoke with admiration – that their captors handed out. Finally, when after some hours' walking I reached less encumbered roads and found my car, I passed thousands, marching four abreast along a railway. The spectacle somehow gave even firmer ground of confidence than the official news of victory which I was to hear at the end of my journey. Seeing is believing. The exact tale must come later.[85]

Philip Gibbs' dispatch for the same day gave more information about the day's fighting around Bazentin Ridge.

For a little while – yes, and even now – it has seemed something rather marvellous. We have broken through the enemy's second line: through, and beyond on a front of two and a half miles, and for the first time since October 1914 cavalry has been in action. . . .
    The attack was to begin before dawn. Behind the lines, as I went up to the front in the darkness, the little villages of France were asleep. . . .
    I described, perhaps at too great length, the bombardment on the night before the 1st July. Then it seemed to me that nothing could be more overwhelming to one's soul and senses. But this was worse – more wonderful and more terrible. . . .
    The moon disappeared soon after 3 o'clock, and no stars were to be seen. . . .
    And at 3.30 there was a sudden moment of hush. It was the lifting of the guns, and the time of attack. Over there in the darkness by Mametz Wood and Moutauban thousands of men, the men I had seen going up, had risen to their feet, and were going forward to the second German line, or to the place where death was waiting for them, before the light came. . . .
    A new sound came into the general din of gunfire. It was a kind of swishing noise, like that of flames in a strong wind. I knew what it meant. 'Enemy machine-guns,' said an artillery observer, who had just come out of his hole in the ground. There must have many of them to make that noise.

At about 4.30 I heard another furious outburst of machine-gun fire in the direction of Longueval, and it seemed to spread westwards along Bazentin-Le-Grand and Bazentin-Le-Petit. I strained my eyes to see any of our infantry, but dense clouds of smoke were rolling over the ground past Contalmaison and between Mametz and Bazentin Woods. It seemed as if we were putting up a smoke barrage there, and later a great volume of smoke hid the ground by Montauban.[86]

The reports of the cavalry charge from the correspondents conjured up romantic images which recall the open warfare experienced in 1914. The *Daily Express* leads 'WITH LANCE AND SABRE':

Three weeks ago had any man told you that before the same measure of time had passed our cavalry would be riding down the Boches you would have doubtless smiled with sympathetic incredulity. Yet this is what actually happened on Friday evening last. It is surely an epoch in the war. No wonder the infantry in their trenches cheered to the echo as the troopers went clattering past them.

'It was like a dash across a polo field,' said an officer to me, 'only our men were all too grimly in earnest to start cheering. We struck between fifteen and twenty of the beggars, and thirty more threw up their hands. Quite a decent little show, the only pity being that it wasn't on a bigger scale, and didn't last longer.' – Reuter special.[87]

It would appear that the cavalry charge had become a sport or piece of showmanship. The reports of the event from the correspondents tended to emphasize a mythical image of the cavalry and the psychological effects on the private soldier's morale rather than the results of the engagement with the German machine-guns. Beach Thomas noted in his dispatch the way that the rumours of the cavalry action in the military bases and hospitals did more for the morale of the soldiers than the actual encounter had achieved physically on the battlefield.

The crowning distinction of this storming of the second German line, this second great battle of July, is marked by the cavalry charge. I never saw such excitement in a man's eyes as among some cavalry I passed in the road at 2 a.m. on Friday morning. There was a rumour of a chance of a possibility of a ride in the open against the enemy. 'At last, at last!' they said.

I thought myself that their chance was one in a thousand, but the unlikely happened. Some fourteen hours later Dragoon Guards and Indian cavalry – the Deccan Horse – did in very truth debouch from behind woods, did leap German trenches, did ride down the enemy in the open cornfields, did take a score and a half prisoners, did carry the right of the advance through to the crown of the ridge besides the Bois des Foureaux or High Wood.

. . . It is already the tale of tales in hospital and camp; and though this ride between the woods of Bazentin and des Foureaux was not of vast strategic importance, it was much more than a pretty incident. It meant that war of movement had in some sense begun. . . .

Less homely and more exciting was the co-operation of an airman with the cavalry in the attempt to destroy a group of supposed machine gunners in a cornfield. The airman bombed and the cavalry followed with a charge. Between the two both gun and gunners ceased to be. Quite how is still in some sort a mystery. But the cavalry charged through, turned and charged back, killing a dozen or so.[88]

These reports did not give the whole picture of events. The results of the cavalry charge were modified to concur with the soldiers' rumours in order to promote greater military loyalty on the Home and Western Fronts.

It was at about 6 o'clock in the evening that some British cavalry came into action. They were the men whom I had seen on my way up to the battlefield, a small detachment of Dragoon Guards and also of the Deccan Horse. They worked forward with the infantry on a stretch of country between Bazentin Wood and Deville Wood, rising up to High Wood, and then rode out alone in Reconnaissance, in true cavalry formation with commander in the rear.

So they rode on into open country, skirting Deville Wood. Presently a machine-gun opened fire upon them. It was in a cornfield, with German infantry, and the officer in command gave the word to his men to ride through the enemy. The Dragoons put their lances down and rode straight into the wheat. They killed several men, and then turned and rode back, and charged again, among scattered groups of German infantry. Some of them prepared to withstand the charge with fixed bayonets. Others were panic-stricken and ran forward crying 'Pity! Pity!' and clung to the saddles and stirrup leathers of the Dragoon Guards. Though on a small scale, it was a cavalry action of the old style, the first on the Western Front since October of the first year of the war.

With 32 prisoners our men rode on slowly still reconnoitring the open country on the skirt of Deville Wood, until they came again under machine-gun fire and drew back. As they did so an aeroplane came overhead, skimming very low, at no more than 300ft above ground. The cavalry turned in their saddles to stare at it for a moment or two, believing that it was a hostile machine. But no bullets came their way, and in another moment it stooped over the German infantry concealed in the wheat and fired at them with a machine-gun. Four times it circled and stooped and fired, creating another panic among the enemy, and then it flew off, leaving the cavalry full of admiration for this daring feat.[89]

Philip Gibbs failed to fully report the outcome of the cavalry charge or, more plausibly, it was concealed by the censors. However, there was a sense that all had not gone so well and that the cavalry had to be rescued from the German machine-guns and the enemy dispersed by aeroplanes.

Lord! Not one in a thousand would have believed it was possible to see this again. When they passed, the infantry went a little mad, and cheered wildly and joyously, as though these men were riding on a road of triumph.[90]

In the war correspondents' dispatches nothing was mentioned of the destruction of the cavalry as it charged through the cornfields towards High Wood. They seemed too preoccupied with the reactions of the troops that the cavalry passed than with what the cavalry actually did. Second Lieutenant F.W. Beadle described what actually happened as the cavalry galloped into action.

> So the German machine-guns were going for the infantry and the shells were falling all over the place. I've never seen anything like it! They [the cavalry] simply galloped on through all that and men dropping on the ground, with no hope against the machine-guns, because the Germans up on the ridge were firing down into the valley where the soldiers were. It was an absolute rout. A magnificent sight. Tragic.[91]

Clearly in the trench warfare which now existed on the Western Front the cavalry had become obsolete in the face of the machine-gun. What was needed on the battlefield was a kind of armoured horse which could resist the piercing bullets of the machine-gun, but also be capable of negotiating the trench system. Two months after the cavalry's ordeal the British would reveal their new secret weapon to break the stalemate: the tank.

By the end of July, as the casualty lists filled more and more newspaper space, prominent people in the Government and on the Home Front began asking questions about the price of war. Haig was asked about the 300,000 casualties by the CIGS[92] at the end of July 1916.

> Whether a loss of say 300,000 men will lead to really great results, because if not, we ought to be content with something less than we are now doing.[93]

Haig replied that it was only 120,000 more than normal.

> Principle on which we should act. Maintain our offensive. Our losses in July's fighting totalled about 120,000 more than they would have been had we not attacked. They cannot be regarded as sufficient to justify any anxiety as to our ability to continue the offensive.[94]

If there had not been such a gulf in the knowledge between the Western and Home Fronts this type of question would not have been necessary. Precisely because the military and the war correspondents had been economical with the true cost of war and why a battle of attrition was essential if the German Army was to be beaten, the Home Front had little understanding of the sacrifice that was required of them. Considering the restrictions on information available to the Home Front and the censoring of the war correspondents' reports, it was not surprising that the general public could not comprehend how the war was progressing. Their only criteria for

A British Mark I tank, built and first used in the Battle of Flers-Courcellette, 1916. It was 32 ft 6 in long.

measuring success on the battlefield were casualties and land gains, which the tactics of 'bite and hold' and attrition battles used by the British military did not stand up to. A more open policy by the military and trust in the Home Front might have avoided this confusion.

By the middle of September 1916 the battle for Flers-Courcelette had begun. This was indeed a historic battle as it witnessed the British Army's first use on the battlefield of the tank, so called as its true nature was hidden under the façade of a water carrier.

For the soldiers who formed up in no man's land on 15 September and advanced at 6.20 a.m. towards Switch Trench it was the start of the third phase of the Somme offensive. The bombardment which preceded the attack lasted forty minutes and was witnessed by Percival Phillips. What is interesting about this dispatch is the description of his journey behind the lines to a vantage point and his honesty in stating that very little could be seen. He does not even bother to try and describe the intensity of the bombardment as no words can do it justice.

When I went up to the line at four o'clock yesterday morning the enemy was trying to sleep through a harassing – but ordinary – bombardment that pricked him at intervals from midnight onwards. His own guns were quiet. Had his airmen been able to gaze down on us in the moonlight they would have carried back a disturbing picture of a great army ready to attack.

The tense calm of the last hour before battle leaves an unforgettable impression. The preparations are finished. Everything is ready for the dawn. Expectant infantry crowd the forward trenches, rehearsing their final orders and locking home their bayonets; gunners pace idly beside their batteries, fingering their watches; empty dressing-stations put out neat piles of bandages, and skilful surgeons wait to mend the wounds of men who are still unhurt. The stage is set for the great drama, and silence, heavy and oppressive, hangs over the waiting army in the field.

You have motored four miles in the chilly night air, past ghostly columns of foot soldiers, guns and wagons drawn up compactly along the winding roads. There is no sound, no movement among them; neither men nor horses turn at the sound of your car. You see a long blur of white faces below the broad-brimmed helmets of steel; interminable rows of shadowy forms weighted down with packs and cartridges; an officer on his horse, peering ahead into the moonlight; a group silhouetted by an electric torch bending over a map at a cross roads; limbers and their seated figures seemingly carved from single blocks of stone; a battalion of infantry beside a hedge, and then another battalion, and still another; infantry winding up the hills and down the valleys and through the sleeping villages, grouped around little churchyards and massive farm buildings, and flowing over the broad fields round about; troops, nothing but troops, dumb, incurious, immobile, waiting in the darkness for the sound of the guns that will blaze them a way through the enemy's country ahead.

Nothing that I can write will convey an adequate impression of such a bombardment as the one that preceded yesterday morning's attack. Try to imagine yourself standing on a pile of broken masonry, looking out over gently rising ground that is utterly destitute of trees, houses, or sign of any living thing. The deafening uproar, louder and more nerve-shattering than any noise you have ever heard, seems to come principally from a gigantic howitzer, which spits flames from a cellar fifty yards away on the right, and two equally formidable brothers which fling their unpleasant shells directly over your head, with an accompanying blast which shakes you to the core. The noise of innumerable other guns massed around you is curiously deadened and unimportant. Directly in front, and as far as you can see to the right and left, the countryside is stabbed by thousands of flashes of fire. It is like the incessant winking of gigantic signal lamps. Each flash means a shell for the enemy. The distant ridge is wreathed in smoke clouds, and high above, German shrapnel breaks spasmodically over the advancing infantry. Of the latter nothing can be seen. There is only the broad expanse of dead grey country pierced by countless gusts of flame as the incomplete picture of the beginning of this great British attack.

What you could see, however, at the very beginning of the battle, was the triumphant supremacy of the British aeroplanes in the sky above. While batteries of calibers were pouring a deluge of red-hot metal into the battered German trenches, squadrons of aircraft passed back and forth unhindered by the wild efforts of the German gunners to drive them off. . . .

I am much afraid that no phase of the advance would appeal to an eye-witness as dramatic, even though he could have followed it step by step. Could you have looked beyond the veil yesterday morning at the creeping barrage and the men who came after, you would have seen nothing more than single figures strolling across the fields, stepping rather carefully as they went. No one ran. They could not. A group might pause for a minute and look round casually, perhaps talk together, and then resume their promenade. Sometimes a group was thinned imperceptibly. You could not have seen men dropping while their comrades dashed ahead. A man was there in the sunlight – and then he was not. The craters swallowed up dead and wounded alike. Just bare fields and a crowd of men out for a morning walk – that was how the attack really looked.[95]

By 7.50 a.m. soldiers had occupied Flers Trench and at 8.20 a.m. Tank D16 entered the village of Flers followed by the infantry from the 122nd Brigade. As this news reached Britain the Fleet Street presses began to run with the headline 'A TANK IS WALKING UP THE HIGH STREET OF FLERS WITH THE BRITISH ARMY CHEERING BEHIND'.[96] The optimism portrayed in the war correspondents' dispatches about tanks driving down the main street in Flers on 15 September may well have reaffirmed soldiers' faith in their commanders. Lyn Macdonald believed that this was probably the best news of the whole battle and indeed of the whole war.[97]

The first reports of the new weapons on the battlefield came from an official communiqué released by Haig at GHQ.

In this attack we employed for the first time a new type of heavy armoured car, which had move of considerable utility.[98]

However, by 18 September these armoured cars had captured the imagination of the war correspondents and the Home Front's newspapers were full of amazing stories of the British 'tank' which had aided the advance through the enemy's third line. Philip Gibbs called them 'ICHTHYOSAURUS CARS' and in his dispatch he described their effect on the morale of the advancing infantry.

Many of them [soldiers] went over, too, in the greatest good humour, laughing as they ran. Like children whose fancy has been inflamed by some new toy, they were enormously cheered by a new weapon which was to be tried with them for the first time – 'the heavily-armoured car' mentioned already in the official bulletin.

That description is a dull one compared with all the rich and rare qualities which belong to these extraordinary vehicles. The secret of them was kept for months jealously and nobly. It was only a few days ago that it was whispered to me.

'Like prehistoric monsters. You know, the old Ichthyosaurus,' said the officer.

I told him he was pulling my leg.

'But it's a fact, man!'

He breathed hard, and laughed in a queer way at some enormous comicality.

'They cut up houses and put the refuse under their bellies. Walk right over 'em!'

I knew this man was a truthful and simple soul, and yet could not believe. . . .

It appeared, also, that they were proof gainst rifle bullets, machine-gun bullets, bombs, shell-splinters. Just shrugged their shoulders and passed on. Nothing but a direct hit from a fair-sized shell could do them any harm.

'But what's the name of these mythical monsters?' I asked, not believing a word if it.

He said 'Hush!'

Other people said 'Hush! . . . Hush!' when the subject was alluded to in a remote way. And since then I have heard that one name for them is the 'Hush-hush.' But their real name is Tanks.

For they are real, and I have seen them, and walked round them, and got inside their bodies, and looked at their mysterious organs, and watched their monstrous movements.

VAST TOADS.

I came across a herd of them in a field, and, like the countryman who first saw a giraffe, said 'Hell! . . . I don't believe it.' Then I sat down on the grass and laughed until tears came into my eyes. (In war one has a funny sense of humour.) For they were monstrously comical, like toads of vast size emerging from the primeval slime in the twilight of the world's dawn.

The skipper of one of them introduced me to them. . . . 'When our soldiers first saw these strange creatures lolloping along the roads and over old battlefields, taking trenches on the way, they shouted and cheered wildly, and laughed for a day afterwards.' And yesterday the troops got out of their trenches laughing and shouting and cheering again because the Tanks had gone on ahead, and were scaring the Germans dreadfully, while they moved over the enemy's trenches and poured out fire on every side. As I shall write later, these motor monsters had strange adventures and did very good work, justifying their amazing existence. . . .

THE TANK'S ADVANCE.

But we had a new engine of war to destroy the place. Over our own trenches in the twilight of the dawn those motor-monsters had lurched up, and now it came crawling forward to the rescue, cheered by the assaulting troops, who called out words of encouragement to it and laughed, so that some men were laughing even when bullets caught them in the throat. 'Creme de Menthe' was the name of this particular creature, and it waddled forward right over the old German trenches, and went forward very steadily towards the sugar factory.

There was a whip of silence from the enemy there. Then, suddenly, their machine-gun fire burst out in nervous spasms and splashed the sides of 'Creme de Menthe'. But the Tank did not mind. The bullets fell from its sides, harmlessly. It advanced upon a broken wall, leaned up against it heavily until it fell with a crash of bricks, and then rose on to the bricks and passed over them, and walked straight into the midst of the factory ruins.

From its sides came flashes of fire and a hose of bullets, and then it trampled around over machine emplacements 'having a grand time', as one of the men said with enthusiasm. It crushed the machine-guns under its heavy ribs, and killed machine-gun teams with a deadly fire. The infantry followed in and took the place after this good help, and then advanced again round the flanks of the monster.

In spite of the Tank, which did such grand work, the assault on Courcelette was hard and costly. Again and again the men came under machine-gun fire and rifle fire, for the Germans had dug new trenches, called the Fabeckgraben and Zollerngraben, which had not been wiped out by our artillery, and they fought with great courage and desperation. . . .

These soldiers of ours were superb in courage and stoic endurance, and pressed forward steadily in broken waves. The first news of success came through from an airman's wireless, which said:– A Tank is walking up the high street of Flers with the British army cheering behind. It was an actual fact. One of the motor monsters was there, enjoying itself thoroughly, and keeping down the heads of the enemy. It hung out a big piece of paper, on which were the words: 'GREAT HUN DEFEAT SPECIAL'.

The aeroplane flew low over its carcase machine-gunning the scared Germans, who flew before the monstrous apparition. Later in the day it seemed to have been in need of a rest before coming home, and two humans got out of its inside and walked back to our lines. But by that time, Flers and many prisoners were in our hands, and our troops had gone beyond to further fields.[99]

Percival Phillips likened the tanks to Trench Dreadnoughts.

Armoured cars working with the infantry were the great surprise of this attack. Sinister, formidable, and industrious, these novel machines pushed boldly into 'No Man's Land,' astonishing our soldiers no less than they frightened the enemy. Presently I shall relate some of the strange incidents of their first grand tour in Picardy; of Bavarians bolting before them like rabbits, and others surrendering in picturesque attitudes of terror, and the delightful story of the Bavarian Colonel who was carted about for hours in the belly of one of them, like Jonah in the whale, while his captors slew the men of his broken divisions.[100]

Beach Thomas' description of the tank was the most entertaining.

They looked like blind creatures emerging from the primeval slime. To watch one crawling round a battered wood in the half-light was to think of 'the Jabberwock with eyes of flame' who 'came whiffling through the tulgey wood and burbled as it came'.[101]

Tanks had superseded the cavalry's place on the battlefield, they had become a rallying point for both the soldiers fighting on the Western Front and the public on the Home Front. The *BEF Times* on 1 December 1916 had an article on the tank's performance called 'How the tanks went over' by their special correspondent 'Mr Teech Bomas'.

In the grey and purple light of a September morn they went over. Like great prehistoric monsters they leapt and skipped with joy when the signal came. It was my great good fortune to be a passenger on one of them. How can I clearly relate what happened? All is one chaotic mingling of joy and noise. No fear! How could one fear anything in the belly of a perambulating peripatetic progolodymythorus. Wonderful, epic, on we went, whilst twice a minute the 17in. gun on the roof barked out its message of defiance. At last we were fairly in amongst the Huns. They were round us in millions and in millions they died. Every wag of our creature's tail threw a bomb with deadly precision, and the mad, muddled, murderers melted. How to describe the joy with which our men joined the procession until at last we had a train ten miles long. Our creature then became in festive mood and, jumping two villages, came to rest in a crump-hole. After surveying the surrounding country from there we started rounding up the prisoners. Then with a wag of our tail (which accounted for 20 Huns) and some flaps with our fins on we went. With a triumphant snort we went through Bapaume pushing over the church in a playful moment and then steering a course for home, feeling that our perspiring panting proglodomyte had thoroughly enjoyed its run over the disgruntled, discomfited, disembowelled earth. And so to rest in its lair ready for the morrow and what that morrow might hold. I must get back to the battle. – TEECH BOMAS.[102]

The *BEF Times* was part of a collection of trench newspapers produced on the Front line by some of the men of the 12th Battalion Sherwood Foresters 24th Division. 'Teech Bomas' is a lampoon of the war correspondent William Beach Thomas and this article on the tank reflected the exaggerations to be found in all the war correspondents' reports to the Home Front.

Not mentioned in the war correspondents' dispatches of 15 September was the actual performance of the forty-two tanks available for the day's battle. It would

People purchasing war bonds at the tank in London.

seem that the tanks had a huge effect on morale and optimism, but their achievement in battle was vexing. Of the forty-two which went forward, only twenty-five actually passed the Front line and at the end of the day seventeen of the twenty-five were destroyed or had broken down on the battlefield.[103] Again the propaganda machine had concealed the truth, but had achieved a colossal boost to morale. Paddy Griffith called this 'Excessive enthusiasm' whereby the newspapers had used the tank 'as an only too rare ray of hope in a generally desolate landscape'.[104]

Nevertheless, because the truth had been exaggerated, there are signs in Philip Gibbs' later dispatches that the war would soon be over.

> 'It's time to finish old Fritz' was the shout of one soldier to another. 'We want to go home for Christmas!'[105]

This must have filtered down to the public on the Home Front, with the success of the tanks and the sweet smell of victory bringing great optimism that the war was nearing a conclusion. But the propaganda had engendered too much optimism and in Philip Gibbs' dispatch at the end of September 1916 there was a stark warning:

> It is only the beginning. People at home must not think that the German army has lost its power of defence and that the great rout is at hand. They are drawing back their guns, but saving most of them. They are retreating, but will still stand again, and dig new trenches and defend other villages. There will be greater and fiercer and more desperate fighting before the end comes, and God alone knows when that will be.[106]

What is interesting about the later stage of the battle is that the Army began to pool its resources. On 26 September the combined endeavours of power of the old and new forms of military hardware and tactics were first observed. On the day in question tanks had been brought forward to facilitate taking Gird Trench, and part of the XV Corps Cavalry Regiments was used to enter Guendecourt. By the end of the day the British forces occupied part of the Gueudecourt–Le Transloy road.

Fighting on the Somme continued into November of 1916. However, because of the weather, the battle ground to a halt, becoming stuck in the mud. Winter had again called time on the fighting for another year.

> Mud, for the men in the line, was no mere inorganic nuisance and obstacle. It took on an aggressive, wolf-like guise, and like a wolf could pull down and swallow the lonely wanderer in the darkness.[107]

NOTES

1. P. Gibbs, *Realities of War* (Heinemann, 1920), p. 24.
2. H.P. Robinson, *The Turning Point: The Battle of the Somme* (Heinemann, 1917), p. 1.
3. J.E. Edmonds, *History of the Great War; Military Operations, France and Belgium, December 1915–1st July 1916* (Shearer, 1986), p. 263.
4. Edmonds, *Great War, 1916* (Shearer, 1986), p. 266.

5. W. Miles, *History of the Great War. Military Operations France and Belgium, 1916. 2nd July 1916 to the End of the Battles of the Somme* (Macmillan, 1938), p. 292.

6. Robinson, *Turning Point*, p. 9.

7. B. Woodhead, *Life in France* (Unpublished, 1916).

8. Robinson, *Turning Point*, p. 7.

9. The code name for 24 June was 'V' and 29 June, the start of the offensive, was to be 'Z'. This all changed with the postponement of the start time.

10. W.B. Thomas, *A Traveller in News* (Chapman & Hall, 1925), p. 109.

11. J. Charteris, *At G.H.Q.* (Cassell, 1931), p. 149.

12. The *Daily Chronicle*, Monday, 3 July 1916 (London).

13. The *Daily Express*, Monday, 11 September 1916 (London).

14. The *Daily Express*, Monday, 3 July 1916 (London).

15. W.B. Thomas, *With the British on the Somme* (Methuen, 1917), p. 63.

16. Robinson, *Turning Point*, p. 14.

17. The *Daily Chronicle*, Monday, 3 July 1916 (London).

18. J. Laffin, *British Butchers and Bunglers of World War One* (Alan Sutton Publishing, 1988), p. 74.

19. The *Daily Chronicle*, Monday, 3 July 1916 (London).

20. The *Daily Chronicle*, Monday, 3 July 1916 (London).

21. Laffin, *Butchers and Bunglers*, p. 74

22. D. Read, *The Power of News, The History of Reuters* (Oxford University Press, 1992), p. 138.

23. Read, *Power of News*, p. 138.

24. Read, *Power of News*, p. 138.

25. R. Blake (ed.), *The Private Papers of Douglas Haig 1914–1919* (Eyre & Spottiswoode, 1952), p. 154.

26. M. Middlebrook, *The First Day of the Somme* (Penguin Books, 1971), p. 263.

27. S. Hynes, *A War Imagined* (Pimlico, 1992), p. 110.

28. M. Bell, *In Harm's Way* (Hamish Hamilton, 1995), p. 236.

29. Thomas, *Traveller in News*, p. 109.

30. N. Lytton, *The Press and the General Staff* (W. Collins Sons & Co., 1920), p. 57.

31. Northcliffe, *At the War* (Hodder & Stoughton 1916).

32. Northcliffe, *At the War*, p. 60.

33. L. Macdonald, *Somme* (Papermac, 1984), p. 173.

34. Blake, *Private Papers*, p. 166.

35. Blake, *Private Papers*, p. 180.

36. C. Repington, *The First World War, 1914–1919. Personal Experiences, Volume I* (Constable & Company, 1920), p. 266.

37. War diaries of the 9th & 10th Battalions, The King's Own Yorkshire Light Infantry. WO-95/21262 124235. Public Record Office (Kew).

38. 64th Brigade. WO-95/2159 130677 (July 1916). And 10th Battalion KOYLI WO-95/2162 124235. Public Record Office (Kew).

39. The *Daily Chronicle*, Monday, 10 July 1916 (London).

40. Thomas, *With the British*, pp. 86–9.

41. The *Daily Express*, Monday, 10 July 1916 (London).

42. The Regimental Aid Post and position of ten bearers of the Royal Army Medical Corps.

43. A clear indication that the bombardment had not done its job as far as the uncut wire in no man's land. See operation orders No. 6 by Lt-Col King. Preparation 3.A.

44. Wave system: a way of advancing in which each battalion was divided up along a front of two platoons in length and ten waves to the rear. Each wave would then advance at timed intervals. See M. Middlebrook, *The First Day of the Somme* (Penguin, 1971), p. 95.

45. The three mines which Private Woodhead mentions were located very close to his position and were set off at 7.28 a.m., 2 minutes before zero hour. In Sausage Valley to the left of Private Woodhead was the Lochnagar mine packed with 60,000 lb of explosives, of which the crater can still be seen today at some 80m across and 22m deep. Across the main Albert–Bapaume road in Mash Valley still to the left of Private Woodhead was the location of Y Sap mine 40,600 lb and to the right of Private Woodhead outside Fricourt were the Triple Tambour Mines under the German Front line.

46. Battalion objectives, see operations orders No. 6 by Lt-Col. King, Commander of the 10th Bn KOYLI.

47. Shelter Wood: objective of 64th Brigade.

48. The 64th Brigade.

49. Derrancourt, 2 miles south-west of the divisional headquarters of Meaulte.

50. Maj.-Gen. D.G.M. Campbell.

51. B. Woodhead, *Life in France* (Unpublished, 1916).

52. War diaries of the 64th Brigade. WO-95/2159 130677. Public Record Office (Kew).

53. Edmonds, *Great War, 1916*, p. 359.

54. Edmonds, *Great War, 1916*, p. 360.

55. War diaries of the 64th Brigade. WO-95/2159 130677. Public Record Office (Kew).

56. Information from: C. McCarthy, *The Somme, The Day-by-Day Account* (Arms & Armour Press, 1993), p. 21.

   R.C. Bond, *The King's Own Yorkshire Light Infantry in the Great War, 1914–1918* (Volume III, Percy, Lund, Humphries and Co., 1928), p. 822.

57. Edmonds, *Great War, 1916*, p. 360.

58. War diaries of the 21st Division. WO-95/2130 130666 (July 1916). Public Record Office (Kew).

59. War diaries of the 64th Brigade. WO-95/2159 130677. Public Record Office (Kew).

60. Edmonds, *Great War, 1916*, p. 313.

61. War diaries of the 64th Brigade. WO-95/2159 130677, (July 1916). Public Record Office (Kew). From orders for 1 July 1916:

   '*Operation orders 6 By Lieut Colonel King, commanding 10th Bn. K.O.Y.L.I.*

   Objective.

   The objective of this Battalion is to seize the easterly side SHELTER WOOD, from BIRCH TREE WOOD to x 22 c.5.2. and consolidate a position in rear thereof, from ROUND WOOD along CRUCIFIX TRENCH (straddling SUNK ROAD) to x 21. d.8.0.

   As soon as SHELTER WOOD is seized word must be sent back and the supporting Battalion, 1st East Yorks, will pass through us and proceed to the second objective which is QUADRANGLE TRENCH.'

62. War diaries of the 9th and 10th Battalions, The King's Own Yorkshire Light Infantry. WO-95/21262 124235. Public Record Office (Kew).

63. P. Gibbs, *The Battles of the Somme* (Heinemann, 1917), p. 71.

64. Woodhead, *Life in France*, p. 13.

65. War diaries of the 9th and 10th Battalions, The King's Own Yorkshire Light Infantry. WO-95/21262 124235. Public Record Office (Kew). Figures vary and in the regimental history of the KOYLI figures are from the 21st Divisional diary.

   'The official "Q" diary of the 21st Div, gives the total casualties in the Battalion for the period 30th June to midnight 3rd July as under; Officers, 12 killed and 17 wounded; other ranks, 50 killed, 265 wounded and 162 missing.' Bond, *King's Own*, p. 824.

66. Gibbs, *The Somme*, p. 71.

67. P. Fussell, *The Great War and Modern Memory* (Oxford University Press, 1975), p. 22.

68. Gibbs, *The Somme*, p. 285. The classical Greek notion of combat is used in dispatch, p. 207.

69. Mallins and McDowell, *The Battle of the Somme* (WO Films Committee, 1916).

70. Mallins and McDowell, *The Battle of the Somme* (WO Films Committee, 1916).

71. Woodhead, *Life in France*, p. 1.

72. Woodhead, *Life in France*. Football match, p. 4; cinema, p. 7; boxing competition, p. 10; concert, p. 12.

73. Gibbs, *The Somme*, p. 155.

74. Gibbs, *The Somme*, p. 158.

75. Gibbs, *The Somme*: Dispatches: 'The death Song of the Germans', 4 July 1916, p. 52. 'The German side of the Somme', 9 August 1916, p. 196. 'The German verdict of the Somme battles', 3 October 1916, p. 330.

76. Woodhead, *Life in France*, p. 4.

77. Woodhead, *Life in France*, p. 11.

78. Middlebrook, *First Day*, p. 227.

79. Gibbs, *The Somme*, p. 235.

80. Bell, *In Harm's Way*, p. 237.

81. High Wood was about 1 mile north-east of Bazentin Le Petit.

82. Macdonald, *Somme*, p. 135.

83. The *Daily Chronicle*, Saturday, 15 July 1916 (London).
84. Lytton, *The Press*, p. 69.
85. The *Daily Mail*, Monday, 17 July 1916 (London).
86. The *Daily Chronicle*, Monday, 17 July 1916 (London).
87. The *Daily Express*, Monday, 17 July 1916 (London).
88. The *Daily Mail*, Monday, 17 July 1916 (London).
89. The *Daily Chronicle*, Monday, 17 July 1916 (London).
90. Gibbs, *The Somme*, p. 123.
91. Macdonald, *Somme*, p. 138.
92. Chief of the General Staff.
93. Blake, *Private Papers*, p. 258.
94. Blake, *Private Papers*, p. 258.
95. The *Daily Express*, Monday, 18 September 1916 (London).
96. The *Daily Chronicle*, Monday, 18 September 1916 (London). This was originally a wireless message from a British airman flying over the battlefield.
97. Macdonald, *Somme*, p. 271.
98. The *Daily Mail*, Saturday, 16 September 1916 (London).
99. The *Daily Chronicle*, Monday, 18 September 1916 (London).
100. The *Daily Express*, Monday, 18 September 1916 (London).
101. Thomas, *With the British*, p. 221.
102. P. Beaver, *The Wipers Times* (Papermac, 1988), p. 133.
103. Macdonald, *Somme*, figures from p. 272.
104. P. Griffith, *Battle Tactics of the Western Front. The British Army's Art of Attack, 1916–1918* (Yale University Press, 1994), p. 163.
105. Gibbs, *The Somme*, p. 258.
106. Gibbs, *The Somme*, p. 302.
107. First published in W. Miles, *History of the Great War, Military Operations France and Belgium. 1916, 2nd July to the end of the Battles of the Somme* (Macmillan, 1938); quoted in C. McCarthy, *The Somme, The Day-by-Day Account* (Arms & Armour Press, 1993), p. 163.

ARRAS, APRIL 1917

With the coming of spring the generals of the Allied forces were planning their 1917 offensives. In December 1916 Lloyd George became British Prime Minister, elected on the promise of a full and final victory and now he needed results.

However, as Paddy Griffith emphasized, the beginning of 1917 did not actually witness the dawn of disillusionment and weariness on the Western Front because a large part of the BEF had only arrived in France during 1916.[1] Haig had been made a Field-Marshal and his full dispatch on the Somme operation, which stressed its achievements, was published in December 1916. Analysed by *The Times* military correspondent, it demonstrated the confidence of the military at this time.

> It will be seen by his description that the objects of this great offensive were not those which the German Press has gratuitously ascribed to him. His objects were to relieve Verdun, to prevent the transfer of German troops elsewhere, and to wear down the strength of the enemy in his front. He claims that these objects were achieved, and, further, that the achievement of any one of them would have been sufficient to justify the Somme battle. He also states that there is evidence to show that the losses of the enemy in men and material were higher than those of the Allies – a point which the enemy's Press at present contests – and he shows us that the enemy's strength was higher in November than in July, and consequently that the object of tying down the enemy on the Western Front was fully attained.[2]

In February 1917 the Germans began their retreat to the newly reinforced Hindenburg line, portrayed in Britain by the war correspondents as a sign of weakness and imminent collapse. This was another sign to the military and Home Front that the Germans had indeed lost the Battle of the Somme and that Haig's attrition policy was working. Today, with hindsight, it is considered that the German Army's retreat placed them in a stronger position as the Hindenburg defences reduced the length of their line and released valuable divisions to increase their reserve troops. Behind them the Germans destroyed anything that might be useful to the Allied troops in order to hinder their advance. Philip Gibbs reports on the desert the Germans had created for the Allies to cross.

> The weather is still favourable to the enemy in his plan of withdrawal. Yesterday there was over all the battlefields such a solid fog, after a night of frost which condensed the earth's moisture, that one could not see fifty yards ahead. Our airmen, if they had thought it worth while mounting, would have stared down into this white mist and seen nothing else. Our gunners had to fire 'off the map' at a time when direct observation would have been most valuable.

At the French Front, left to right: General Joffre, President Poincaré, George V, General Foch, General Haig.

I do not recall having seen anything so uncanny on this side of the front as the effect of our men moving in this heavy wet darkness like legions of shadows looming up in a grey way, and then blotted out. The fog clung to them, dripped from the rims of their steel helmets, made their breath like steam. The shaggy coats of horses and mules plastered with heavy streaks of mud were all damp with little beads of moisture as white as hoar-frost.

Nothing so far in this German movement has been sensational except the fact itself. Fantastic stories about gas-shells, battles, and great slaughter in the capture of the enemy's position are merely conjured up by people who know nothing of the truth.

The truth is simple and stark. The enemy decided to withdraw, and made his plans with careful thought for detail in order to frustrate any preparations we might have made to deal him the famous knock-out blow and in order to save his man-power, not only by escaping this great slaughter which was drawing near upon him as the weeks passed, but by shortening his line and so liberating a number of divisions for offensive and defensive purposes. He timed this strategical withdrawal well. He made use of the hard frost for the movement of men and guns and material, and withdrew the last men from his strongholds on the old line just as the thaw set in, so that the ground lapsed into quagmire more fearful than before the days of the long frost, and pursuit for our men and our guns and our material was doubly difficult. He destroyed what he could not take away, and left very little behind. He fired many of his dug-outs, and left only a few snipers and a few machine-gunners in shell-holes and strong posts to hold up our patrols while the next body of rear-guard outposts fell back behind the

barbed wire in front of the series of diagonal trench lines which defend the way
to Bapaume. In Gommecourt our troops found only one living man, and he was
half dead and quite blind. He had been wounded twenty-four hours previously
by a bomb from one of our scouts and had crawled back into a dug-out. It is
astounding, but, I believe, quite true, that he knew nothing about the
abandonment of Gommecourt, even when it had been achieved. He would not
believe it when our men told him. He had lain in his earth-hole wondering at the
silence, believing himself deaf as well as blind, except that he could hear the
crash of shells. He was frightened because he could hear no movement of his
fellow-soldiers.

The German scheme is undoubtedly to delay our advances as much as
possible and at the cheapest price to himself, so that much time may have
elapsed (while his submarines are still at work, and his diplomats, and his
propaganda) before we come up to him with all our weight of men and metal
upon the real lines to which he is falling back. By belts of barbed wire between
the lines of retirement, down past Loupart Wood, and then past Grevillers and
Achiet, and outside Bapaume, as well as by strong bodies of picked troops
holding on to these positions until the last moment before death, capture or
escape, and by massing guns eastward of Bapaume in order to impede our
pursuit by long-range fire from his 'heavies,' and to hold the pivot while his
troops swing back in this slow and gradual way, he hopes to make things easy
for himself and damnably difficult for us.[3]

The seasoned war correspondents, who had spent the winter back in Britain
turning their dispatches into instant history books, reappeared on the Western Front
in March. Beach Thomas was no exception.

After three months absence from the front I find a startling change in the
relation of our Army to the enemy's; and this German retirement – none the less
a retirement because deliberate and highly organised – away from a dreaded
attack is only one sign and symptom out of very many. The change is
principally this: that we are fighting better and the German is fighting worse, at
most points in the line. . . .

Of course the German retreat has accentuated this sense of superiority. As the
German retires he sets all manner of traps with intent to cut off our patrols who
feel forward over ground that is still everywhere a mosaic of trenches – a maze
of which only the enemy have the key. . . .

The position to-day is this. The enemy, 'flitting' along these spidery avenues
of communication, has reached a more or less regular line, defended by wire,
resting on high ground north of Gommecourt on his right and on Le Transloy
ridge on his left. This means that the first phase of the retirement is over. The
enemy has shortened his line, can release a few troops – of which he is seriously
in need – and take a breathing space.[4]

The Arras offensive had been a plan originally conceived in 1916 as a
supplementary attack to the Battle of the Somme. This had been postponed because

of the vast casualties experienced on the Somme. Now it was being revived to form part of General Nivelle's plans for a French offensive in April. The British and Canadian involvement at Arras and Vimy Ridge was to act as a distraction, occupying the Germans while the French made preparations for their major attack further south.

The British offensive began on Easter Monday, 9 April 1917 at 5.30 a.m. after five days of bombardment on this 12 mile front. However, what made this offensive different and probably the main reason for the early successes on the first day was the introduction of the 'creeping' barrage. This new artillery technique provided a steady, forward-moving barrage behind which the infantry could follow. It witnessed a shift in artillery tactics from the destructive fire of the Somme to neutralizing fire, as described by Griffith.

> Its aim was not to cut wire, destroy batteries or collapse enemy dug-outs, but simply to persuade the enemy's infantry to cower in the bottom of its trenches, and stay there, for the duration of the attack.[5]

The 'creeping' barrage thus gave the enemy in their trenches no time in which to prepare themselves between the bombardment and the coming onslaught of advancing infantry. This was to solve the problems experienced on the Somme when the artillery barrages lifted to let the advancing troops through thus allowing the Germans enough time to position their machine-guns on the trench parapets.

The first day's offensive saw the capture of Vimy Ridge by the Canadians and the British pierced the Hindenburg line, taking the second line of German defences in under two hours. Reports from the war correspondents celebrate the 'SPLENDID BRITISH ADVANCE'[6] and look forward to more successes in 1917. Beach Thomas obviously had not witnessed much of the opening offensive from his vantage point and resorted to describing his journey to the Front.

> At 5.30 this morning Sir Douglas Haig by deliberate choice threw the weight of the British Army against perhaps the strongest force of the enemy ever yet concentrated in such a fortress.
>
> Near Arras our troops leapt to the attack in the midst of such artillery fire as the world has never seen. It was accompanied by an onslaught of strange engines of war, while overhead, as soon as the clouds allowed, our aeroplanes, moving at 130 miles an hour, rushed to tackle any German machines they could find. . . .
>
> It is useless to try and describe the momentum behind the lines. As we moved up in the darkness past tramping men and bivouacs and the enormous apparatus of war, the flashes reflected from the low clouds lit the road and field continuously, but later the bombardment flickered and wavered, and when I reached the observation point the fireworks were almost normal. . . .
>
> From this vantage-point, where the full panorama from Vimy to Tilloy was etched in the flames, I write immediately after watching the first storming. It is too early to give more than partial news, but the famous divisions directly in front of me, both of which I had before seen throw themselves on an entrenched and buttressed enemy, went straight through to their goal. . . .

A Canadian being decorated on the field of battle.

LATER

Returning towards the front at noon, I saw everywhere proof that the day had gone from good to better. . . .

The troops who, I understand, took the Vimy Ridge and Thelus spoke scornfully of the enemy's fighting. 'They call themselves Reserve Guards and can't fight better than that!' said one soldier. . . .

The toughest fighting was immediately east of Arras, especially at the railway triangle. When we had taken it a tank was seen perched across one of the cusps of line. But many places thought strongest and most formidable, notably the redoubt called the Harp, were captured, with many prisoners, in our stride.

North of St. Quentin we took three more villages. The position is still fluid, and prisoners still appear moving westward across the skyline.[7]

The Times correspondent was also experiencing problems actually seeing the battle in progress from the special vantage point which had been chosen by the military. Perhaps this was another time-wasting exercise to keep the correspondents away from the real battle down below.

I have just returned to the telegraph base from seeing as much of the opening phase of the battle as it is possible to see of an action on a wide front. Details of the progress of the fighting after our first assault are yet lacking, but we know that we have broken the German lines everywhere and that prisoners in good numbers are already coming in.

It was like the days of the beginning of the Battle of the Somme again, and the Battle of Arras, if that is what it is to be called may prove no less disastrous to the Germans. . . .

It was too dark, nor was I near enough, to see the infantry actually going over, but though one had to imagine the dim figures in greyness down below the sight was very thrilling. . . .

Such a battle as has begun this morning cannot be fought without heavy casualties. We must be reconciled to that in advance. But the enemy will suffer more than we, and we shall break him here as we broke him on the Somme. The Army has no doubt or misgiving. Its worst fear is that the enemy will not stay and fight.

CANADIANS OVER VIMY CREST
Later
From all parts of the line come reports of brilliant successes. During the afternoon I have been visiting the headquarters of various units engaged, both Home troops and Canadians, seeing the wounded in the clearing stations. Everywhere is the same in triumph.[8]

It was not until a few days later, when the smoke and dust had settled on the battlefield, that the war correspondents were able to give a fuller account of the fighting around Arras. Two days later, Philip Gibbs' dispatch attempted to piece together the events of the first day and the Canadians' triumphant capture of Vimy Ridge.

The enemy has lost already nearly 10,000 prisoners and more than half a hundred guns, and in dead and wounded his losses are great. He is in retreat south of the Vimy Ridge to defensive lines farther back, and as he goes our guns are smashing him along the roads. During the night the Canadians gained the last point called Hill 145, on the Vimy Ridge, where the Germans held out in a pocket with machine-guns, and this morning the whole of the high ridge, which dominates the plains to Douai, is in our hands, so that there is removed from our path the high barrier for which the French and ourselves have fought through bloody years. Yesterday before daylight and afterwards I saw this ridge of Vimy all on fire with the light of great gun-fire. The enemy was there in strength, and his guns were answering ours with a heavy barrage of high explosives. This morning the scene was changed as by a miracle. Snow was falling, blown gustily across the battlefields, and powdering the capes and helmets of our men as they rode or marched forward to the front. But presently sunlight broke through the storm-clouded countryside by Neuville-St.-Vaast and Thelus and La Folie Farm, up to the crest of the ridge, where the Canadians and Highlanders of the 51st Division had just fought their way with such valour. . . .

The Canadian attack yesterday was astoundingly successful, and carried out by high-spirited men, the victors of Courcelette in the battles of the Somme, who had before the advance an utter and joyous confidence of victory. On their right were the Highland Brigade of the 51st Division who fought at Beaumont-Hamel, and who shared the honour of that day with the Canadians, taking as many prisoners and gaining a great part of the ridge. They went at dawn, through the mud and rain which made scarecrows of them. They followed close and warily to the barrage of our guns, the most stupendous line of fire ever seen, and by 6.30 they had taken their first objectives, which included the whole front-line system of German trenches above Neuville-St.-Vaast, by La Folie Farm and La Folie Wood, and up by Thelus, where they met with fierce resistance. . . . The Canadian casualties on the morning of attack were not heavy in comparison with the expected losses, though, God knows, heavy enough, but the German prisoners were glad to pay for the gift of life by carrying our wounded back. The eagerness of these men was pitiful, and now and then grotesque. . . .

By three o'clock in the afternoon the Canadians and the Highland Brigades had gained the whole of the ridge except the high strong post on the left of Hill 145, captured during the night. Our gun-fire had helped them by breaking down all the wire, even round Heroes' Wood and Count's Wood, where it was very thick and strong. Thelus was wiped utterly off the map. This morning Canadian patrols pushed in a snow-storm through Farbus Wood, and established outposts on the railway embankment. Some of the bravest work was done by forward observing officers, who climbed to the top of Vimy Ridge as soon as it was captured, and through the heavy fire barrages reported back to the artillery all the movements seen by them in the country below.[9]

From this point the battle slowed down with very few gains. The 4 mile gap which had been created in the German line on the first day was not fully exploited by the

The belfry and town hall at Arras following the British bombardment, July 1917.

British Army and was soon plugged with German reinforcements. Advances were further hampered by snow blizzards and on 15 April Haig ordered an end to the offensive. Taylor pithily summed up the progress of the Battle of Arras after the initial successes.

> Then the old story was repeated. The offensive was pushed on too long at the same place. The Germans brought up reserves. Once more the line settled down thicker and stronger than before. The only achievement of the Battle of Arras was a fresh butcher's bill: 150,000 British casualties, 100,00 German.[10]

The day after the Arras battle was laid to rest, General Nivelle's French offensive began in earnest on the Aisne. This achieved little except to exhaust the French Army beyond its breaking point. Mutinies followed and General Nivelle was soon to disappear from the scene in disgrace.

However, for the British military command the Battle of Arras was an important lesson in the use of artillery and 'bite and hold' trench-warfare tactics in combination with the technological developments such as the 'creeping' barrage. These advances had boosted the confidence of the military to a point where it felt quite comfortable in its new role and this encouraged a more open policy towards the press.

The war correspondents had become a valuable asset to the military, communicating directly with the Home Front and deflecting difficult criticism. During this time the British press had demonstrated its full support of the military and that they were fighting for the same goals and aims. They had surrendered their press freedoms to censorship and even turned a blind eye to the true reality of war, and now the military was ready to fully embrace the correspondent within its inner organization.

By the time the war correspondents were reporting the next major British offensive on the Western Front their status within the Army had again changed. With the entry of the USA into the war and Lloyd George in charge on the Home Front, the military authorities had to open up their operations to public scrutiny. This was to take the form of a new openness towards the war correspondents already at GHQ, the results of which filtered through to the Home Front during the Battle of Messines Ridge.

NOTES

 1. P. Griffith, *Battle Tactics of the Western Front. The British Army's Art of Attack, 1916–1918* (Yale University Press, 1994), p. 84.
 2. *The Times*, Saturday, 30 December 1916 (London).
 3. The *Daily Chronicle*, Monday, 5 March 1917 (London).
 4. The *Daily Mail*, Monday, 5 March 1917 (London).
 5. Griffith, *Battle Tactics*, p. 142.
 6. The *Daily Mail*, Tuesday, 10 April 1917 (London).
 7. The *Daily Mail*, Tuesday, 10 April 1917 (London).
 8. *The Times*, Tuesday, 10 April 1917 (London).
 9. The *Daily Chronicle*, Wednesday, 11 April 1917 (London).
10. A.J.P. Taylor, *The First World War* (Penguin Books, 1966), p. 175.

Section Three

COMPLETE SURRENDER,
JUNE 1917 TO
NOVEMBER 1918

COMPLETE SURRENDER

In February 1918 Hamilton Fyfe of the *Daily Mail* returned to France from reporting on the Russian Front. He was astounded by the difference in treatment now afforded to the war correspondents on the Western Front compared with his last visit in 1914.

> I have been driving and tramping these last few days over the battlefields of the Somme, through the countryside that I left in October 1914 – a countryside as fair and prosperous as any in Europe.
>
> I saw the first three months of the war here, in spite of the difficulties which in those days hedged about the trade of a war correspondent. We were like Ishmaels – every man's hand was against us. Yet we managed to see a good deal. Now I return to find the path of the newspaper man grown smooth. Every arrangement possible is made which can help him to do his work. More than that, he is lodged and fed in conditions which, remembering Russia and Rumania – recalling, too, how we fared sometimes those first three months even in France – I call the height of comfort.[1]

Since the beginning of the war Hamilton Fyfe had served as a correspondent with the French, Russian, Romanian and Italian armies and in 1917 had embarked on a lecture tour of Spain and Portugal discussing the war and the Russian Revolution. Fyfe had also been part of Northcliffe's British war mission to the USA along with William Beach Thomas in November 1917.

Circumstances certainly had improved for the war correspondents since they had been branded as outlaws in 1914. During the period of 'official correspondence' the war correspondents had had to overcome the military's and War Office's distrust of them. They achieved this by becoming part of the military's façade which concealed the reality of war from the Home Front. Their dispatches assisted the generals to stay in control by deflecting criticism and persuading the Home Front to accept the military's point of view. The press had already gone through a process of surrendering to the military and War Office's demands, which included relinquishing their freedom to report the full truth of war and choosing to work under the military censorship rules and regulations. The war correspondents had now become part of the military structure and must, therefore, have had access to sensitive and official secrets which they chose not to use in their dispatches.

The correspondents' loyalty to the military had been proved and their reward was a new openness that was first experienced before the Battle of Messines Ridge in June 1917. Before the start of the battle the war correspondents were assembled and given a full lecture on the coming offensive by General Harington. Known to all as Tim, in June 1916 Harington had become the Major-General of the General Staff for the Second Army under General Plumer. Together, Plumer and Harington were responsible for the organization of the surprise attack on Messines Ridge. Therefore, for the first time one of the main architects of a battle was discussing his plans with the accredited correspondents on the eve of the offensive. The war correspondents were given information that in the wrong hands could have spelt disaster for the British offensive at Messines Ridge. This illustrated the scale of the military's new policy of openness towards the press.

Beach Thomas attended this first lecture of its kind and was shocked by the military's honesty and sincerity towards the correspondents with regard to the battle plans.

> His candour on this occasion left me aghast. War correspondents had multiplied much by this time. With American and French and Italian correspondents we composed almost a mob. But General Harington had decided to have his say, to put all his cards on the table. He sketched the great battle of the morrow, described exactly how the waves of troops were to go forward and where. He gave us elaborate barrage maps, and maps with brown, green and blue lines marked. At the end he said, 'If we do not succeed to-morrow it will be all our own fault, for the army has given us every-thing we asked for.' We were a long way from Mr Churchill's doctrine in 1914 that the war was to be fought in a fog and the only place for a war correspondent was in London.[2]

Philip Gibbs was also at the same lecture, hosted by Sir John Harington, and which lasted for over an hour.

> He put down all his cards on the table, with perfect candour, hiding nothing, neither minimizing nor exaggerating the difficulties and danger of the attack, pointing out tactical obstacles which must be overcome before any chance of success, and exposing the general strategy in the simplest and clearest speech. I used to study him at those times, and marvelled at him. After intense and prolonged work at all this detail involving the lives of thousands of men, he was highly wrought, with every nerve in his body and brain at full tension, but he was never flurried, never irritable, never depressed or elated by false pessimism or false optimism. He was a chemist explaining the factors of a great experiment of which the result was still uncertain. He could only hope for certain results after careful analysis and synthesis. Yet he was not dehumanized. He laughed sometimes at surprises he had caused the enemy or was likely to cause them – surprises which would lead to a massacre of their men. He warmed to the glory of the courage of the troops who were carrying out his plans.
>
> 'It depends on these fellows,' he would say. 'I am setting them a difficult job. If they can do it, as I hope and believe, it will be a fine achievement. They have been very much tried, poor fellows, but their spirit is still high, as I know from their commanding officers.'
>
> At the end of one of his expositions Sir John Harington would rise and gather up his maps and papers, and say: 'Well, there you are, gentlemen. You know as much as I do about the plans for to-morrow's battle. At the end of the day you will be able to see the result of all our works, and tell me things I do not know.'[3]

This new openness towards the war correspondents was to last to the end of the war. Their dispatches displayed the effects of this policy, appearing to be better informed about the facts and figures of the major offensives in 1917 and 1918. During the offensive for Messines Ridge the war correspondents' dispatches contained detailed information about the preparations which we still use today, for example, the amount of explosives used in each of the twenty mines. Being able to gain access to this kind of information would have been unheard of during the Somme, when the correspondents only knew of mining activities when they exploded and then had to guess at the power behind them.

Although the military openness improved the quality of the technical details in the war correspondents' dispatches it did not go so far as to expose the real face of battle to the Home Front. Even if the military had tried to bring the reality of the fighting to the Home Front by 1917 the gap between the image and actuality of the war was too great. During 1917 the Home Front was itself struggling against food shortages and air raids. John Terraine discerned the end to the Home Front's 'limited liability war' during this period.[4] The Somme had demonstrated the human cost of warfare and now the British public had to adjust to food queues and rationing brought about by the German submarine campaign and the increased danger of aerial bombardment because of their improved aircraft design and reliability. Harassed themselves by the effects of war, the Home Front were to experience 'battle fatigue' at news from the Western Front, which meant that even with the military trying to bridge the information divide their action came far too late. The Home Front was now engaged in its own real battles and sacrifices which diverted its attentions from the Western Front.

The censorship regulations affecting the war correspondents having been somewhat relaxed at this time, accounts of the fighting during Passchendaele indicate the hopelessness of the situation through their descriptions of the weather. This would not have been permitted at the time of the Somme. During the Somme the dispatches of the war correspondents tended to be far too optimistic thus not matching the results achieved. Having had their fingers burnt in 1916, the war correspondents were certainly more careful to avoid producing over-confident dispatches before the results of battle were known. Yet it is debatable whether the Home Front fully appreciated this change as they were distracted by their own problems of survival.

Even though the dispatches of the war correspondents became more realistic, at the same time the casualty lists published in national newspapers began to disappear. Full casualty lists of all ranks had been printed in the *Daily Telegraph* and *Morning Post* up to 1916, and *The Times* stopped this practice at the end of 1917. This appears strange when the Army and War Office had relaxed their attitude towards the press and also when this relationship was not always guaranteed to facilitate the Home Front's access to information.

Terraine described the start of 1917: 'It was a year of new men, new situations, new desperation.'[5] This might explain why the openness of the military and War Office towards the press developed at this time. In June 1916 Lord Kitchener, Secretary to the War Office, was drowned on his way to Russia and was replaced by Lloyd George. In December Asquith resigned as Prime Minister and was succeeded

The King (far left) at the Front outside a captured German dugout.

by Lloyd George and General Joffre, Commander of the French Army, was ousted by General Nivelle. They all endeavoured to contribute fresh ideas and solutions in order to bring about an early end to the war.

The real reason for Haig's new policy of openness towards the press in 1917 was probably an attempt to deflect the increasing criticism from the Home Front, especially the politicians and the War Ministry, of the losses incurred during his offensives. During the Somme Northcliffe had been brought out to the Western Front to try and improve Haig's image and diminish the challenge to his command. Again, after the German's March offensive of 1918, Haig's position was in danger from a group of individuals including Lloyd George, Henry Wilson, Lord Milner and Sir John French.[6] People on the Home Front increasingly demanded from the Government detailed information of British actions and the daily routine of war. Consequently, by using the press, Haig had a means of communicating directly with the people at home and a way of counteracting the doubts and charges levelled at him by the politicians.

Haig's personal characteristics, as examined by Tim Travers in his book *The Killing Ground* may, in some part, explain why it took so long for the military to respond to the needs of the war correspondents. It would appear that Haig was a solitary and aloof figure who had difficulty communicating with others. Travers suggested that Haig's inward-looking character prevented him from being able to accept new ideas, change and innovation.[7] This might explain why distrust of the war correspondents never really disappeared and why Haig was never able to develop a warm and long-standing relationship with the press. Haig left Charteris, Head of Intelligence at GHQ, to deal with the press and only very occasionally did the correspondents meet Haig at arranged press interviews and functions. This was a relationship of necessity between Haig and the war correspondents, which disappeared after the war ended.

Lloyd George and the War Office were also beginning to understand the value of the press working for the common good. Having worked with William Aitken, MP for Ashton-Under-Lyne, at the War Office in 1916, Lloyd George rewarded Aitken for his part in the downfall of the Asquith government with a peerage. Now known as Lord Beaverbrook, proprietor of the *Daily Express* and the *Globe*, he had been using his skills and connections in journalism, business and government to become an influential force in wartime politics. During the period when there were no accredited correspondents on the Western Front Beaverbrook had become the Canadian Government representative at British GHQ and published dispatches under the title 'Canadian Eyewitness'.

During this phase of the war Lloyd George developed an official propaganda machine run by the War Office. This was brought about partly by the American entry into the war in April 1917, which made the façade of military openness a priority. In 1917 Northcliffe went to the USA to head the British War Mission and was later to become head of enemy propaganda in 1918. In February 1918, after the removal of Buchan, Beaverbrook became the first Minister of Information which G.S. Messinger described.

Under Aitken the government's publicity efforts increased greatly in extent, intensity, and sophistication, and the growing influence of propaganda in numerous areas of national and international activity eventually caused an animated parliamentary debate – the first of its kind during the war.[8]

At this time Lloyd George was trying to absorb the press lords into the War Office machinery and increase his hold over them. The Minister of Information was at the centre of this policy which began to embrace all forms of communications including painting, a photographic bureau, and cinema and news reel divisions with the aim of influencing the war in Britain's favour.

There was a correlation between the war correspondents' relationship with the military and the tactical developments in modern warfare. During the latter stages of the fighting, from the German spring offensive of 1918, the nature of battle once again changed to a flexible, mobile war. Accordingly the tactics and value of land altered to accommodate these changes, which in turn required that the Home Front be educated in order to accept them. In the early stages of the war the Home Front would judge the success of a battle by the amount of land gained or lost and the size of the casualty lists published in some national newspapers up until the end of 1917. By the end of the war the correspondents were acting as educators, informing the Home Front of changes in the direction of the war and how its success should be measured.

This phase of the war finally demonstrated to the press, military and War Office that they were all on the same side with the same aims and goals – to bring about victory for Britain. Before 1917 they had worked against each other, now the foundations had been established for the press and military to work together.

NOTES

1. The *Daily Mail*, Tuesday 5 February 1918 (London).
2. W.B. Thomas, *A Traveller in News* (Chapman & Hall, 1925), p. 120.
3. P. Gibbs, *Realities of War* (Heinemann, 1920), p. 50.
4. J. Terraine, *The First World War, 1914–1918* (Leo Cooper, 1983), p. 128.
5. Terraine, *First World War*, p. 124.
6. T. Travers, *The Killing Ground. The British Army, the Western Front & the Emergence of Modern Warfare, 1900–1918* (Routledge, 1993), p. 241.
7. Travers, *Killing Ground*, pp. 102–10.
8. G.S. Messinger, *British Propaganda and the State in the First World War* (Manchester University Press, 1992), p. 123.

MESSINES RIDGE, JUNE 1917

In May 1917 the British accredited war correspondents moved to a château in the town of Cassel and stayed there for the whole of the Passchendaele campaign. The town was quite close to the Front line and liable to receive the odd stray enemy shell. From here it was a only brief walk to the battlefield, as noted by William Beach Thomas.

> It was a short run from there into Ypres; and not much of a walk over the Pilkem ridge into full view of battle.[1]

Messines Ridge runs to the south of the Ypres salient and is about 150 feet high. It was in German hands in early 1917 and gave the enemy a clear view of all the surrounding countryside. The Germans consequently could see everything that went on in the British trench system below them. Haig, therefore, wanted to secure the high ground before beginning a major offensive near Ypres. Problems with the French forces, who were still recovering from Nivelle's failed offensive and trying to keep mutinous troops in order, meant that Haig's attack had to be made in isolation. The preparation for this prelude to the main Flanders offensive had already taken two years to execute and its implementation was now the responsibility of General Plumer and his Second Army. However, for the first time the preparations were to include a detailed briefing to the waiting correspondents by those who planned the offensive.

Since January 1917 a special battalion of miners had been tunnelling under the ridge, digging over 8,000 yards of galleries, ready to lay nearly a million pounds of explosives to form twenty mines. The official history described the Messines Ridge offensive as a unique operation with the longest preparation time of any offensive on the Western Front and indeed of the entire war.

> The obstinacy and duration of the underground warfare in the preparation of these mines, the depth and length of the galleries driven, the weight of the charges laid and the length of time they remained tamped and wired, makes this mining offensive the most notable undertaken in conjunction with any battle or campaign of the war.[2]

Plumer, unlike other generals of the British Army at the time, was open to suggestion and encouraged discussion while he was planning the Messines Ridge offensive. It was to be a classic siege operation of the 'bite and hold' type taking as much preparation time and as many materials as necessary in order to minimize the loss of life. The objectives were adjusted several times in the planning stages as a result of discussions with corps and divisional commanders and in an attempt to take account of changing local conditions. Once these had been resolved the infantry involved were trained behind the lines with a mock-up scale model of Messines Ridge.

Special training areas at the back of each corps sector, on ground resembling that to be crossed on the day of assault, had been marked with tapes and coloured flags to show the various farms, woods, strongpoints and objectives. The assault brigades carried out at least half a dozen rehearsals over these areas, the men, wearing full kit, practising every detail, including the methods of communication and the move forward of brigade and battalion headquarters; artillery brigades rehearsed with the infantry brigades they were to support. A large model of the Ridge, the size of two croquet lawns, was constructed near Scherpenberg for all those taking part, down to platoon commanders, to study; many of the divisions, too, made clay models of their particular sector.[3]

The correspondent at the *Express*, Percival Phillips, after witnessing the beginnings of the battle for Messines Ridge, came across this model as he returned to GHQ with reports of the real thing.

The battle itself was rehearsed bit by bit. The infantrymen who followed the equally well trained artillerymen's barrage this morning had been drilled for their journey by practice trips far from the scene that left nothing to chance, . . . They had a wonderful model of the ridge – covering more than an acre of ground and true in every detail of contour and adornment – which could be studied for hours. I came on this remarkable miniature reproduction of the ridge on my way back from witnessing the attack early this morning.[4]

The bombardment for the offensive began on 21 May with a total of 2,266 guns and howitzers assembled for the operation and was intensified in weight from 31 May. However, at a conference on 30 May Haig became worried that the Germans might evacuate their Front line before the day of assault. He therefore urged Plumer to blow the mines before the proposed zero day. Plumer kept his nerve and refused to detonate before the proposed time. Zero day was 7 June and zero hour was set for 3.10 a.m., when twenty mines would be simultaneously exploded under the German Front line positions.

On the evening before the battle the accredited war correspondents were brought to the Second Army's Headquarters for a lecture on the strategies for Messines Ridge by General Harington. They were given all the facts and figures behind the preparation for this great offensive. Lytton, a correspondent censor with GHQ present at this first lecture of its kind commented:

The first of these lectures took place the day before the Messines offensive, and General Harington began his lecture with the momentous words, 'Gentlemen, I don't know whether we are going to make history tomorrow, but at any rate we shall change geography.'[5]

On the day nineteen of these mines exploded on time and could be felt like an earthquake back in the south of Britain. Even the Prime Minister Lloyd George was woken in the early hours of the morning of 7 June so that he could experience the force of the blast in England.

BATTLE DIN HEARD IN LONDON.
MR. LLOYD GEORGE CALLED TO LISTEN.
Mr Lloyd George, who was staying at Walton Heath on Wednesday night, was called at three o'clock yesterday morning in anticipation of the explosion with which the battle opened and of the exact hour of which he had been notified.

He and others heard clearly the tremendous shock. Sleepers in the district were awakened by it, and even in London some heard shortly after 3 a.m. what they judged to be heavy guns across the channel, till the account of the firing of the ponderous mine told them what it really was.[6]

The articles which appeared in the newspapers all had vivid descriptions of the simultaneous mine explosions and were remarkably close to the truth. Some of the detailed information given by General Harington had enlightened the dispatches with figures on the number of mines and their composition and the length of time taken to prepare for this offensive.

One problem that now faced the war correspondents was how to write about the ever intense shelling in new ways, having exhausted all the clichés during the bombardment of the Somme in July 1916. Perry Robinson of *The Times* attempted to fully describe the impact of the force of the blast.

I watched the attack from a very advantageous position, but the dim light of the early dawn, and, still more, the volumes of smoke which enveloped the whole battlefield, made it impossible to see what was happening. From what one can learn from the various quarters, however, the attack was perfectly successful every-where, and, while there was hard fighting from the start on many parts of the line, our casualties on the whole are extremely light, and everything which we had set ourselves to win was won even more rapidly than we had dared to hope. . . .

How many mines went up at once I do not exactly know, but it was nearly a score. Many of these mines were made over a year ago, and since then had lain under German feet undiscovered. In all, I believe over 600 tons of high explosives were fired simultaneously. Can you imagine what over 600 tons of explosives in 20 or so blasts along an arc of 10 miles looks and sounds like? I cannot describe it for you. Personally, I can only vouch for having seen nine of the great leaping streams of orange flame which shot upwards from that part of the front immediately before me, each one of the nine a huge volcano in itself, with as many more volcanoes going off at the same moment beyond them, hidden by their flames and out of sight, and each vast sheet of flame as it leaped roaring upwards threw up dense masses of dust and smoke, which stood like great pillars towering into the sky, all illuminated by the fires below.

It had been broad daylight for two hours when I came away, and still the guns had not for a moment ceased and still to the eastward the smoke cloud grew more dense.[7]

Philip Gibbs also had difficulty in finding a new way to characterize this amazing bombardment.

It is my duty to write the facts of it, and to give the picture of it. That is not easy to a man, after seeing the bombardments of many battles, has seen just now the appalling vision of massed gun-fire enormously greater in intensity than any of those, whose eyes are still dazed by a sky of earthquakes shaking the hill-sides, when suddenly, as a signal, the ground opened and mountains of fire rose into the clouds. There are no words which will help the imagination here. Neither by colour nor language nor sound could mortal man reproduce the picture and the terror and the tumult of this scene.[8]

William Beach Thomas reported from the battle, dazed by the magnitude of the opening bombardment. Once again the classic pattern of the war correspondent's day at the start of an offensive was detailed. This started by watching the opening bombardment in the morning, before going to GHQ to send the initial dispatch back to London. Then in the afternoon the war correspondent spent time travelling to the rear of the Front line meeting and talking to the wounded and prisoners, before returning to the GHQ via divisional Headquarters picking up the results of the day's fighting. Lastly in the evening a full report of the day's events and results would be sent to London.

This morning General Plumer's army, which for nearly two years has fought a fine stonewall battle, took in hand its biggest and boldest attack of this war. I come back from the sight of it dazed and battered by the fury of engines of war, new and terrible and grouped in untold mass.

I have seen several of the heaviest bombardments ever conceived by scientific imagination; none of them approached this in volume or variety or terror, and one moment in it will live for ever in the mind of all who were within range as a spectacular miracle of the world. An hour before dawn, as we stood over the dim valley, where the black tree-tops looked like rocks in a calm sea, we saw what might have been doors thrown open in front of a number of colossal blast furnaces. They appeared in pairs, in threes, and in successive singles. With each blast the earth shook and shivered beneath our feet. 'It is worse than an earthquake,' said someone who had known one of the worst.

Thunderclouds of smoke rose in solid form to immense heights from Hill 60, from Wytschaete Wood, and other places, and while our eyes were full of the spectacle a thousand guns opened. Was ever such a signal for such an upheaval? The air shook as the earth shook, and where the earth and air met incredible explosions set the world on fire. . . .

The attack stretched from Observatory Ridge through St. Eloi, Hill 60, Wytschaete, Petit Bois, Plugstreet [Ploegsteert] Wood, and a score of famous

The 'fighting fifth' (Northumberland Fusiliers) after the Battle of St Eloi.

places – in all a ten mile stretch, over an area where the German line sags in a great bend between the jutting headlands of Ypres and Armentières. . . .

Later

The battle of Messines Ridge, as the sequel to the Battle of Vimy Ridge, will be almost the greatest battle in our history, if we keep what we have won. At the moment that I write our skilled observers see German divisions in mass gathering for the attack, but whatever may happen in the future it remains that we took what we meant to take exactly as we meant to take it and at the precise minute when we meant to take it.

When the Anzac troops went to storm the crown of this famous ridge the enemy stopped them not at all; all they waited for was the advance of their own barrage, and some of the more ardent spirits would not wait for this, but dodged forward among their own shells and while still among them sent up hilarious rockets announcing their arrival. While some were digging with gusto and skill on the back of the ridge others pushed well down the slope, where at the moment their adventure is in full career.

Seldom was a great victory more cheaply won than the capture of Messines. It yielded as many prisoners as casualties. Personally, after watching the bombardment and writing of it, I was able to go forward and meet both prisoners and wounded walking back from Messines.

Night

All the fresh news of the battle enhances its completeness. The only single spot in the whole of the ten-mile front where we have been checked is a corner of

Battle Wood. The fighting was very furious for what is known as the White Château, but our men refused to recognise its strength and forced their way through in spite of the odds. The many woods, especially round Wytschaete, were strongly fortified, notably Radius Wood, where some of the concrete dug-outs were capable of holding a company.[9]

The effect of nineteen mines exploding under the German Front line was overwhelming and deadly as nearly 10,000 German soldiers were killed or buried alive in an instant. With the objectives set at only short distances these were all captured before the effect of the surprise simultaneous explosions of mines had worn off. Within three hours the Second Army had secured the whole ridge and the next day war correspondents were already roaming about the captured German Front line. Percival Phillips, exploring the battlefield, was astonished to find patches of ground untouched by the effects of war just half a mile behind the German Front line.

We hold all the ground won in yesterday's successful attack on the Messines Ridge and the ground beyond it. There have been no counter-assaults, and the enemy artillery has been comparatively quiet.

This morning German infantry was seen massing near Warneton, behind their new lines of defence, but our guns were quickly turned on them and the formations were dispersed. We have slightly improved our new positions at several places, taking more prisoners in the area east of Messines.

The thing that impressed me most was the contrast between this battlefield and that of the Somme. After the fierce fighting last summer there was not a blade of grass or any living thing in the valleys or on the hills we wrested from the enemy, but here I came upon little patches of grass and a few stunted trees half a mile behind the German front lines, and this side of Wytschaete, in view of our observers – like oases in the desert – . . .[10]

During this battle it is difficult to judge the effect that the military's new openness towards the war correspondents had on the quality of the dispatches published in the newspapers. This is mainly because the offensive was such an overwhelming success and, consequently, there was little information that the military authorities felt should be suppressed or censored. However, the dispatches do seem more informed on the numbers involved in the preparation of battle. This new openness would eventually be put to the test in the Third Battle of Ypres, commonly known as the Battle of Passchendaele, when the outlook was not as good.

For the moment the military were basking in the glory of victory at a time when the Home Front needed a morale boost because of their own troubles. However, as A.J.P. Taylor questioned, did the preparatory work outweigh the results which were achieved at Messines Ridge?

It was a remarkable success, and a beautiful exercise in seige warfare. But it had disquietening aspects. Two years of preparation and a million pounds of explosive had advanced the British front at most two miles. How long would it take at this rate to get to Berlin?[11]

Bullecourt, 14 May 1917.

NOTES

1. W.B. Thomas, *A Traveller in News* (Chapman & Hall, 1925), p. 119.
2. J.E. Edmonds, *History of the Great War. Military Operations, France and Belgium, 1917, Volume II* (HMSO, 1948), p. 35.
3. Edmonds, *Great War, 1917*, p. 34.
4. The *Daily Express*, Friday, 8 June 1917 (London).
5. N. Lytton, *The Press and the General Staff* (W. Collins Sons & Co., 1920), p. 97.
6. The *Daily Chronicle*, Friday 8 June 1917 (London).
7. *The Times*, Friday, 8 June 1917 (London).
8. The *Daily Chronicle*, Friday, 8 June 1917 (London).
9. The *Daily Mail*, Friday, 8 June 1917 (London).
10. The *Daily Express*, Saturday, 9 June 1917 (London).
11. A.J.P. Taylor, *The First World War* (Penguin Books, 1966), p. 190.

THE THIRD BATTLE OF YPRES, 1917

After the successes at Messines Ridge in June 1917 Haig had been pushing to follow this up with another offensive in Flanders advancing towards the Belgian coastal ports. However, the effects of the Somme on the Home Front meant that the Government was in no mood to go through another long, drawn-out offensive with little gain and long casualty lists.

Haig, therefore, had to actively promote his plans for this major offensive of breaking through to the Belgian coast to the War Cabinet and come up with reasons why the British Army should fight, rather than wait for American back up in 1918. With this in mind, Haig exaggerated the importance of capturing the ports of Ostend and Zeebrugge, which the British Army only needed in order to advance 30 miles from their present position. These were thought to be the main German U-boat ports for the area, which simply was not true. The official history suggested that Haig's recruitment of Jellicoe and his support for the offensive influenced the War Cabinet's decision to go ahead with the preparations in Flanders.

> Admiral Jellicoe emphasized the need to occupy the Belgian coast before the winter. He stated categorically that it was useless to discuss plans for next spring, as we should be unable to continue the War into 1918, owing to lack of shipping, unless we could clear the Germans out of Zeebrugge before the end of the year. . . .
> In a later conversation with General Smuts, Admiral Jellicoe said that he had, if anything understated the case; he remarked to Sir Douglas Haig that 'if the army cannot get the Belgian ports, the Navy cannot hold the Channel and the war is lost'.[1]

Haig reasoned that this offensive was required, that the French General Petain had pleaded for them to divert the German pressure from a mutinous French Army and that it was Britain's last chance to win the war before American troops arrived. Everybody except Haig, it would seem, was opposed to an Ypres offensive, which included his own generals and his French Allies. His plans appeared to overlook the fact that the Ypres salient had become the most heavily fortified part of the whole German line and that the Flanders region often became muddy with heavy rainfall.

At a meeting of the War Cabinet in June the politicians were not informed of the negative nature of a Flanders offensive, and the problems which this might create in that region. Haig manipulated the Cabinet and they accepted his point of view with the promise of the chance for a complete victory before the end of the year. However, at this point Haig was only given the approval to proceed with preparations for an offensive. By the time the War Cabinet gave their assent on 25 July for the full-scale offensive, Haig was already into the final barrage stage for a 31 July start.

The bombardment began on 17 July with a barrage of over 3,000 guns and was intensified from 28 July for three days and nights concentrating on the known German battery positions. Rather than the desired effect of destroying any resistance in front of the British troops and their objectives, the bombardment weakened the local infrastructure in a waterlogged area.

As the region was prone to flooding because of the clay soil and high water table it had been criss-crossed with a network of drainage channels and dikes. This had been done to prevent Flanders from becoming a swamp. The bombardment from the amassed guns shattered this delicate network of waterways which meant that any heavy rainfall had the potential to turn the battlefield into a quagmire. The muddy bog created by shellfire was to become the British Army's worst enemy, slowing down their advance and drowning the wounded soldiers before they had a chance to reach the dry land of the casualty clearing stations. The bombardment also served to warn the German Army of an impending offensive on their Front, taking away any element of surprise and giving the enemy valuable time to strengthen their defences.

A dispatch from Beach Thomas on 27 July 1917 described the heavy artillery fire which indicated to the enemy that an offensive is imminent. The gas shells being sent into Ypres were likely to contain mustard gas, which was the enemy's latest weapon and was first used by the Germans on 12 July. This must have had a very disruptive effect on the Allies' preparations and may have even led to the postponement of the start of the offensive to the end of July. Denis Winter went as far as to say that British records of the impact of mustard gas were destroyed to conceal the embarrassment it caused.[2] It would seem likely that this was the case and however open the military were with the war correspondents the effects of mustard gas were not about to be disclosed so close to the start of the Flanders offensive.

Ypres having suffered two years of war.

The war was never much hotter along our front, though no battle is being fought. We live in a storm of artillery that shocks the air over 100 miles of country – British artillery and German artillery – and the belt of war grows deeper and deeper. A 15in. shell or two fell recently 20 miles from the front line; thousands of gas shells were poured into Ypres; heavy shells were concentrated during the day at Coxyde, on the coast, 5 miles behind Nieuport, and at night at Oost Dunkerque (near Coxyde), which I saw bombarded for the first time in 1914. The back areas at a score of places, untouched for two years, are almost daily searched, at intervals little stretches of front-line trench are blotted out by sudden storms of fire, sometimes preparatory, sometimes without sequel, as near Armentières a few days earlier.[3]

Following heavy rainfall zero day on 31 July saw the clay ground transformed into a muddy swamp, having been thoroughly churned up by the shellfire. At 3.50 a.m. nine British and six French divisions attacked on a 15 mile front from the River Lys to the River Yser. The objective was to remove the Germans from Pilckem Ridge opening a gap through which the cavalry could be sent to gallop towards the Belgian coast. From the general plan in the official history it would appear that Haig had envisaged a rapid campaign on the short and sharp scale of Messines Ridge. It was planned to be close to the Belgian coast by 7 August.

Sir Douglas Haig did not contemplate a prolonged campaign in the Ypres district and hoped that the Fifth Army would be approaching the Roulers-Thourout railway, fifteen miles from the start in time for the coastal operation by the Fourth Army to catch the high tides on the 7th or 8th August. Then the original offensive, joining hands with the coastal attack and landing, would be continued from the line Thourout–Ostend towards Bruges and the Dutch frontier, south of the Schelde.[4]

Far from being a short and sharp campaign, three months later, after a series of battles throughout August, September and October, the British and Empire troops finally reached one of the original objectives. Passchendaele was reached in November and the distant objectives of Ostend and Zeebrugge on the Belgian coast had been all but forgotten. The offensive became another great battle of attrition with Haig convinced that the Germans' morale had been shaken and a collapse was due at any moment.

A plan can never be regarded as more than a general guide for a campaign. Sir Douglas Haig had frequently pointed out and in writing, as already mentioned, that the enemy must first be 'worn down' by battle; the only question was whether the Empire forces could afford this wearing-down process; it was to be reduced if possible.[5]

After the first day parts of the British Army had advanced nearly 2 miles on the left, progress being made in the direction of Pilckem Ridge and St Julien. However, in the sector around the Menin Road progress fell short of its second objectives before the continuing rain postponed the next attempt to reach the coast. With many British dead and wounded, Haig's main achievement in the first day's battle was the furthest advance produced compared with any previous engagement on the Western Front. However, this could not compensate for the weather, which deteriorated, turning the Third Battle of Ypres into a crawl across a vast swamp for little gain and much suffering.

Reports of the first day's fighting from the war correspondents had an optimistic air about them: 'that it is too soon to talk of results, but the first day has gone well'. It was a time to inform the Home Front of the vast preparations and bombardments that made this offensive possible. Gibbs' dispatch of 31 July had all these classic qualities and more – the weather was against the offensive and the lightly wounded were just not as cheerful as in previous battles.

The battle which all the world has been expecting has begun. After weeks of intense bombardment, not on our side only, causing, as we know, grave alarm throughout Germany and anxiety in our enemy's command, we launched a great attack from Lys to Boesinghe. We have gained ground everywhere, and with the help of French troops, who are fighting shoulder to shoulder with our own men, in the northern part of the line above Boesinghe, we have captured the enemy's positions across the Yser Canal and thrust him back from a wide stretch of country between Pilckem and Hollebeke. He is fighting desperately at various points, with a great weight of artillery behind him, and has already made strong counter-attacks and flung up his reserves in order to check this sweeping advance. Many Tanks have gone forward with our infantry, sometimes in advance and sometimes behind, according to the plan of action mapped out for them, and have done better than well against several of the enemy's strong points, where, for a time, our men were held up by machine-gun fire.

So far our losses are not heavy, and many of these are lightly wounded, but it is likely that the enemy's resistance will be stronger as the hours pass, because he realizes the greatness of our menace, and will, beyond doubt, bring up all the strength he has to save himself from a complete disaster. During the past few weeks the correspondents in the field have not even hinted at the approach of the battle that has opened to-day, though other people have not been so discreet, and the enemy himself has sounded the alarm. But we have seen many of the preparations for this terrific adventure in the north, and have counted the days when all these men we have seen passing along the roads, all these guns, and the tidal wave of ammunition which has flowed northwards should be ready for this new conflict, more formidable than any of the fighting which raged along the lines since April of this year. . . .

The weather was against us, as many times before a battle. Yesterday it was a day of rain and heavy, sodden clouds, so that observation was almost impossible for our flying men and kite-balloons, and our artillery was greatly hampered. The night was dark and moist, but luck was with us so far that a threatening storm did not break, and our men kept dry.

One can always tell from the walking wounded whether things are going ill or well. At least, they know the fire they have had against them, and the ease or trouble with which they have taken certain ground, and the measure of their suffering. So now, with an awful doubt in my mind, because of the darkness and the anxiety of men conducting the battle over the signal-lines, and that awful drum-fire beating into one's ear and soul, I was glad to get first real tidings from long streams of lightly wounded fellows coming along from the dressing-station.

They were lightly wounded,[6] but pitiful to see, because of the blood that drenched them – bloody kilts and bloody khaki, and bare arms and chests, with the cloth cut away from their wounds, and bandaged heads, from which tired eyes looked out. One would not expect good tidings from men who have suffered like these, but they spoke of a good day, of good progress, of many prisoners, and of an enemy routed and surrendering.[7]

The *Daily Express* promised 'GRAPHIC DESCRIPTION OF THE FIRST DAY'S FIGHTING', from its correspondent Percival Phillips. Phillips talked about 'hard fighting at certain points' which surely should have been wiped out by the 'bombardment of unprecedented strength'.

The Battle of Flanders began at four o'clock this morning, and the first day has gone well for the Allies. We attacked along the Ypres salient and south of it simultaneously, with a French army immediate left. There has been hard fighting at certain points, but many redoubts and other strong points were captured with very little resistance.

A well-screened gun on the Somme Front.

The enemy divisions suffered severely not only in the preliminary bombardment, which was of unprecedented strength and severity, but wherever they showed resistance to our infantry. . . .

More than a general summary of our first progress is not yet possible. We know, however, that the day has been a success, thanks not only to the English, Scottish, Welsh, Australian, and New Zealand troops engaged, but also to our aeroplanes, which hold a complete mastery of the sky in this battle area, to our gallant tanks, which appeared in unusual numbers in the grey dawn this morning and to the marvellous work of the gunners, who first flattened out the defences which we took to-day. . . .

The first advance at dawn gave us new ground averaging a thousand yards in depth in the salient. We took it 'like clockwork,' as I heard one expert express it. Before six o'clock in the morning the British and French divisions engaged had gone still further into the area of obliterated farms and blasted woods, keeping contact perfectly, the last Tommy on our left and the last poilu on the French army's right being in touch as grey and khaki went forward shoulder to shoulder over the fields.

Six o'clock found our men 2,000 yards from the starting point at many places, and even further at others. They had encountered a little resistance in some places. The Guards found some machine gunners hidden in abandoned gun-pits at a crossing on the railway embankment at Pilckem Ridge. They dealt with this post swiftly and went on to their destination. . . .

Progress was faster and smoother on the left of the salient, the ground being better than on the right, where the corrugated surface of a series of slight hills with many waterlogged trenches between made an advance a tedious and laborious task. Largely for this reason there was more opposition on the right. The Guards were able to finish certain work expected of them well before noon, by which time Pilckem Ridge was solidly in their hands. . . .

A strong enemy counter-attack had been launched at ten o'clock against the Allied armies at their junction, but it has been held well in check, and up to that time no other German counter-attack had been attempted. . . .

Very few wounded had reached the casualty clearing stations in the Guards' area by ten o'clock, and the number was far less than expected. At every headquarters I visited I heard the same statement – 'Casualties very light'. One division thought it had more prisoners than wounded men. . . .

The preparation for this battle was an artillery bombardment of stupendous strength, delivered by a concentration of batteries which must have been many times that of the enemy guns grouped against the British front. For nearly a fortnight this formidable armament was directed against the German trenches in the salient of Ypres and around it, the defences behind the roads of approach, and in fact every part of the battlefield and abutting territory. . . .

They knew what was coming. The artillery duel was beyond all description. At times all the guns in Flanders were shouting in unison, and amid this infernal tumult our men dug and drilled and did many fine and heroic acts.[8]

What Beach Thomas stumbled on during the first day's fighting around Ypres was the new style of German defence. This new defence system was probably the main reason for the slow progress of the Allied troops in the Third Battle of Ypres. Gone were the days when the Germans placed all their troops in the Front line to defend it to the last man. The Front line had been replaced with concrete gun emplacements and pillboxes built at intervals along the line where the soldiers could shelter in time of bombardment. When barrages stopped, the German battalions within the pillboxes could take up their positions at the gun emplacements and wait for the advancing troops. The line was only thinly held, keeping the main bulk of the German troops behind the Front line in order to use a strong counter-attacking force. Therefore, the attacking soldiers had to attack these machine-gun emplacements and pillboxes before they could take the Front line. Even then the Front line would be no more than a boundary of shell craters, and the attackers would then be liable to numerous counter-attacks from troops who had been little affected by the 'unprecedented strength' of the British bombardments.

> War Correspondents' Headquarters, France, Tuesday. – The intolerable suspense of many days, even weeks, ended this morning with the outbreak of one of the greatest battles of history. All was on a plan, immense beyond credence. Tanks moved up as frequent as toads after summer rain, themselves not a little resembling giant toads. Guns, great and small, lurked literally in thousands, and the bridging apparatus alone suggested a vast army. Just before the battle one division alone built seventeen bridges in an afternoon. For ten days our guns had pounded the enemy with such effect that, as we know the crew of one German battery had to be replaced nine times and the guns of a battery five times. Four days ago our aeroplanes were loosed like a fleet of destroyers, and they swept clean the ocean of air over the battle front.
>
> HAVOC LET LOOSE.
> I watched this morning the outbreak of the storm that all this and more portended. Gas shells were rained on the enemy early in the night. Then, after the usual monotonous hush on both sides, full havoc was at last let loose. Bombardments, drumfire and barrage fire have all been described to death, and even this, which transcended all, may be left to imagination. It seemed as if 10,000 shells a minute were fired. The enemy knew our intention, and was waiting. It was the third battle of Ypres. . . . The ground was too shallow and wet for the enemy to drive his deep shafts for spacious dug-outs. Instead he had built a number of thick concrete and iron 'pill-boxes' so near the surface that some were thrown up and tossed over still almost intact by our burrowing shells. Never was a bolder storming plan. Every man and every thing had to cross a broad river canal the enemy knew. They had registered every bridge, and none save airmen could cross to the enemy's side except by one of these registered bridges, pounded every day and night by a powerful and expert artillery.[9]

It is surprising that the details about the conditions faced by the soldiers were not censored in the war correspondents' reports. These articles and dispatches were not at all like those describing previous offensives on the Western Front, which tended to be wholly optimistic. The detailed description of the terrain which the soldiers had to brave indicated the helplessness and futility of battle as the weather worsened. The truthfulness of these accounts is shocking, particularly when compared with those detailing the Battle of the Somme. The latter battle was portrayed as a heroic show of strength and determination against an evil enemy and Passchendaele as one of the British Army's most costly disasters in history. Lytton, Head of Censorship at GHQ during part of the Flanders offensive, noticed a change in the message put out in the correspondents' dispatches.

> During the Flanders offensive they spoke of the angelic patience of the men and of their great sufferings; they did not actually say that the task was impossible, but they gave clearly the impression that to fight the whole German army, on that narrow strip of land between the Belgian inundations (on the north) and the industrial valley of the Lys (on the south) in torrents of rain, was almost hopeless.[10]

The report of the second day's fighting towards the goal of Passchendaele again demonstrated how the weather was affecting the progress. In Beach Thomas' dispatch even the so-called triumphs of the first day's advance were overshadowed by the squalid conditions in Flanders. It would appear that what the enemy and the British were now fighting was the worsening weather.

> Floods of rain and a blanket of mist have quite doused and cloaked the whole of the Flanders plain. The newest shell-holes, already half-filled with soakage, are now flooded to the brim.
>
> The chief triumph of the afternoon of the battle had been the moving forward of the guns. You might have thought that some of our field guns were cavalry going forward to the chase.
>
> The rain has so fouled this low, stoneless ground, spoiled of all natural drainage by shell-fire, that we experienced the double value of their early work, for to-day moving heavy material was extremely difficult and the men could scarcely walk in full equipment, much less dig. Every man was soaked through and was standing or sleeping in a marsh. It was a work of energy to keep a rifle in a state fit to use.
>
> The weather possibly arrested some counter-attacks, and certainly prevented all observation, but the enemy has the advantage of retiring on guns long since snug in their concrete beds, and profits by a certain number of concrete dug-outs. No aircraft could leave its shed, no guns stir across country, and even the infantry were immobilised almost to the state of tree-stumps.
>
> This windless milky downpour, beginning soon after midnight, lasted throughout to-day, increasing in volume. The utter completeness of our yesterday's victory made the rain less momentous, for all had been done that we wanted to do. We had not only won what we sought pat to the moment; we had also given ourselves time to make many trenches firm, and extend posts, and complete all junctions of troops during daylight in spite of heavy German shelling and counter-attacks. One unit on the flank of our principal advance

made a great daylight raid subsidiary to the advance and captured 40 prisoners, while on the left the Guards captured two garrisoned farms without the help of the artillery.[11]

Percival Phillips was somewhat more optimistic about the progress of the fighting, implying that most of the advance had been carried out before the weather turned for the worse. Even so the dispatch still mentioned lakes and streams which must have exhausted the soldier trying to cross them and slowed down the advance.

The weather changed for the worse last night, although fortunately too late to hamper the execution of our plans. The rain was heavy and constant throughout the night. It was still beating down steadily when the day broke chill and cheerless, with a thick blanket of mist completely shutting off the battlefield. During the morning it slackened to a dismal drizzle, but by this time the roads, fields, and footways were covered with semi-liquid mud, and the torn ground beyond Ypres had become in places a horrible quagmire.

It was pretty bad in the opinion of the weary soldiers who came back with wounds, but it was certainly worse for the enemy holding fragments of broken lines still heavily hammered by the artillery and undoubtedly disheartened by the hardships of a wet night in the open after a day of defeat. . . .

Our easier advance on the northern side of the salient was due to the more open character of the ground. Although waterlogged, like the rest of the plain of Flanders, with many small ditches among the fields, there were few impediments in the form of wooded tracts or copses where the enemy could get a foothold.

East of Ypres, where our progress has been less rapid, the battlefield bristles with obstacles of an unusual character. It abounds in patches of wood and copse, interlaced by shallow streams and pools of water, which in some places extend to dimensions of small lakes. . . .

The British troops now lying under a pitiless rain before Polygon Wood and its neighbouring fragments of forest are back on familiar ground, for every foot of it was contested when the Hun drove down from Zonnebeke, but little of it is recognisable to-day. You could not trace their line in the mud and wreckage of the Flemish farms, for they are lying in craters and other impromptu shelters, like the enemy beyond, and the battle front which forty-eight hours ago was sharp and clear between layers of broken wire now straggles deviously through the debris on and around the slopes above. There are few distinguishing landmarks which enable me to give a picture of this part of the field.[12]

By 3 August the British offensive had ground to a halt and was therefore postponed until the weather had improved. This was to be the pattern for the next three months. A series of long, slow crawls of the British Army to Passchendaele, witnessing a chain of attacks which ended in men drowning and guns and machinery disappearing in the sea of mud. Philip Gibbs described the situation at the end of the third day's offensive.

The weather is still frightful. It is difficult to believe that we are in August. Rather it is like the foulest weather of Flemish winter, and all the conditions which we knew through so many dreary months during three winters of war up here in the Ypres salient are with us again. The fields are quagmires, and in shell-crater land, which is miles deep round Ypres, the pits have filled with water. The woods loom vaguely through a wet mist, and road traffic labours through rivers of slime. It is hard luck for our fighting men. But in spite of repeated efforts the enemy has not succeeded in his counter-attacks, after our line withdrew somewhat at the end of the first day south and south-east of St. Julien.

The general position remains the same. The weather remains the same, and the mud and the discomfort of the men living under incessant rain and abominable shell-fire do not decrease; nevertheless, they have smashed up attack after attack, and their spirit is unbreakable. The enemy is suffering from the same evil conditions, and his only advantage is that perhaps he has better cover in which to assemble his men, and that, owing to his defeat, he is nearer to his base, so that they have not so far to tramp through the swamps in order to get up supplies of food for guns and men. As usual, we have behind us a wide stretch of shell-broken ground, which, in foul weather like this, becomes a slough.[13]

The graphic descriptions of the hopeless conditions and problems encountered that the newspapers were publishing on a day-to-day basis make it difficult to understand why General Haig continued to push forward. However, Haig believed the progress of the battle was adequate, as was revealed in a note sent to the War Cabinet on 4 August.

. . . Sir Douglas Haig described the fighting of the 31st July as 'highly satisfactory and the losses slight for so great a battle'.[14]

On 16 August the British renewed the offensive over a 9 mile front, north of the Ypres–Menin Road after failing to capture the Gheluvelt Plateau on 10 August. Again the weather was unkind and rain continued to flood the battlefield, although the troops managed to capture the ruins of Langemarck. Percival Phillips recounted the horrendous journeys that the troops made just to reach the enemy around Langemarck.

The battle of Flanders was resumed early this morning, when the British and French armies struck heavily on a wide front north and east of Ypres.

Considerable ground has already been gained in the region round St. Julien and Langemarck. Indications point to our being firmly established in Langemarck village and beyond it, while further south the attack has developed in the direction of Polygon Wood and adjoining patches of woodland strongly held by the enemy. Fighting still continues along this broad front.

I talked to-day with a number of wounded men engaged in the fighting in Langemarck and beyond, and they were unanimous in declaring that the enemy infantry made a very poor show wherever they were deprived of their supporting machine guns and forced to choose between meeting a bayonet charge and flight. . . .

The mud was our men's greatest grievance. It clung to their legs at every step. When a heavily-laden infantryman pulled one boot free he carried great cakes of clay with it, and even with the cowering Prussians plainly visible in their craters he had to stop and shake free his feet.

The approaches to Langemarck were mere bogs at the best – actual ponds at the worst. Successive rainstorms had flooded the fields. In some places, wherever there were gullies water lay at the bottom, and the roads of pre-war days have wholly disappeared in a desert of shell-holes and the debris of three years' trench life. . . .

The infantry had to pick their way slowly, ever so slowly, through the slime and the water and carefully surround these isolated redoubts as they loomed through the fog, flinging their bombs until the inmates came out or were killed, as pleased them best.

Frequently they had to pause to pull their comrades from the treacherous mire – figures embedded to the waist, some of them still trying to fire their rifles at a spitting machine gun – and yet, despite these almost incredible difficulties, they saved each other and fought the Hun and went through the floods to Langemarck. . . .

It is too soon to talk of them individually or to learn in detail of their work in the attack, but I can assure you that all the men I saw in the dressing stations to-day were full of confidence and firm in their belief that they had helped to give the Hun another hard blow. Give them dry ground and they ask no more.[15]

There was a heavy price to pay for little gain against the Germans' skilful resistance and with the failure Haig decided to transfer the main part of the offensive. Haig changed the principal role of the advance from Gough and the Fifth Army to Plumer and the Second Army. This held up further advances until 20 September.

In September, while the fighting continued towards Passchendaele, there was an ongoing campaign in the newspapers to name the regiments that were involved. Pressure from the general public had slowly built up in Britain as many wanted more information on their county's regiments. Early in 1916 when the war correspondents met with Haig and Charteris the freedom to mention the names of units involved had been a main topic of discussion. From William Beach Thomas' recollections on the subject it seemed to have been an ongoing discussion between Charteris and the war correspondents at GHQ ever since. Every time in the past the military had come up with the same argument for withholding this information.

The standard answer was that no name must be mentioned that would hint to the enemy the constitution of our battle line. For this reason no name was 'released,' was allowed to be published, unless there was evidence or a reasonable presumption that the enemy already knew what division faced them.[16]

Australians parading for the trenches.

However, as Thomas revealed, the effects of this policy were unfortunate in that the English regiments forfeited their battle recognition and glory to the larger overseas garrisons.

> The reason was sound enough as far as it went, but it had some unfortunate results. The only divisions that remained in one corps continuously were the Canadian and Australian. The enemy were supposed always to know which corps was in front of them. The unit was too big to be concealed. So it came about that after most engagements the war correspondents were informed that they could mention Canadians and Australians. This had the effect of piling up the impression that the whole burden of fighting was on the shoulders of the overseas troops.[17]

The headlines in the *Daily Mail* on 10 September were 'THE CENSORED ENGLISH SOLDIER' and 'NAME THE REGIMENTS'.

> The reticence of the British military censorship, which almost uniformly suppresses mention of the English units while occasionally recording the deeds of the Scottish, Irish, Canadian and Australian regiments, is assisting the Germans in a peculiarly mischievous form of propaganda in foreign and Allied countries. The enemy is now pretending that English troops are so rarely referred to because they never do anything. England's part in the war, these German slanders allege, is to make profit and to drive others to fight. The casualty list tells a different tale, but it is not read abroad.

Appeals have been made to the high authorities who are responsible for the policy pursued, as yet with little success, though we note that the Northumberlands are mentioned by Sir Douglas Haig in last night's report. The correspondents are not allowed to telegraph names of regiments unless they have been passed by the censor. Mr. Beach Thomas, who so ably represents The *Daily Mail* at the western front, has asked that proper honour might be given to English units. . . .

Every page of this war is full of heroic episodes; not a county but has its deeds and its legends of sacrifice. The extent and sorrow of those sacrifices is shown by the lengthening lists in our English churches and college chapels and before our shrines of those who have given everything that man can give for a noble cause. But who knows of those lists outside England?[18]

During the resumption of the offensive on 20 September, for the first time the military authorities allowed the county names of the English regiments to be published in war correspondents' dispatches. Now the Home Front were able to follow their counties through the ensuing battles thanks to the open policy of the War Office in response to the war correspondents' requirements. Beach Thomas' dispatch of 22 September named regiments involved in the battle for the first time.

Yesterday's victory came out in clear and complete outline under the bright sunlight of this morning. Never had so far-flung a line advanced together in so effective a comradeship as in yesterday's battle. The Surreys, Yorkshires, Australians, South Africans, Scottish, Lancashires, Kents and many others in one united front went straight to their objectives without a check in spite of a turbulent country and a fighting enemy.[19]

Perry Robinson also had the opportunity of naming some of the regiments which had been passed by the censor. However, he took a different view to that of Beach Thomas and the *Daily Mail*. He thought that lists of this kind could not do justice to all the many soldiers involved in a battle and would penalize those who had not attained objectives through no fault of their own.

Some Durhams here behaved magnificently, and took large numbers of prisoners, as did also the Kentish and Surrey regiments.

But to mention all troops which behaved as well as troops can behave would be to give a list of our whole order of battle. There were Northumberland Fusiliers and Royal Fusiliers and Riflemen, and fine things are told of the Royal Scots and more than one light infantry regiment. But, as many times before, I say again that any list like this is unjust. Some troops must be omitted. One cannot name all regiments engaged, but can only mention those whose fame happens to have reached one's ears, or who had some especially famous position on the front of their attack, and this is cruel to others who fought, perhaps, less conspicuously, but may have done it with even greater gallantry.

It is enough to say that our men fought splendidly, as they always do, so that one hears no criticism, no tale of hesitation, or mention of any single straggler.[20]

From this point the offensive continued on and off throughout October and into November. Meanwhile in Britain, as a result of the growing casualty lists, questions were being asked about the purpose of this continuing attrition. The Home Front witnessed the Germans being pushed back only yards at a time in return for heavy losses. So small were these gains that the public had to be educated on the 'meaning of victory' and reminded of Haig's objectives. Perry Robinson commented on this.

> We out here are wondering whether you at home properly appreciate the magnitude of the recent victory. If not it is probably our fault, because we have found it so difficult to explain.
>
> The Germans in their wireless point as evidence of the significance of our success to the 'extraordinarily small amount of positive British gains'. This is their old game, which perhaps impresses the ignorant among their own people and neutrals. For a long time they sought to represent each of our attacks as 'an attempt to break through'. We have never attempted to break through. It is not that kind of war. But wherever they were strongest, wherever they had their most formidable positions and had most troops assembled to kill there we have struck and grasped their positions and killed.
>
> It is the same in the recent battle. Here on the end of the ridge on the Menin Road the Germans had staked their best troops to try and avert our menace against that ground. To-day we hold the ground, and look down laughingly on all their positions beyond, and no one knows better than the German Higher Command how bitterly their sacrifice has been in vain.
>
> Our 'extraordinarily small positive gain' is only about one mile deep on a front of five or six. But that one mile, or rather the few acres in the centre of that mile, must have cost the Germans not less than a hundred thousand men in all their fighting here.[21]

These were the reasons for Haig's battle of attrition and this article could be viewed as a piece of propaganda which attempted to deflect attention from the original aim of the offensive of reaching the Belgian coast. The Third Battle of Ypres, the Home Front was assured, was never 'an attempt to breakthrough', but an exercise to kill as many Germans as possible.

Battles through to November included Polygon Wood (26 September to 3 October), Broodseinde (4 to 7 October), Poelcappelle (9 to 10 October), Passchendaele (12 to 13 October and 26 October to 10 November), and the weather continued to make the conditions worse than ever. The headlines told the same old tale and summed up the advance from August to November: 'VICTORY IN THE MUD',[22] 'AUGUST MUD. APPALLING CONDITIONS OF BATTLEFIELD',[23] 'BATTLE IN THE MUD AND FLOOD',[24] 'VIOLENT RAIN CHECKS A NEW HAIG PUSH', 'DEADLY BATTLE FOR PASSCHENDAELE',[25] 'HAIG AGAIN ROBBED BY RAIN',[26] and 'BATTLE IN SWAMP. BRITISH WADE TO THEIR GOAL'.[27]

In November the Canadian troops reached the village of Passchendaele, and from the description by Percival Phillips of what was left of the village it is difficult to understand how this could be considered the crowning glory after three months of persistent attacks.

Our line swung forward without a check. I hear that within twenty minutes the Canadians were rooting out the occupants of Passchendaele cellars. They met a hot machine-gun fire from the church, supported by isolated gun crews in adjoining emplacements, but nowhere did they have to take these defences with the bayonet.

The Canadians brought up their Lewis guns and killed many of these fugitives. They went through the dug-outs with their bombs and dragged out little groups of prisoners. Judging by the stories I heard this morning, there may have been two hundred taken this morning, not more. The line of the objective was strongly garrisoned, and as the number of dead lying about would not account for all the remainder, the only theory is that the others escaped when the attack began.

Nothing remains of the village except two ragged fragments of the solid church tower and rods of iron and concrete over the crypt, raised a few feet above the broken ground. It seems that the Canadians pushed round the eastern side of the village, along the Moorslede and Roulers roads, and up the highway towards Westroosbeke, and made a line in conjunction with the troops on the left who approached Meetcheele.[28]

Passchendaele Ridge, however, was the high ground which pulled the British soldiers out of the quagmire and on to dry land. Gibbs outlined the importance of the ridge to the Home Front on 6 November.

It is with thankfulness that one can record to-day the capture of Passchendaele, the crown and crest of the ridge which made a great barrier round the salient of Ypres and hemmed us in the flats and swamps. After an heroic attack by the Canadians this morning they fought their way over the ruins of Passchendaele and into the ground beyond it. If their gains be held the seal is set upon the most terrific achievement of the war ever attempted and carried through by British arms.

For at and around Passchendaele is the highest ground on the ridge, looking down across the sweep of the plains into which the enemy has been thrust, where he has his camps and his dumps, where from this time hence, if we are able to keep the place, we shall see all his roads winding like tapes below us and his men marching up them like ants, and the flash and fire of his guns and all the secrets of his life, as for three years he looked down on us and gave us hell.

What is Passchendaele? As I saw it this morning through the smoke of the gun-fire and a wet mist it was less than I had seen before, a week or two ago, with just one ruin there – the ruin of its church – a black mass of slaughtered masonry and nothing else, not a house left standing, not a huddle of brick on that shell-swept height. But because of its position as the crown of the ridge that crest has seemed to many men like a prize for which all these battles of Flanders have been fought, and to get to this place and the slopes and ridges on the way to it, not only for its own sake but for what it would bring with it, great numbers of our most gallant men have given their blood, and thousands – scores of thousands – of British soldiers of our own home stock and from overseas have gone through fire and water, the fire of frightful bombardments, the water of the swamps, of the becks and shell-holes, in which they have plunged and waded and stuck and sometimes drowned.[29]

Haig was now satisfied with the results and called a halt to the proceedings on 10 November. The troops in Flanders then began to strengthen their newly acquired defences and dug-in for the winter.

After the fighting around Passchendaele had faded away the war correspondents found themselves at the centre of some criticism on the way their dispatches portrayed the fighting at the Third Battle of Ypres. The historian Leon Wolff believed that the newspaper reports were too optimistic to describe such attacks as victories. He attributed this style of reporting to the rigid censorship regulations which controlled the war correspondents.

> In England and America the newspapers also described the attack as a victory. It is true that their correspondents (billeted in the old town of Cassel perched on a hill a few miles deep in the Salient) were in a difficult position, both for observing and reporting. Censorship was rigid. Negative attitudes were frowned upon. Military Intelligence officers headed by Brigadier-General Charteris exerted great pressure upon them. G.H.Q. resented aspersions upon its omniscience and efficiency, nor did most of these officers see any reason why the war had to be reported anyway. Measures were taken to keep the civilian writers in line. Top men like Perry Robinson of The Times, Philip Gibbs of the Daily Chronicle, Beach Thomas of the Daily Mail, all knew their jobs and what was happening. But the most they could do was refer to the patience and suffering of the men without implying that affairs were disgraceful or impossible.[30]

Wolff misunderstood the relationship between the press and military at this stage of the war. At the beginning of the war the military did not see why war should be reported, but by 1917 it had invested time, officers and material to cater for the war correspondents' requirements. To blame the military's control over the war correspondents for the lack of reality in their dispatches fails to acknowledge the reporters' own sense of morality and self-censorship.

During the Flanders campaign of 1917 Neville Lytton had become the master censor of the British Army which gave him responsiblity for all press units attached to the BEF. He declared that at this point the dispatches of the war correspondents required virtually no censorship attention from his department and that had there been no military regulations imposed on journalists these reports would have changed little.

> They were fully aware that their duty was to inform the near relatives at home of the doings of their men folk, and they spared no pains to get the truth. . . . They were not always in the front line, but every day one or other of them was in a forward area, and at the same time they had the necessary tact to get on the friendly side of the staffs of all units. They knew that I had not the smallest wish

that they should not tell the truth as fully as possible, and they informed me on several occasions that, had there been no censorship, they would have written in just the same strain. If any one ever cares to consult the duplicate files of the correspondents' despatches, he will see that there are no big alterations and that many articles went home untouched by my censors.[31]

It would appear, therefore, that the self-censorship of the war correspondents was a major factor in the style of their dispatches, combined with the military regulations.

At the other extreme, Haig believed that during the Flanders campaign some of the war correspondents' dispatches and descriptions tended to exaggerate the horror of battle. Writing after the war in 1920, Philip Gibbs challenged Haig's claims based on his own experiences as a war correspondent reporting at the Third Battle of Ypres.

As a man who knows something of the value of words, and who saw many of those battle scenes in Flanders, and went out from Ypres many times during those months to Westhoek Ridge and the Pilckem Ridge, to the Frezenburg and Inverness Copse and Glencorse Wood, and beyond to Polygon Wood and Passchendaele, where his dead lay in the swamps, and round the pill-boxes, and where tanks that had wallowed into the mire were shot into scrap-iron by German gun-fire (thirty were knocked out by direct hits on the first day of battle), and where our guns were being flung up by the harassing fire of heavy shells, I say now that nothing that has been written is more than the pale image of the abomination of those battle-fields, and that no pen or brush has yet achieved the picture of that Armageddon in which so many of our men perished.[32]

Gibbs was apparently happy to conform and indeed have confidence in his own self-censorship, but with hindsight he seemed to admit that he might have been mistaken.

Historians looking back on the battle see only the heavy British losses and the great misery Passchendaele caused. This is amplified, with hindsight, by opinions of the Battle of Cambrai, which took place in late November 1917. After initial success (in fact the first day saw the best results at that point in the war in one day's fighting) the offensive failed because there were no fresh reinforcements to exploit the gap created. Had the reinforcements already been thrown into Passchendaele and were therefore exhausted? Liddell Hart believed this was the case.

These attacks had at least done something to restore prestige, if they could have little strategic effect on a campaign which was foredoomed, and in which both the time and the scope for extensive penetration had long since vanished. Unhappily the Higher Command decided to continue the pointless offensive during the remaining weeks before the winter, and thereby used up reserves which might have saved the belated experiment of Cambrai from bankruptcy.[33]

What is even more illogical with regard to the 4½ miles of land gained in the Third Battle of Ypres is that it was so eagerly given up during the Germans' spring offensive of March 1918. The official history examined the question that the exhaustion of the British at Passchendaele resulted in the success of the German onslaught on 21 March 1918.

It put forward the theory that the German achievement might have been a complete victory had it not been for their exhaustion caused by the virtual destruction of their best divisions in the Flanders offensive.

> Perhaps what was of more importance was that the trained German reserves had almost totally disappeared: so that sick men and half-trained lads of 18 and under had to be thrust into both the war-hardened divisions already in France and into the less experienced and less sternly disciplined divisions brought to France from the Russian Front.[34]

The official history stated that the offensive had achieved its aims of ensuring the security of the French Army, which needed time to build up its morale and sort out its internal troubles.

NOTES

1. J.E. Edmonds, *History of the Great War. Military Operations, France and Belgium, 1917, Volume II* (HMSO, 1948), p. 102.
2. D. Winter, *Haig's Command* (Penguin Books, 1992), p. 95.
3. The *Daily Mail*, Saturday, 28 July 1917 (London).
4. Edmonds, *Great War, 1917*, p. 124.
5. Edmonds, *Great War, 1917*, p. 130.
6. Added to the text at this point in blue ink is a comment from a previous reader, 'and many covered with horrible blisters caused by "mustard gas" and spitting gobs of blood which were their lungs coming up in bits. I saw and was there!' The anonymous commentator who felt the need to set the record straight in this copy of Philip Gibbs' book from Merton Public Libraries added to the title page that Gibbs is 'The one sided Writer'. It is remarkable that somebody bothered to write in the margin at all and that the war correspondents, years after the event, still provoked strong comment from a former soldier of the First World War. This can only add weight to Denis Winter's theories on the suppression of the effects of mustard gas from military records.
7. The *Daily Chronicle*, Wednesday, 1 August 1917 (London).
8. The *Daily Express*, Wednesday, 1 August 1917 (London).
9. The *Daily Mirror*, Wednesday, 1 August 1917 (London).
10. N. Lytton, *The Press and the General Staff* (W. Collins & Co., 1920), p. 114.
11. The *Daily Mail*, Thursday, 2 August 1917 (London).
12. The *Daily Express*, Thursday, 2 August 1917 (London).
13. The *Daily Chronicle*, Saturday, 4 August 1917 (London).
14. Edmonds, *Great War, 1917*, p. 177.
15. The *Daily Express*, Friday, 17 August 1917 (London).
16. W.B. Thomas, *A Traveller in News* (Chapman & Hall, 1925), p. 123.
17. Thomas, *Traveller*, p. 123.
18. The *Daily Mail*, Monday, 10 September 1917 (London).
19. The *Daily Mail*, Saturday, 22 September 1917 (London).
20. The *Daily News and Leader*, Saturday, 22 September 1917 (London).
21. The *Daily News and Leader*, Wednesday, 26 September 1917 (London).
22. The *Daily Express*, Friday, 17 August 1917 (London).
23. The *Daily News and Leader*, Saturday, 18 August 1917 (London).

24. The *Daily Mail*, Wednesday, 10 October 1917 (London).
25. The *Daily Mail*, Saturday, 13 October 1917 (London).
26. The *Daily Mail*, Saturday, 27 October 1917 (London).
27. The *Daily Mail*, Saturday, 27 October 1917 (London).
28. The *Daily Express*, Wednesday, 7 November 1917 (London).
29. The *Daily Chronicle*, Wednesday, 7 November 1917 (London).
30. L. Wolff, *In Flanders Fields* (Penguin, 1979), p. 267.
31. Lytton, *The Press*, p. 114.
32. P. Gibbs, *Realities of War* (Heinemann, 1920), p. 387.
33. B.H. Liddell Hart, *History of the First World War* (Pan Books, 1972), p. 334.
34. Edmonds, *Great War, 1917*, p. 367.

CAMBRAI, NOVEMBER 1917

Just ten days after British troops finally reached Passchendaele village the battle for Cambrai began. On 20 November 1917 nineteen British divisions of General Byng's Third Army and three tank brigades successfully broke the Germans' Hindenburg line and advanced over 5 miles. They had created a gap in the German defences and unlocked the door to open warfare on the scale of 1914, before the trench systems. Yet within two weeks of this great advance by the British, fortunes had been reversed and the Germans regained all the land captured and more. The British troops had been humiliated and forced to withdraw to a more defensible line.

At the news of the greatest victory in 1917 on 23 November the Home Front had celebrated by ringing church bells. As Paddy Griffith revealed, the first day's successes at Cambrai were an oasis in the gloom of exhausting fighting that had marked the year.

> This was better than the first day at Arras or Messines, and it certainly made a most welcome change after four frustrating months at Passchendaele. One can readily understand the psychological boost it gave to the British public, who fell to ringing their church bells for the first time in the war.[1]

A fortnight later there began a public outcry as the Home Front were left wondering what could have happened after their celebrations turned into a hollow victory. They wanted to know the full facts of the battle and looked for someone to blame, partly out of their own ignorance of the reality of war and the apparent reversal of fortune on the Western Front. In December an official inquiry was launched by the House of Commons with the aim of finding out the truth about Cambrai.

At the time the war correspondents believed that they had kept the public fully informed of the events surrounding Cambrai and there had been no secrets hidden from the public. However, it would appear from remarks made by Philip Gibbs that the public laid part of the blame at the feet of the war correspondents for not reporting the truth from the battle zone.

> All would have been well if we had been able to hold the captured ground, and there would have been no irony in the ringing of the joy-bells in London. But within ten days the enemy came back with a tiger's pounce. . . . It still seems a mystery to the British people. They still imagine that some fearful secret lurks behind all this in spite of all the detail given by myself and other war correspondents. That one of our generals should have been caught in his pyjamas seemed to them incredible, and for some queer reason that simple fact stuck in their minds and seemed to confirm their worst suspicions, though I

know many officers who have slept many times in their pyjamas in trench dugouts without mishap and closer to the enemy than this general, whose headquarters were at that time far behind the front line. There is no mystery about that set-back in the Cambrai salient, and I have told the facts in full detail.[2]

As was now standard procedure, before the battle commenced the press camps, which now numbered four in total (British, American, Allied and Neutral), were assembled and briefed on the coming offensive. The war correspondents listened to the highly confidential information given by the Third Army's Chief of Staff, General Louis Vaughan who explained the nature of the surprise attack and its limitations. From Philip Gibbs' description of the press conference it is evident that the war correspondents were astounded at the candid style of General Vaughan's dialogue. The press were under no illusions about the difficult task ahead.

That charming man, with his professional manner, sweetness of speech, gentleness of voice and gesture, like an Oxford Don analysing the war correspondence of Xenophon, made no secret of the economy with which the operation would have to be made.
  'We must cut our coat according to our cloth,' he said.[3]

In the early morning of 20 November, infantry and 381 tanks assembled on a front of about 6 miles. The battlefield was 45 miles south of the ill-fated Ypres salient and chosen for its dry, hard ground, which was more suited to the tanks. At the allotted time of 6.20 a.m. the tanks and infantry in mass formation advanced forward towards the German line without a preliminary bombardment to announce their intentions. This meant that the ground was not pitted with shell craters and allowed the tanks to move more smoothly across no man's land. Many books explain that without a preliminary bombardment an element of surprise was created over the Germans and led partly to the success of the early Cambrai offensive. However, Denis Winter challenged this idea, posing the question

If the Germans knew about past battles in advance, how could they have possibly remained in ignorance of 100 guns and 400 tanks moving towards the Cambrai sector?[4]

If this was the case, it should be taken into account that the German command would have been preparing for the imminent offensive just as much as the attacking British troops. This would have been on the same scale as the Third Battle of Ypres, sending fresh reinforcements to the area and keeping the mass of the troops away from the Front line to create a counter-attacking force.

However, in no time at all the massed formation of tanks and infantry broke the Hindenburg line, crossing the three lines of the German defensive system and into the open countryside. At the end of the first day the British troops had advanced nearly 5 miles and blown a hole 4 miles wide in the German defences.

The news of this initial success reached the Home Front via the war correspondents' dispatches on 22 November. As with other offensives, on the first day the correspondents stood overlooking the battlefield, waiting for the charge to begin. When the battle got under way, as with most battles before, the correspondents could see very little of the actual fighting and had to imagine the chaos below them. At this stage of the war this situation had more to do with the war correspondents' safety than a conscious effort on the military's part to keep them away from the action. Perry Robinson commented on what he could see on that dull November day.

> For myself I watched what it was possible to see of the attack from a point where Havrincourt Wood lay on my right and the dark bulk of Bourlon Wood further away on my left front, crowning the eminence which is said to dominate Cambrai itself. . . .
>
> It was, however, as always, impossible to see in the dim light and rolling smoke either tanks or figures of infantry. Above all the murk and glitter and chaos one could see the red rockets, the German signals of distress, tossing skyward. One knew that they were calling piteously for help from their guns, but very little help came.[5]

Philip Gibbs, at the same vantage point as Perry Robinson, relied on his acute hearing to try and understand the battle by sound alone.

> The enemy yesterday morning had a bitter surprise, when, without any warning by the ordinary preparations that are made before battle, without any sign of strength in men and guns behind our front, without a single shot fired before the attack, and with his wire – broad belts of hideously strong wire – still intact, our troops suddenly assaulted him at dawn, led forward by a large number of Tanks, smashed through his wire, passed beyond to his trenches, and penetrated in many places the main Hindenburg line and the Hindenburg support line beyond.
>
> It was a surprise to the enemy, and, to be frank, it will be a surprise to all our officers and men in other parts of the line, and to my mind it is the most sensational and dramatic episode of this year's fighting, ingeniously imagined and carried through with the greatest secrecy. Not a whisper of it had reached men like myself, who are always up and down the lines, and since the secret of the Tanks themselves, who suddenly made their appearance in the Somme last year, this is, I believe, the best-kept secret of the war. The enemy knew nothing of it, although during the last twenty-four hours or so certain uneasy suspicions seem to have been aroused among his troops immediately in front of the attack. . . .
>
> . . . We caught the enemy 'on the hop,' as the men say, and in spite of uneasy moments in the night they had no proof of what was coming to them and no time to prepare against the blow. Some thousands of prisoners have been taken, and most of them say that the first thing they knew of the attack was when out of the mist they saw the Tanks advancing upon them, smashing down their wire, crawling over their trenches and nosing forward with gun-fire and machine-gun fire slashing from their sides. The Germans were aghast and dazed. Many hid down in their dug-outs and tunnels, and then surrendered. . . .

As I stood looking down on the battle, seeing only the gun-fire and nothing of the infantry in the thistles, though I was very close, I heard the awful sweep of machine-gun fire from the flanks of the Tanks. It was answered by machine-gun fire from the enemy redoubts in Lateau Wood, where there was heavy fighting going on, and in Flesquieres village on the height of the crest in front of where I stood by Beaucamp, and from the direction of Havrincourt. It was a very dreadful sound, in one steady blast of fire from many of those weapons – from hundreds of them – and broken into by the sharp staccato hammering, like a coffin-maker with his tacks, from a single machine-gun closer to our captured ground. Hardly a shell-burst came from the enemy's side . . . It was clear at a glance that the enemy was weak in artillery. One of our battalions, the Royal Fusiliers, gained their objectives without a single casualty. Other battalions of English county regiments had very light losses, and they were mostly from machine-guns bullets. At the field dressing-station on the southern part of the attack they had only received 200 walking wounded by eleven o'clock in the morning – five hours or so after the battle began. . . .

I am not allowed to give our exact gains to-day, and it is not well perhaps that the enemy should know them just now. But in a little while I hope to tell the whole story from start to finish, when it will, I hope, gladden people who have been sadly tried by bad news of late from other fronts. In strategy, it seems to me the battle may prove the best adventure we have had, and the enemy was utterly deceived.[6]

George Dewar, a new face to the British press camp, had temporarily replaced Beach Thomas for the *Daily Mail* because Northcliffe, as part of the War Mission to America, had borrowed Thomas for a lecture tour of the USA. Dewar, aged fifty-five, editor of the *Saturday Review* and close friend of Beach Thomas, was no stranger to the Western Front having made repeated visits to the British Army's Front during 1916 and 1917. He had also been a guest of the French Army at Verdun and of the Italian Army in the Julian Alps. In one of his dispatches from Cambrai he noticed the effect the dry ground was having on the tanks' progress and compared it with the countryside around Flanders during that offensive.

The tanks were in no danger of being bogged, as they must be in the frightful quagmires of Flanders.

They could move across nice, firm, thirsty soil in which such plants as the yarrow, cow parsnip, and ragwort, and great masses of docks and darnels flourish. On some of this ground one noticed that the tank in passing scarcely left its stamp. Such soil is the very thing for tanks so long as the weather holds up – it has several times threatened us rather ominously this afternoon, by the way – and it is excellent too for the movements of troops.[7]

While the celebrations were in full swing on the Home Front following news of the early successes and the correspondents' enthusiasm about the new tactics of battle used by the British military, on the Western Front things were not going to plan.

Problems had developed, as the tanks advanced faster than the infantry, thus leaving them behind. The infantry were being caught in the wired areas by German machine-gun fire and the tanks, being so far ahead unaided, were easy pickings for the German batteries. Behind this initial assault the British had very few fresh reinforcements to exploit the gap created to its full potential on 20 November. The British commanders had only forty-eight hours in which to take advantage of the break in the Hindenburg line as German reinforcements were already being rushed to the area by train to plug the gaps.

On the second day of the offensive British troops were still advancing and got as far as Bourlon Wood and captured Fontaine-Notre-Dame. This was a further mile and a half from the previous day's advance. However, this opportunity was rapidly disappearing for the British and with it the supposed surprise of battle. The British troops were suffering from exhaustion and the tank brigades were fast running out of machines and men. By the evening of 22 November a fresh German division from the Eastern Front was already in place to close the gap and strengthen the line.

By 24 November, a day after the church bells had been ringing in celebration around Britain, it was clear from the war correspondents' dispatches that all was not well. Under the headline of 'WHY FONTAINE-NOTRE-DAME WAS LOST', Herbert Russell, the Reuters' correspondent, endeavoured to explain the halt to this victorious advance.

> War correspondents' headquarters, Friday.
> During the last twenty-four hours we have made no further general advance on the main front of our attack, the chief activity is being done by the transport, engineers, and artillery, who are catching up with the rapidity of our rush into enemy territory.
> Fontaine-Notre-Dame, from which we have fallen back, is completely dominated from the heights of Bourlon to the west on the one side, and exposed to enemy fire from across the canal on the other. It made an excellent salient, but it could not be held until there had been a general advance on either side.[8]

The cavalry had made a move through the gap in the Hindenburg line but was brought to a halt by German machine-guns, and the infantry, who had not been trained in the art of open warfare, could do nothing. The German Army was now fighting back fiercely after the initial shocks and preparing in the distance for a massive counter-attack. This is reflected in the stark dispatches of the war correspondents in which there is no attempt to hide the fierce fighting and loss of land in 'over optimistic' language.

> The first great surprise of our attack across the Hindenburg line is over, and the free open fighting, when the cavalry, Tanks, and infantry rounded up the enemy in French villages, has now been followed by closer fighting of the old style, with attacks and counter-attacks, ground gained and ground lost on both sides, while the enemy is making a strong stand with local forces and units hurriedly brought up in order to gain time for the arrival of stronger reinforcements. He is massing men and guns in Cambrai, and preparing to hold a line of defence

Canadian prisoners of the Germans follow the tank.

round that city if he is forced still farther back from his present positions. The battle has continued to-day, and our troops and Tanks have been engaged in heavy fighting round Bourlon Wood, and at Fontaine-Notre-Dame, to the east of it, which we lost yesterday for a time, after a sharp counter-attack upon our Seaforth Highlanders, who entered it on Wednesday night with Tanks. It is a tragedy for the poor civilians there that after a brief spell of liberty which they used to provide the Tank crews with coffee, some of them, if not all of them, fell again into the hands of the enemy.

Tanks and cavalry co-operated in this attack, and the Tanks were a most powerful aid, and cruised round and through the village, where they put out nests of machine-guns. The cavalry then went on into Anneux; but the first patrol had to retire because of the fierce machine-gun fire that swept down the streets, and it had to be attacked and taken again the day before yesterday.[9]

By 26 November it was evident that the British were abandoning parts of the trench systems captured on the first day of the offensive. The following day the British Army were forced to break off the engagement and troops and tanks withdrew from Fontaine. It would seem that hopes of reaching Cambrai had been shattered. From 28 November, the German barrage began to rain down on the British in Bourlon Wood, preparing the way for a massive counter-attack two days later. The Germans rapidly broke through the British positions and advanced almost 3 miles, capturing many guns and soldiers on their way.

The enemy this morning has made a determined effort to drive us back from our newly captured positions, and at about 7.30, after a very violent bombardment, with the use of many gas-shells, delivered a heavy attack with massed storm-troops against our lines round Bourlon Wood. Going up towards the Front before knowing that this new battle was impending, I saw the enemy's fierce bombardment of our lines and other signs of intense conflict. Places where I have been during the past ten days watching this open warfare around Bourlon Wood without seeing much hostile shelling except on the immediate line of attack or counter-attack, were now being swept by fire, and the sky was full of black smoke-clouds of German shrapnel and with the shrill whine of it. It was obvious that the comparative quietude of the days following our last attack on Fontaine-Notre-Dame has been used by the enemy to bring up more guns and store up supplies of ammunition, in order to support the new attack to-day. It was remarkable to see the range and intensity of his fire, and he was shooting as far back as Bapaume, which is now a long way behind our lines. Many squadrons of our aeroplanes were overhead. The enemy's thrust against our positions round the forest of Bourlon was supported by masses of men, who succeeded in driving through for some distance on the west side of the forest, but were checked and driven back by our troops, who fought with the utmost gallantry and self-sacrifice. The battle is still in progress there, but from the latest reports it seems that the enemy has had to retire, after most bloody losses.

Sir Julian Byng's strategy and victory when our troops broke through the Hindenburg line and swept into the country round Cambrai challenged the enemy to open warfare. He has apparently accepted the challenge. It will be a new opportunity for generalship.[10]

By December it was clear to the military and the Home Front that all had not gone well. It had become a time for the military to salvage what defences they had left and rebuild during the winter months. On the Home Front it was a period in which to uncover and examine the truth of the battle. This search for a scapegoat may have been a way of disguising their own ignorance through self-interest. The correspondent George Dewar suggested it was up to individuals to draw their own conclusions from the offensive. They had been given a fairly realistic account of the battle from the war correspondents of the events surrounding Cambrai, but the early censorship rules, established between 1914 and 1917, had created a reality gap which could not be closed. The war correspondents had provided as much of the truth about the battle as they could without infringing the censorship rules. However, those on the Home Front, who endured much of the war with insufficient news of events, then experienced a period of over-optimistic reporting, and finally, when inundated with a mass of realistic information, their reaction was to wave their hands in disbelief.

I do not modify a word I have written of the splendid skill and striking power of our offensive of November 20, which yielded us 10,000 prisoners and Bourlon Wood. That success stands, to apply a famous phrase, but neither must we question or belittle the strength and daring of this huge enemy army on the west. People at home must draw their own moral out of this new German thrust. My present duty is to give as good an account of it as I can. It will be some days before we can clear up the confusion of various accounts. The same tale in detail twice running from actors and observers of a swift, furious onslaught like this is no common experience.[11]

The Home Front were looking for answers from the generals as the British Army settled down for another bleak winter in the trenches with no end in sight to the hostilities. As always it was the correspondents who tried to inject some comfort into their reports of recent events at Cambrai, and also to look forward to the future.

December 6.
The Commander-in-Chief has announced this afternoon in his official communiqué the news of our withdrawal from part of the ground captured in our advance on November 20, in order to avoid holding the sharp salient made by Bourlon Wood and our line running down east and west of it. This operation has been very secretly done, and was carried out with the finest courage and discipline by our troops after the plan was decided. It was not an easy or safe thing to do, and its success depended on the enemy's complete ignorance of our intention and the valour of the rear-guards holding on to positions to the last possible moment, ready to fight hard until the main bodies of troops had withdrawn to our present line of defence. Any premature discovery might have led to immediate pressure of the enemy against our forward posts and considerable danger to those falling back behind them. So far from this happening the enemy was thoroughly deceived as to our intentions, and long after the withdrawal had been effected on our left yesterday morning, he put down a heavy bombardment on the abandoned trenches near Moeuvres, and afterwards launched a strong infantry attack on those positions, watched at a distance by our men, who chuckled at this furious advance upon mythical defenders. It seemed a huge joke to our men, whose sense of humour was sharpened by their sense of safety. . . .
   The events between November 20 and our strategical withdrawal from Bourlon Wood to the present line form one of the most thrilling and extraordinary episodes in the history of this war. It began when Sir Julian Byng's audacious and cunning plan of attack without preliminary bombardment and with large numbers of Tanks stupefied the enemy and opened a wide breach in the Hindenburg line through which our infantry and cavalry passed out into the open country round Cambrai, and did amazing things which have not yet all been told – as, for instance, the story of the German prisoners that some of our troopers actually rode into Cambrai itself on the first night of victory.
   Ten thousand prisoners were taken by us, and it is believed that, but for certain elements of bad luck, Cambrai might have been ours, though it was not within our expectations. The enemy was quick in hurling up guns and reinforcements and developed violent counter-attacks. In all those he lost prodigiously in men, and the number of his casualties must have been extravagantly high, even according to accounts given by his own prisoners. After all this fighting and one day of vicissitudes, during which the enemy had the luck to get through a weak place in our advanced lines and overrun some of the country we had gained, we had withdrawn to a strong position on ground

seized from the enemy in a cheap and easy way. Here we remain secure, with good observation and strong lines behind us.[12]

Another offensive had ended in stalemate as winter took hold of the battlefields. However, as a result of the Cambrai offensive both the Germans and Allies developed new tactics. These were to become the key to the German and Allied successes on the Western Front during the German spring offensive in March and the Allied offensive in the summer of 1918.

NOTES

1. P. Griffith, *Battle Tactics of the Western Front. The British Army's Art of Attack, 1916–18* (Yale University, 1994), p. 164.
2. P. Gibbs, *Open Warfare, The Way to Victory* (Heinemann, 1919), p. 4.
3. P. Gibbs, *Realities of War* (Heinemann, 1920), p. 397.
4. D. Winter, *Haig's Command* (Penguin Books, 1992), p. 118.
5. The *Daily News and Leader*, Thursday, 22 November 1917 (London).
6. The *Daily Chronicle*, Thursday, 22 November 1917 (London).
7. The *Daily Mail*, Thursday, 22 November 1917 (London).
8. The *Daily Mail*, Saturday, 24 November 1917 (London).
9. The *Daily Chronicle*, Saturday, 1 December 1917 (London).
10. The *Daily Chronicle*, Saturday, 24 November 1917 (London).
11. The *Daily Mail*, Monday, 3 December 1917 (London).
12. The *Daily Chronicle*, Friday, 7 December 1917 (London).

THE GERMAN OFFENSIVE, 1918

The nature of the war at the beginning of 1918 was changing as one power left the fighting and another joined. Russia was in crisis and revolution, it could not continue fighting on the Eastern Front for fear of imminent collapse. On 3 March 1918 the Germans and Russians signed a peace treaty to end hostilities on the Eastern Front. The Treaty of Brest-Litovsk had grave implications for the Allies. The German Army was now free to fight the war on one front; German troops from the redundant Eastern Front could be transferred to the Western Front and support a major offensive to end the war in Germany's favour. In only a few weeks the German fighting strength had increased by 30 per cent on the Western Front.[1]

However, the Germans needed to be quick to gain the advantage before the mass of American troops and war materials arrived on the battlefield. Although the Americans had declared war on Germany in April 1917 it took many months for their total war potential to be achieved. It was believed that the full impact of the American war machine would not be felt on the Western Front until 1919 at the earliest. As in European countries, the American economy and industry had had to adapt to meet the demands of the war – troops needed to be trained and given the hardware to fight. All this took time, a gap in which the German Army had the best and maybe only chance of achieving a victory which would end the war in her favour.

While activity increased on the German side of the Western Front with a build up of new ammunition dumps, more aeroplanes and battery positions, it was clear to the British Intelligence that an enemy offensive was imminent. Therefore, the British military began to brace itself and tried to alert the Home Front to the apparent dangers through the dispatches of the war correspondents.

In late February 1918 the newspapers published the war correspondents' dispatches which had been written with the express aim of forewarning the Home Front of the approaching German offensive. These contained the evidence collected by Military Intelligence and included interviews from newly captured German prisoners, articles on the enemy's new gas weapons and news that German tanks had been sighted close to the battlefield. Headlines included 'READY FOR THE HUNS', 'HUNS TALK OF OFFENSIVE', and 'GERMAN TANKS SEEN ON FRONT'.[2] Hamilton Fyfe, correspondent for the *Daily Mail* while Beach Thomas was still in America, sent back a dispatch in which he had talked to recently taken German prisoners.

Visiting a portion of our line which is not far from the Cambrai area, I was told that one of the German tanks had been seen some distance behind their front. . . .
This one was being exhibited to a crowd of soldiers, who seemed to be following

it about with admiring wonder. Whether they will follow it with equal alacrity over No Man's Land remains to be seen.[3]

Philip Gibbs also reported the sighting of German tanks close to the front.

Meanwhile it is certain that the enemy is preparing to bring Tanks into action. We knew some time ago that he was training some of his troops to attack behind them, and some of our observers have seen a Tank behind the enemy's lines. It was lumbering around with a body of German infantry on each side of it. This year may see Tanks against Tanks, and many curious alterations in tactics resulting from this moving machine-gun emplacement; but we have a long start in experience and technique, and the advantage should be immensely on our side.[4]

These warnings of the imminent dangers of a German attack given by the war correspondents on behalf of the military throughout February and early March had little effect on the Home Front or its morale. The information gap between the Home Front and France was such that the general public did not understand the seriousness of these threats. Gibbs explained how the articles were received.

Flanders had made no difference to national optimism, though the hospitals were crowded with blind and maimed and shell-shocked.
  Nobody believed the war correspondents. Nobody ever did believe us, though some of us wrote the truth from the first to last as far as the facts of war go apart from deeper psychology, and a naked realism of horrors and losses, and criticism of facts, which did not come within our liberty of the pen.[5]

Just as the Home Front could not understand the Cambrai set-back in November of 1917, it did not believe the war correspondents' stark predictions for 1918. Maybe they were suffering from 'battle fatigue' after nearly four years of war and had their own struggles to deal with. More likely is that the years of 'Eyewitness' and 'official correspondence' had taken their toll on the credibility of the military and war correspondents.
  However, the political/military bickering between Lloyd George, Robertson and Haig over the number of reserves kept in England and the reorganization of the British Army might have been a catalyst. In January Haig had been ordered by the War Cabinet to take over part of the French Front without any compensating reinforcements and Lloyd George and Robertson decided to limit the number of reserves sent out to France. In light of this the alarmist dispatches of the war correspondents could have been a tactic on the military's behalf to scare Lloyd George into a change of mind over the reserves issue.[6] It is certain that when Philip Gibbs wrote of the impact these dispatches had on the Home Front he was unaware of the wider political issues.
  The main preparations for the spring offensive began on 9 March with the Germans launching a series of bombardments on the Western Front, which Martin Gilbert described as 'Their largest and most essential gamble of the war'.[7] Two days before the Germans launched their offensive Percival Phillips wrote in his dispatch

about the increase in shelling from the enemy. However, he put this down to the 'increased wealth' of the Germans since the end of fighting on the Eastern Front. What is interesting is the comment on the long-range shells which were falling well behind the Front line. This was no accident and was an attempt to disrupt the communication lines between Front line trenches and military authorities. The *Daily Express'* headline proclaims 'FUTILE SHELLING OF THE LAND BEHIND OUR LINES', although it failed to realize that this bombardment was going to cause an almost total breakdown in the communication infrastructure when the German advance began.

> The enemy seems determined to emphasise his increased wealth in weapons and the ability to waste ammunition now that the Russian front has vanished. Back areas that have not been troubled by high explosive since we bent the German line back beyond the ridges of Passchendaele and Messines are again feeling the old familiar shock of falling shells.[8]

On 21 March 1918 at 4.30 a.m. some 4,000 German guns began the hurricane bombardment of the British defences around the Somme. The main attack was on a front, 42 miles in length, between Gouzeaucourt and Barisis, with the aim of cutting off the British forces from their French allies. What the Germans had learnt at the Battle of Cambrai was now put to the test on a much larger scale. This new approach used a sudden artillery bombardment of gas and smoke shells, followed by the rapid infiltration of storm troops into the British Front. The day even saw the first nine German tanks in action on the battlefield.

By the end of the day the new German tactics had succeeded and, aided by the morning mists, their advance had moved forward 4½ miles through the crumbling British defences. Confusion set upon the British Army as troops who had very little experience or training of open warfare were propelled from their trenches. Liddell Hart considered the complacency of the British in their trench systems as a major factor in the success of the German advance.

> The main cause of the subsequently rapid flow-back lay in the frequent breakdown of control and communication. During three years of trench warfare an elaborate and complex system, largely dependent on the telephone, had been built up, and when the static suddenly became fluid the British paid the inevitable penalty of violating that fundamental axiom of war – elasticity.[9]

The *Daily Express* leads on 22 March, announcing the grim news that, 'GERMAN OFFENSIVE OPENS ON A WIDE FRONT' and '50 MILES OF OUR LINE ATTACKED ON A VASTER SCALE THAN EVER BEFORE'.[10]

> An attack, which appears to be the beginning of the great German offensive, was made against the British front west and south-west of Cambrai to-day.
> The German army attacking south of the Scarpe seems to have delivered its first blow principally in the triangle of Arras–Cambrai and Bapaume–Cambrai roads, while the German army south of Cambrai is striking in the region of the Scheldt Canal . . .

It is impossible to give more than the vaguest outline of the fighting in this despatch. Between four and five o'clock this morning the preliminary wire-cutting bombardment was begun between the Scarpe and Vendeuil, south of St. Quentin, and the first infantry waves appear to have attacked soon after daylight. I hear of fighting at Bullecourt and in the region of Hargicourt and Villers Guislain, where the German storm troops are endeavouring to thrust forward the left jaw of the gigantic pincers. The German effort is being made with great vigour and determination. . . .

If this battle proves to be the real German effort against the British front we must expect hard and continuous fighting. The enemy has trained his troops well in open warfare, and they are well supported by light and heavy artillery and a host of trench mortars intended to move forward steadily with the advancing infantry. I see no cause for anxiety in the news we have received thus far. The first day of any battle does not yield very clear accounts of its development, but by to-morrow we should know whether this great offensive, on which the enemy has lavished such a wealth of material and labour, has given him an initial success.[11]

The dispatches were unclear at this time about the true scale of the German offensive. There were rumours and unconfirmed reports from all over the British fighting fronts of which correspondents such as Philip Gibbs were quick to make sense.

A German offensive against our front has begun. At about five o'clock this morning the enemy began an intense bombardment of our lines and batteries on a very wide front – something like sixty miles – from the country south of the Scarpe and to the west of Bullecourt in the neighbourhood of Croisilles, and as far south as our positions between St.-Quentin and our right flank on the Oise.

After several hours of this hurricane shelling, in which it is probable that a great deal of gas was used with the intention of creating a poison-gas atmosphere around our gunners and forward posts, the German infantry advanced and developed attacks against a number of strategical points.

Among the places against which they seem to have directed their chief efforts are Bullecourt – the scene of so much hard fighting last year by the Australians, Scottish, and London troops – Lagnicourt, and Noreuil (both west of Cambrai), where they once before penetrated our lines and were slaughtered in great numbers, the St.-Quentin Ridge, which was on the right of the Cambrai fighting, the two villages of Ronssoy and Hargicourt, south of the Cambrai salient, and the country south of St.-Quentin.

It is impossible to say yet how far the enemy will endeavour to follow up the initial movement of his troops over any ground he may gain in the first rush, or with what strength he will press forward his supporting divisions and fling his storm-troops into the struggle. But the attack already appears to be on a formidable scale, with a vast amount of artillery and masses of men, and there is reason to believe that it is indeed the beginning of the great offensive advertised for so long a time and with such ferocious menaces by the enemy's agents in neutral countries. If so it is a bid for a decisive victory on the Western Front, at no matter what sacrifice, and with the fullest brutalities of every engine of war gathered together during the months of preparation and liberated entirely for this front by the downfall of Russia.

To-day I can give no details of the fighting, but will reserve all attempts to give a clear insight into the situation until my next message, when out of the hurricane of fire now spreading over sixty miles or more of the battlefields there will come certain knowledge of the fighting. At the moment there are only scraps of news from one part of the Front and another, unconfirmed rumours, reports of ground given or taken, and the vague tidings of men hard pressed, but holding out against repeated onslaughts. It would be a wicked, senseless thing to make use of these uncertain fragments from many sources, and some hours must pass before it becomes clear how much the enemy has gained by his first blow and how much he has failed to gain against the heroic resistance of our troops. The immediate endeavour of the enemy seems obvious. It is an enlargement of his strategical plan in the attack of November 30 against the lines we held after the first Cambrai battle, and it covers the same ground, on a much wider boundary. He appears to be assaulting both wings of the salient between the Scarpe and the south end of the Flesquieres Ridge in order to cut off all the intervening ground, which includes Havrincourt Wood and Velu Wood, the line south of Morchies and Beaumetz, and a stretch of the country east and south-east of Bapaume, down to St.-Quentin and the Oise, which he abandoned to us in his retreat last March after the battles of the Somme. By a rapid turning movement from both wings he would hope to capture many of our men and guns. It is a menace which cannot be taken lightly, and at the present moment our troops are fighting not only for their own lives, but also for the fate of England and all our race. . . .

The main street of Combles.

The heart of all the people of our race must go out to these battalions of boys upon who our destiny depends, and who now, while I write, are making a wall with their bodies against the evil and the power of our enemy.[12]

The German advance was on such a vast scale that it caused problems for the war correspondents who now had to travel many miles between their telegraphic base and the scene of the fighting. Many valuable hours could be wasted by the correspondents trying to find the centre of the storm, travelling between the Somme and Flanders. On the first day of the offensive Perry Robinson was already preparing to visit the sector with most activity.

These reports came from points as wide apart as the neighbourhood of Croisilles, Bullecourt and Lagnicourt, on the north, to the region of Ronssoy and Hargicourt on the south. It is impossible to say as yet how much this movement portends, except that it has the appearance of a considerably larger operation than has taken place this year. I am leaving for the sector of the line where the chief activity appears to be taking place.[13]

The problems of the war correspondents were to worsen during the retreat of the British across the Somme as the news changed every hour. Perry Robinson, in a dispatch on the state of play, had to apologize to his readers for the disjointed nature of his report.

You will understand that it is not easy to give a connected account of the details of a conflict of such enormous scope, into which the Germans on a 50-mile front have already thrown in a minimum of 600,000 men of the infantry divisions alone. Every hour the situation changes, and the great line sways and reels as, at one point or another, the Germans force new penetration, or we hurl them back again from the ground they thought they had won.[14]

By 27 March the British Army had found its feet and the German advance had begun to slow down. Taylor pointed out that this was due to the nature of transport forces involved in getting Allied reserves to the battlefield faster than the attacking infantry moved forward on foot.[15] For a time it had seemed that the French and British troops might split after a 10 mile gap appeared, as the two Allies retreated in different directions. In order to stop this on 26 March both Allies agreed to appoint General Foch as the Commander of the Allied Armies in France to coordinate the armies. The newspaper reports from 27 March were calmer and less alarmist, although the German threat was still a serious one. It had become time to reassure the Home Front that all had not been lost.

Our battle front fluctuated very little in the past twenty-four hours, and at a number of points between the Scarpe and the Somme we have repulsed the enemy. Fighting slackened perceptibly in this region yesterday, and the lull imposed by the necessity of relieving worn out German divisions and moving forward heavy guns continued to-day, save at isolated points, where the enemy sought to improve local advantages.

He has been terribly punished on the old battlefield of the Somme. Our batteries have been threshing the billowed slopes of the Ancre valley and the broad expanse of ruined trench and craterland lifting to the height of Thiepval and reaching out to the dead villages around Bapaume. The guns have given the massed army of General von Below no rest. His men can find no shelter from the shells that fall thickly on every patch of open ground between the nests of rotting redoubts and half-obliterated refuges of Germans who died under the first Somme bombardments nearly two years ago. . . .

The war of movement has been responsible for an extraordinary crop of false rumours of the wildest description, many of which are undoubtedly of enemy origin. False reports as to the situation are industriously circulated, but the confidence of the populace has been restored by the exposure of many false-hoods.

The people are reassured by the calm demeanour of our troops. When a column of infantry rested to-day at the end of a village street some of the men produced the inevitable football and began kicking it joyously about a field. The peasants, who were packing their belongings and preparing to move, stopped to watch the game, and one woman was heard to say to her neighbour: 'If the English can play football we need not be alarmed.'[16]

The German advance had been so extensive that within a week of the offensive beginning they had advanced nearly 40 miles towards Amiens. By 30 March the Germans were 11 miles from Amiens when a successful counter-attack by British and Empire troops slowed down and halted them.

This advance appeared formidable, especially when the British command were expecting such an attack to happen in the early part of 1918. Haig had believed that the attack would take place further north than the Somme and had therefore concentrated his reserves around the Channel ports to defend them. However, Haig was not as far from the truth as the situation would have us believe. Ludendorff's plan for the Somme was a kind of distraction for the British to move their focus away from the Ypres salient. Then when the desired effect had been achieved by the German Army, Ludendorff moved the centre of the offensive northwards to Passchendaele.

On the morning of 28 March the German offensive expanded northwards towards Arras, which happened to be where Haig had strong reserves. Here the German Army achieved little and the Home Front had a lesson from Hamilton Fyfe on how to view the current situation on the Western Front. Yards that had been fought over to the death in 1917 no longer mattered in this period of open warfare and the public had to be educated about this point.

The only important development of to-day's fighting is the attack on the Arras front, which began with the usual bombardment from 5 o'clock onwards and was followed by an advance of infantry in great strength.

The enemy has a very large number of troops here and he is using them with the same prodigal vigour which has marked his efforts elsewhere. We fell back from foremost positions on part of the front attacked and in spite of heavy casualties, after stubborn fighting on and around Telegraph Hill, near the Arras–Cambrai road, the enemy gained a little ground on a front of about 2,000 yards, not that he measures his gains in territory. A prisoner, a man of high intelligence, said that no one in the German Army wanted merely to gain ground. This was not the aim of the High Command. Their aim and the desire of all Germans was to reach a decision and end the war. 'The defeat of the British,' he said, 'is what we hope for. We do not want to go a certain distance and then dig ourselves in and go on for another two years.'

Since that is the enemy view, let us be equally sensible. Let us not worry about this or that village, captured only for the time being. Let us not gaze gloomily at the map and say, 'Another thousand yards gone.' That is not the way to look at a battle on this scale. What we must do is to consider which army is more likely 'to stick it out' and to put in the finishing blows.[17]

On 5 April the Germans halted their offensive on the Somme and preparations were made to move the onslaught north to Flanders. Again on 9 April the offensive was renewed with the aim of driving back the British and Belgian troops, opening up the road to Calais and the Channel ports.

The attack centred around Neuve Chapelle which was defended by a Portuguese division who were badly in need of rest. Sweeping away the Portuguese soldiers, the German troops punched a hole in the Allied line which was 30 miles wide and 5 miles deep. Little of this impending disaster can be found in the reports from the war correspondents on the first day of the Battle of Lys, probably because this information had not yet reached them, rather than because of the work of the press censor's blue pencil. Hamilton Fyfe of the *Daily Mail* reported

The fresh stage of the German offensive for which we have been waiting began this morning.

The enemy has attacked us upon an 11 miles front in the flat, muddy country north of Lens and south of Armentières. He has chosen this time to strike from a point where his line bulges, probably in the hope of penetrating far enough to force us to fall back from one or another of the salients which occur in our line above and below the new battlefield.

It may be this is only a diversion intended to attract reserves from other sectors so as to make the operations farther south easier for the enemy, or it may be that he means to try to carry on both sets of operations at once. . . .

Between 8 and midnight he is calculated to have sent over 60,000 gas shells.

Then after an interval the bombardment began at 4.5 a.m. on the front chosen for the attack and on sectors north and south of it. It continued on Armentières until 11 o'clock.

Again there was a mist in this damp country. It was especially dense, and about 8 o'clock the defenders of our positions saw the German infantry looming through it. The Germans made their most violent effort at the extreme right of our battle-front, where the Hill of Givenchy, the only hill in the neighbourhood, was their objective.

A little distance to the north of this our Portuguese Allies are engaged. The latest report I can get about them is that they were fighting hard in the middle of the day. Near Givenchy about noon we got a batch of 80 prisoners. At the same time at least one point in our forward line was still holding out. The brave garrison of a post in the middle of the marshes on the canal bank were cheerfully defending it, with good hope of success.[18]

Philip Gibbs' dispatch sought to turn the bad news round by focusing on the cost in lives to the enemy of this advance, rather than dwelling on the rapid retreat of the Portuguese.

A heavy and determined attack was begun against us this morning a considerable distance north of our recent battles, on about eleven miles of front, between Armentières and La Bassée Canal. So far as news comes to us up to this afternoon, the enemy has succeeded in driving through our outpost lines, while our troops are holding him by Givenchy on the right and about Fleurbaix on the left.

This new attack was preceded by a long, concentrated bombardment, which has gradually been increasing during the last day or two, until it reached wild heights of fury last night and early this morning. The enemy has used poison-gas in immense quantities, and it may be estimated that during the night he flung over 60,000 gas-shells in order to create a wide zone of evil vapour and stupefy our gunners, transport, and infantry if they were caught without their masks, which is improbable. His gun-fire reached out to many towns and villages behind our lines, like Béthune and Armentières, Vermelles and Philosophe, Merville and Estaires, and this did not cease round Armentières until 11.30 this morning, though farther south, from Fleurbaix, his infantry attack was in progress at an early hour, certainly by eight o'clock, and his barrage lifted in order to let his troops advance. The strength of his attack is not yet known with any certainty, but three divisions are in that area, including the 44th Reserve, the 81th and the 10th Ersatz, and it is probable that he has other forces engaged.

Part of our line was held by Portuguese troops, who, for a long time, have been between Laventie and Neuve-Chapelle holding positions which were subject to severe raids from time to time. They are now in the thick of this battle, most fiercely beset, and unfortunately giving ground too rapidly.

Suddenly the enemy has struck, and the centre of strife for a moment has shifted. It is an awkward ground for attack and bad weather for such ground, because the enemy has to advance across dead-flat marshes, cut through and through by an intricate system of canals, which must be all flooded now, after heavy rain and shell-fire, which has broken the banks. All the enemy's efforts this morning do not seem to have carried him far through those marshes, and up to the time I write his storm-troops are being held back and shattered by machine-gun fire before Givenchy, outside an outpost in the marshes sap, and at a place called Picantin, in front of Laventie. If he gets no farther, his venture will be futile except as a demonstration in order to weaken our reserves by further casualties and increase the strain on our main defence. Meanwhile his own losses must be reaching prodigious figures. To-day again many of his men lie dead in those swamps by Neuve-Chapelle.[19]

After the fall of Armentières and the capture of Messines Ridge on 11 April, Haig called for and indeed pleaded with his army to fight it out to the last man. It would appear that the situation had become so grave that Haig felt it necessary to appeal to his troops. This plea was published in the newspapers on 13 April and it told the Home Front so much more about the situation in France than the war correspondents could do or were allowed to.

To all Ranks of the British Army in France and Flanders:
Three weeks ago to-day the enemy began his terrific attacks against us on a fifty-mile front. His objects are to separate us from the French, to take the Channel ports and destroy the British Army.

In spite of throwing already 106 divisions into the battle and enduring the most reckless sacrifices of human life, he has as yet made little progress, towards his goals. We owe this to the determined fighting and self-sacrifice of our troops. Words fail me to express the admiration which I feel for the splendid resistance offered by all ranks of our Army under the most trying circumstances.

Many among us now are tired. To these I would say that victory will belong to the side which holds out the longest. The French Army is moving rapidly and in great force to our support.

There is no other course open to us but to fight it out. Every position must be held to the last man; there must be no retirement. With our backs to the wall and believing in justice of our cause, each one of us must fight on to the end. The safety of our homes and the freedom of mankind depend alike upon the conduct of each one of us at this critical moment.[20]

A church service conducted before battle.

This plea had been addressed to the ranks of the British Army, who already had their backs to the wall, and therefore maybe it was an appeal with the Home Front directly in mind. The soldiers on the Western Front were perhaps too preoccupied with fierce fighting to be able to read Haig's message and perhaps it was an attempt to damage Lloyd George's reputation in relation to the decision to withold reserves from the battle zone in January 1918. Haig's plea certainly made the Home Front aware of the bleak reality of the fighting in France and Belgium. It was a stark warning that desperate times were ahead. Liddell Hart commented

> To the British public, and even perhaps to the British forces, this message came like a thunderclap, awakening them to the graveness of the danger and seeming almost to convey a warning that hope had gone and only honour remained – to go down fighting with their faces to the foe.[21]

More bad news was to follow as the familiar place names etched on the public's consciousness and fought over desperately during the Third Battle of Ypres were evacuated and recaptured by the enemy. Passchendaele was reoccupied on 16 April without a fight, which seems particularly poignant after all the effort and sacrifice made by the Allied troops to capture it in November 1917.

Having been constantly informed during 1917 of just how important Passchendaele Ridge was to the British Army, the Home Front again had to be re-educated about the nature and tactics of open warfare. They had to understand why the ridge was given up so freely, that warfare had so evolved as to make the value of the ridge redundant. The onus fell on the correspondents. Percival Phillips explained

> Our withdrawal from Passchendaele and the ground for which so many men of the Empire have died causes the deepest regret, but it has not discouraged the soldiers, who know that in open warfare trench positions lose their former value, and that the people at home will regard the sacrifice in the same sensible way.[22]

Later Phillips went on to highlight the benefits of open warfare compared with the trench system, when Passchendaele had been a prized possession.

> Now that they occupy their old posts on that crest the Flanders plain is again at their feet, but save on the clearest days even the most powerful glass is of comparatively little value in registering distant targets. When our trenches hugged the base of the ridge we suffered from close observation. Open warfare, however, frees the British line from this disadvantage.
> Messines Ridge is a greater thorn in his flesh. Passchendaele and the battlefield this side of it is more of an obstacle to the enemy than a help – the wilderness must be reclaimed, and troops sent forward in the hope of reaching Calais are far beyond good billets of any kind.
> Our men know from experience the difficulty of creating cover and maintaining dry shelters in this desert. It is a vast graveyard. Wherever one digs the mingled wreckage of human bodies and accumulated filth of three and a half

years of warfare are unearthed: the water cannot be drunk, and even food seems
to be contaminated when deposited in these surroundings.[23]

These dispatches promoted a propaganda message, to persuade the Home Front to
understand and accept the military point of view when things were not going well.
Hamilton Fyfe explained to the Home Front how to re-evaluate the lives of sacrificed
soldiers of the Passchendaele salient.

The evacuation of the salient at Passchendaele need not be regretted. It would
have been cause for uneasiness if we had held on here. It is regrettable, of course,
especially if we reckon the lives lost last year in taking this ground as having
been sacrificed for it, but that is not the right way to reckon. The lives were not
given to take this ground, but to beat the Germans. This ground was incidental.
The other is the essential point, and we shall do better in this respect now we
have liquidated a difficult obligation. Do not be hypnotised by the map.[24]

By 18 April the Germans had gained 10 miles from the British since the offensive
had moved north on 9 April. The progress of the Germans was now grinding to
another halt. Later, on 24 April, the Allies' morale was boosted by the first tank-to-
tank battle on the Western Front. The German troops, aided by thirteen tanks, took
the village of Villers-Brettonneux, but as the newspapers reported, what became seen
as important was the superiority of the British tank. The *Daily Express* celebrated the
fact with the excessive enthusiasm mentioned by Griffith[25] in the report entitled
'BATTLE OF THE TANKS. FIRST FLEET ACTION WON BY THE BRITISH'.

By Percival Phillips, Thursday night.
For the first time British and German tanks have met in battle, and the victory is
ours. They fought yesterday in the open fields round Villers-Brettonneux, east
of Amiens, where the enemy made a determined and, for the moment, a
successful attack on that town and high ground round it.
    The German tanks led the attack, swinging on the town from the north-east
and from the south, and in their wake came infantry with their machine guns
and heavy mortars and light artillery.
    Altogether there were four or five tanks. They were bulky, ungainly creatures,
quite unlike the British tank in appearance, with a broad, squat turret containing
quick-firing guns. Hidden in the thick mist until very close to our trenches, they
crawled up in the wake of an intense barrage about six o'clock in the morning.
The first intimation some of our troops had of the new enemy was when one
loomed through the smoke near the monument south of the town and dropped
into a shallow valley or gully running parallel with our trenches. Having gained
it, the tank turned north, and travelled towards Villers Brettonneux, flattening
the parapets and firing its guns at the infantry. A British captain who was nearly
run over crouched against the ground and in his rage fired his revolver against
the broad flank of the beast as it lurched past.
    British tanks came up during the morning. The German tanks saw them
approaching, and started forward through the shell-fire to engage them.

They concentrated their guns on one British tank, but others came to the rescue, and in the brief duel that followed one enemy tank was put out of action by an opponent of less bulk and lighter armament and the others scuttled away.

Later in the day a light British tank had a most successful engagement with German infantry which had penetrated to the neighbourhood of Cachy village, south-west of Villers Brettonneux. Fresh battalions of the new 77th Division were seen forming up in the open for another attack. A light tank, which, as the Germans know to their sorrow, is rather more agile than its elder brethren, slid swiftly across the fields and laid these battalions low. It came back, its sides covered with blood. Its commander had charged the Germans repeatedly and run down many of them, as well as killing a greater number with his guns. The survivors were completely demoralised.

The lesson of this first engagement between German and British tanks seems to be that we have nothing to fear from the enemy despite the greater size and armament of his machine. Their crews plainly showed their unwillingness to stand when invited to fight out to a finish.[26]

Hamilton Fyfe, although not a witness to the events, explained how the war correspondents' news pool system worked.

I hear that our tanks, when they came into action in the afternoon, did terrible execution. They caught the Germans preparing to attack near Cachy, the farthest point of their advance, and they went among them. These were light tanks with a considerable speed. When they returned their sides were red with blood. They had shot down many with their guns and they had crushed many others to death by knocking them down and running over them.

The one fight between tanks of which I have had first-hand evidence ended decidedly to our advantage. Some German tanks of large size, with big turrets, attacked two of our 'female' tanks and disabled one. Then a British 'male' tank came up and knocked out one of the Germans. The other rolled away while this combat was going on. They evidently did not like the fierce look of the British 'males'.[27]

Then the Home Front had some good news at last, to be reminded that not all hope had been lost in the British Army. This was to be followed up the next day when the British recaptured Villers-Brettonneux and took 600 German prisoners.

Once again Ludendorff called off the offensive on 29 April. It was wearing the German troops down and they had become exhausted. Their morale was low mainly because they had not achieved the decisive break in the Allied lines which had been expected.

Taylor put forward an interesting additional idea, which may have influenced the failure of the German troops to capitalize on their advances. He implied that the German soldiers became discouraged when they saw the quality of life and lavish supplies which the British held behind their lines.[28] This observation was further expanded by Liddell Hart.

Propaganda and censorship could hide the difference so long as the front was an inviolable wall of partition. But when the Germans broke through the British lines and into the back areas the truth was revealed to the German troops.[29]

The idea was that as the German soldiers advanced further forward behind the former British lines they became even more demoralized to the extent that they believed they had already lost the war. As it was, it took another month before Ludendorff ordered the continuation of the offensive moving down to the Aisne.

The German offensive took off again in the early hours of 27 May with amazing results. They managed to advance 10 miles in a single day, which had not been witnessed on the Western Front since the early days of August 1914. Fourteen German divisions broke through on a 24 mile front in the French sector between Soissons and Rheims after a preliminary bombardment made up of 4,000 guns.

It was such an unexpected attack that the British command had sent four battle-fatigued divisions down to this quiet sector for a rest. Now they found themselves in the path of the advancing German Army once again. By midday the enemy had crossed the Aisne, and by 3 June German troops were within 40 miles of Paris, crossing the Marne. However, the Germans had still failed to break the Allied line, which bulged around the enemy on three sides causing them to over-extend themselves.

The *Daily Express*, to emphasize the magnitude of the German advance, explained to its readers that the Germans were nearer to Paris than Brighton is to London.[30] Distance was becoming a major difficulty to the war correspondents, as the events were now taking place all along the Western Front. The main centre of the fighting had moved down to around Soissons and the war correspondents were based in GHQ behind the main British Front. They, therefore, had to make do with rumours and information from official reports for their dispatches. Hamilton Fyfe for the *Daily Mail* commented:

> The enemy has become active again at several points. Whether at any of these points he means to resume his offensive with all the strength at his disposal is doubtful. At present these attacks may be merely feints to screen his real intention and to induce us to expect the coming blow in the wrong place. . . .
>
> British troops were involved in the affair only to a very small extent on the left of the French. They were just at the edge of the infantry action. Of course they had been included in the bombardment. This extended very far beyond the front upon which the infantry were thrown in.
>
> At the same time the British troops holding a sector on the River Aisne between Rheims and Laon were attacked in some force. The French on their flanks were also drawn into this operation. I understand that fighting is going on and that the German effort is of a determined character, more serious than that which was made in Flanders.[31]

Perry Robinson detailed what vague information there was available in order to piece together the new offensive.

The attack between Soissons and Rheims was made on a front of nearly 30 miles from Vauxaillon, to the north of Soissons, to Brimont above Rheims, and which distance approximately 12 miles on the right were held by British divisions.

The reports which reach here show that the British divisions seem to have held their ground with the utmost stubbornness. The extreme left of the British line was compelled to swing back, which it appears to have done methodically, pivoting on the left centre and fighting hard all the way. The left centre, centre, and right, up to a late hour were holding almost the original positions, subsequently falling back slowly on to the Aisne in conformity with the movement on their left.[32]

The distance between the battlefields of Soissons and the British GHQ slowed down the news reaching the Home Front and the full reports of the British and French retreat to the Marne did not appear in the newspapers until 4 June. Percival Phillips pieced together what he called a successful retreat of the British Army. Such was the success of this rear-guard action that it became too late to blow up bridges across the Aisne and part of the Army was cut off.

I believe that some twenty-five German divisions attacked on the morning of May 27, all of which had been fighting previously in the north. Up to May 30 more than forty divisions are said to have been identified on the battlefront west of Rheims, including reinforcing divisions from the army of General Von Hutier. The front held by the British extended on both sides of Crainne, and it is said that the great weight of infantry flung against our troops in the vicinity of the town was supported by about one hundred tanks.

When the enemy infantry attacked the British remained at their posts until the former had nearly crossed No Man's Land – at this point about two thousand yards deep – and continued to fire until the first wave was nearly upon them, when they retired, having blown up any of their trench mortars which they could not get away. Simultaneously with the appearance of the German infantry the air was filled with hostile aeroplanes, which attacked our troops with bombs and machine guns. . . .

Some of the bridges could not be blown up in time. The first aim of the enemy was to reach the Aisne regardless of casualties, and he succeeded in doing this before the day was very far advanced. Some British troops falling back on the river found the Germans there before them. The Aisne Canal, which runs parallel with the river, proved a serious obstacle to some of our men, who were unable to cross, and were cut off. . . .

The British troops which succeeded in crossing the Aisne continued their rear-guard battle southward over high ground towards the valley of the Vesle, about five miles distant. They continued to be hard pressed, and it was not possible to make a long stand north of the Vesle. There was further fighting around Fismes and St. Gilles before they came out of the battle.[33]

Under the headline 'BRITISH BRAVERY ON AISNE' Perry Robinson put forward the theory that the British had not been taken by surprise. They had just run out of time to complete the bridge blowing, which might have stopped the enemy crossing the Aisne.

> We are beginning to hear some of the details of the experiences of the British divisions which have been fighting so gallantly between Rheims and Soissons.
>
> None the less, we were not taken by surprise. We saw quite clearly on the evening before that the attack was coming, and our men stood to all night of May 27 waiting for the performance to begin. It was about one o'clock in the morning when the enemy bombardment began with a torrent of high explosive shells of all calibers along the entire front. . . .
>
> For a time the German bombardment consisted wholly of high explosives. Then came a period of gas shelling. This, again, was succeeded by a burst of high explosive, and that again by another period of gas. During the last part of the bombardment, before four o'clock, everything came together, including great quantities of various gas and high explosive. The infantry attack was delivered about four o'clock, with, it is estimated, about a hundred Tanks on the Craonne sector of the British front alone. . . .
>
> . . . Our line fell back systematically, fighting almost yard by yard. Men of the 50th Division about Craonne were almost too reluctant to give way, for when ultimately somewhere about noon they reached Maizy, on the Aisne, they found that place with the bridge there already in the hands of the Germans, and here it was that most such unwounded British as were taken prisoner were compelled to surrender. Arrangements had been made for blowing up all the bridges over the Aisne, but at Maizy and apparently some other points the work was not completed in time.[34]

Localized fighting continued in the French sector throughout June with the Germans trying to extend their gains. However, it was not until 15 July that Ludendorff launched his fifth offensive of 1918, on a 50 mile front of the Marne. This time the art of surprise eluded the Germans and two days later the Allies embarked upon a counter-stroke advancing 4½ miles.

For the war correspondents with the British Army it was a lean time as the centre of the fighting was on the French Front. Their dispatches filled less and less column space, sometimes reduced to a short paragraph, making way for news from the French fighting Front and the accredited war correspondent with the French Army. This situation was not to change until in August the British once again went on the offensive during the Battle of Amiens.

NOTES

1. B.H. Liddell Hart, *History of the First World War* (Pan Books, 1972), p. 384.
2. The *Daily Mail*, February, 1918 (London).
3. The *Daily Mail*, Monday, 25 February 1918 (London).
4. The *Daily Chronicle*, Monday, 25 February 1918 (London).
5. P. Gibbs, *Realities of War* (Heinemann, 1920), p. 403.
6. See T. Travers, *The Killing Ground. The British Army, the Western Front & the Emergence of*

Modern Warfare, 1900–1918 (Routledge, 1993), p. 221.

7. M. Gilbert, *First World War* (HarperCollins, 1995), p. 406.
8. The *Daily Express*, Wednesday, 20 March 1918 (London).
9. Liddell Hart, *First World War*, p. 395.
10. The *Daily Express*, Friday, 22 March 1918 (London).
11. The *Daily Express*, Friday, 22 March 1918 (London).
12. The *Daily Chronicle*, Friday, 22 March 1918 (London).
13. The *Daily News and Leader*, Friday, 22 March 1918 (London).
14. The *Daily News and Leader*, Monday, 25 March 1918 (London).
15. A.J.P. Taylor, *The First World War* (Penguin Books, 1966), p. 220.
16. The *Daily Express*, Thursday, 28 March 1918 (London).
17. The *Daily Mail*, Friday, 29 March 1918 (London).
18. The *Daily Mail*, Wednesday, 10 April 1918 (London).
19. The *Daily Chronicle*, Wednesday, 10 April 1918 (London).
20. The *Daily Mail*, Saturday, 13 April 1918 (London).
21. Liddell Hart, *First World War*, p. 399.
22. The *Daily Express*, Thursday, 18 April 1918 (London).
23. The *Daily Express*, Friday, 19 April 1918 (London).
24. The *Daily Mail*, Thursday, 18 April 1918 (London).
25. Excessive enthusiasm for tanks, see P. Griffith, *Battle Tactics of the Western Front. The British Army's Art of Attack, 1916–18* (Yale University Press, 1994), p. 163.
26. The *Daily Express*, Friday, 26 April 1918 (London).
27. The *Daily Mail*, Friday, 26 April 1918 (London).
28. Taylor, *First World War*, p. 221.
29. Liddell Hart, *First World War*, p. 399.
30. The *Daily Express*, Monday, 3 June 1918 (London).
31. The *Daily Mail*, Tuesday, 28 May 1918 (London).
32. The *Daily News and Leader*, Wednesday, 29 May 1918 (London).
33. The *Daily Express*, Tuesday, 4 June 1918 (London).
34. The *Daily News and Leader*, Tuesday, 4 June 1918 (London).

THE ALLIED OFFENSIVE, 1918

At 4.20 a.m. on 8 August 456 tanks moved forward across the Somme on a day which was to become known as 'The black day of the German Army'. This was the beginning of the Battle of Amiens, an attempt by the British Allies to push the German Army back across the Somme battlefields. There was no preliminary artillery bombardment, but aided by a thick mist the British advanced nearly 6 miles.

More important than the actual gains of 8 August was the psychological effect on the German Army who up until this point had been striving for victory on the Western Front. This battle made the German command and soldiers realize that their aspirations of a total victory had been blighted. What followed was the self-demoralization of the German Army, as Ludendorff concluded that the war would have to be ended by negotiation. Victory had eluded them.

From this point onwards until the armistice in November the Allies continued their advance and the Germans retreated to safer defensive positions. For the war correspondents this four-month period became a nerve-shattering time as they tried to contend with the ever-changing position of the British Army. Conditions were rapidly altering all over the Western Front and the war correspondents had scarcely the resources to cover every event in detail. The *Daily Mail*, in an article on Beach Thomas by his close friend George Dewar, explained the pressures that the war correspondents had to deal with every day.

War correspondents like Beach Thomas, whose clean-cut cameos of the great advance enabled millions of the British public to visualise it almost in detail in its earlier stages, have a very difficult task to-day with battle fronts anything from 12 to 60 miles long – and with the Press officer's orderly very likely knocking and waiting at attention at their door at 5.30 p.m. for the last few slips of their 'copy'. From 4.30 a.m. (and sometimes earlier) to 5.30 p.m. they must be more or less hard at it.

There is a great deal of nonsense talked about the superiority of the old school of war correspondents. The truth is they were not supermen at all and they worked under far less stress than Beach Thomas must to-day. I knew Charley Williams well; I also knew Archibald Forbes a little. Neither, believe me, would have done to-day's war news an atom better than Beach Thomas, Philip Gibbs, Percival Phillips, or Perry Robinson in their respective papers are doing it now in this glorious thrust by the British and French armies.[1]

Beach Thomas himself confessed that between August and November 1918 it was a stressful time for a journalist in France.

Relief at the end of war was enhanced for the war correspondent by a purely selfish feeling. As the advance was pushed forward over country shattered and robbed of all convenience in the way of hotels or telegraph lines, he was forced to longer and longer journeys up and back. Day after day he was not less then seven hours in a motor-car, and a car that was pressed to the utmost possible speed, that often started in the dark and ended in the twilight. Between the two journeys he saw what was to be seen of battles, of bandages, of the country and the people in it, he searched out prisoners – and once, at any rate, one of them was just missed, along with the prisoners, by German shrapnel. He wrote at what speed was possible, anywhere, and anyhow; and often had not a moment's leisure so much as to read through the words. . . . Three of my colleagues at one time could scarcely endure to enter a motor-car except under compulsion. So worn were their nerves.[2]

The results of the first day of the Battle of Amiens were to lift the spirits of the Home Front, with headlines such as 'SMASHING BLOW AT THE HUN',[3] 'GREAT ADVANCE. 9 MILES AT ONE POINT'[4] and 'UNPARALLELED SCENES OF THE GERMAN ROUT'.[5] Beach Thomas told the amazing story.

From dawn to midday we watched along the cliff of the Somme one of the greatest single feats of arms in the annals of the British Army, and the arms were of the strangest and most various sorts.

On the ground were our iron horses on caterpillar feet; 300 ft. above flew airmen whose impudent audacity has never been excelled.

Seldom did an adventure end more triumphantly or begin in greater strain. A diary of those waiting hours roughly jotted down at the time and place will show how the crisis felt, and incidentally how much had to be overcome to realise that triumph.

It was not yet light when we passed through a village heavily shelled earlier in the night. Two dead horses, a broken ambulance, and the fresh rubble of several houses told some part of the tale. Soon we reached one of the best observation posts ever provided by nature for a battle drama, but darkness and mist clinging like face cloths to the face was over everything and increased the strain felt by the waiting soldiers. Everyone's spirits rose as zero approached. It was now certain as normal signs could make it that the enemy was unaware.

At 4.25 the silence broke into splinters, and even the darkness and mist seemed to open at the clap of our preparatory barrage. A gunner observer who had fought through the Somme and Flanders said as he lifted a telephone in his dug-out, 'It is the best I ever saw, and yet not half the guns were registered.'

This thunder continued like one protracted clap for just four minutes. As it halted and checked for a moment in order to be lifted farther back on the enemy we knew that the infantry and tanks had charged. But nothing whatever was visible, and the mist now came down thicker than ever and, though it was clear above, one could see scarcely 40 yards along the earth. Aeroplanes nevertheless seemed to hum overhead in about equal numbers with the shells.

At 5.45 appears the first group of prisoners, about two score – a very punctual group. I never before saw prisoners quite like them. They were spick and span, no dirt or heat, no bloody sconces or limp limbs. Only their uniforms and bayonets suggested war. They had apparently surrendered to the barrage itself in sheer admiration without effort to fire.

At 9.30 we all felt that open warfare was beginning, and I could see across Hamel village such movement of men and machines as I never saw before. Not a single German shell fell in their neighbourhood.

At 10 the picture of the battlefield and the sense of triumphant movement were magnificent. The weather is and has been ideal. First the cloaking mist absolved the need for smoke, and as the first enemy lines were won progressive clearness came in time for us but too late for the enemy.

It was hard for me to leave the scene, as the visibility was improving every moment and the panorama was becoming incomparable, but it was time to go farther back and hear the more precise details of the vague but stirring things I had seen.

LATER

A general view of the scope and issue of the battle is already possible, though the day is still young. Good news travels faster than bad in battles. The Germans know less than we do. . . .

The tanks, which did magnificent work, helped the speed, but the prime credit still belongs to the dash and training of the infantry. They smothered the German infantry as the gunners smothered the German gunners. They showed great ingenuity through the half-open warfare which succeeded the first assault, in manoeuvring round machine-gun nests, and in hiding themselves, octopus-like, in their own smoke. Their movement was so quick and concerted that the enemy had little time to give to removing his guns.

It is reported that all along the line field guns were overrun, and that a particularly large group of them were captured north of the Somme near Chipilly, where escape was impossible, thanks to the sharp bends of the Somme River, of which the reaches thereabouts are a series of S's. I believe more guns, and of course more machine guns, have been captured than can be catalogued in a day or two. A few were used against the enemy quite early in the day.

The feature of the day was the extinction of the German artillery. Its answer to our barrage was rather slow and patchy, though up to standard in some places, notably north of the river, where the concentration and efficiency were both greater; but it lasted a very short time in its first degree of excellence.[6]

Perry Robinson compared the day's events to those of the previous great battles during the last three years of war.

Troubles are multiplying for the Germans to-day, with the French co-operation, we launched the first offensive on a large scale that we have made this year, recalling the great attacks of the Somme battle, of Arras, or of Flanders. It was admirable in its organisation and execution, taking the enemy completely by surprise. Capture both of prisoners and guns will be very large.

In a little more than two hours after the start we had heard of the capture of the whole tier of nearer villages. On the right the French before noon were in possession of villages on the south side of the Avre, while fighting was then in progress on the northern bank. Since then we have continued to advance apparently along the whole front, and more villages are now in our hands.[7]

Today this comparison appears strange as the great battles such as the Somme and Flanders mentioned by Robinson evoke more of a sense of wasted lives and futility eighty years after the events. These images of battle have been constructed with hindsight and with much more informed knowledge than the Home Front and war correspondents had at the time.

A day after the first assaults the British war correspondents were exploring the battlefields, which up until 8 August had been no man's land. Unfortunately for Philip Gibbs, who had been reporting from the Front since August 1914, he was absent on sick leave and had to be content with reading about the correspondents' adventures during this astounding juncture. While he recovered on the Home Front, veteran correspondent Henry Nevinson stepped up to take his place until Gibbs' return at the end of August. Perry Robinson out in what had been no man's land described his trek through the wreckage of war. It is strange that he was only able to see enemy dead from his position on the battlefield, but perhaps the mention of British dead might have distressed the Home Front at a time of triumph.

I have spent much of the day from early morning until noon walking over parts of the battlefield; having first the extraordinary experience of being able to pass in a motor-car not only over what yesterday was No Man's Land, but over the trenches of the front German system, and from my seat in the car look down on the enemy dead below. When the road became impassable by reason of the shell-holes made by our guns one could stray at large over the great deserted plain, while the guns thudded intermittently and our aeroplanes wheeled overhead.[8]

The battle was advancing across familiar territory and through villages of the Somme, which held painful memories of 1916 for the Home Front. While the Allies maintained their pressure, Ludendorff recommended to the Kaiser that immediate peace negotiations were the best option to save Germany from total humiliation.

The battle now extended across a large area of the British Western Front and the war correspondents divided up the fighting line between themselves, each travelling to a different section to seek out the latest information and soldiers' stories. At the end of the day when all the war correspondents met back at their billets the information from each section would be pooled before they all wrote their dispatches. Beach Thomas travelled further north during this time to witness the beginning of a German retreat. The British Army were advancing ever closer to Armentières, which they had abandoned in the early spring.

An Australian heavy gun at work.

I left the Somme this morning for the neighbourhood of the Lys, and found that a wide and deliberate retreat of the enemy is proceeding steadily and that nowhere are his steps more worth following than in Merville, entered by English troops on Sunday and Monday and now well behind our front line, which has moved forward a maximum depth of three and a half miles in the last few days on a 7-miles front.[9]

On the Somme the Second Battle of Albert commenced, with Albert being recaptured on 22 August. On the first day Percival Phillips described how the enemy were swept away by the rapid progress of the British Army.

Out of the chill white fog that lay damp and heavy on the old battlefield between Arras and the twisted valley of the Ancre there came at dawn to-day fresh disaster for the Hun.

Tanks, long feared and the subject of vague prophecy, appeared at last as the vanguard of a new British advance. They lumbered into village ruins ribbed with machine guns and across dangerous valleys similarly swept by lead, melted away the thin outposts of the enemy, chased fugitives and captured not a few, and sent a deep thrill of apprehension across the desert wastes of the Somme country that reached the nerves of a German army commander somewhere beyond Bapaume. Following the tanks came British infantry, reclaiming with unexpected ease and swiftness these poor remnants of the French hamlets and fields around them.

It was a complete surprise, this blow at sunrise in a blanket of fog, which has driven deeper our line into the wilderness between Arras and Bapaume.

The road to Bapaume, Albert.

Delivered on a front of between ten and eleven miles as the front then ran, with the northern limit of advance roughly Moyenneville and the southern Irles, in the angle of the Ancre just above Miraumont, it hurled – this is not an exaggeration – the German battalions back on the first impact to the massive embankment of the Arras–Albert railway.

Forward of them were machine-gun outposts organised in depth, and entrenched infantry covered by a good deal of old and some new wire. The total depth of these defences from the railway embankment to the outposts in Bucquoy and in front of Ayette was from two and a half to three miles. The ground is rough and broken, there are treacherous gullies and hidden pits likely to impede tanks and disturbing to foot soldiers at the best of times. Village ruins rising out of this tangle of grass-covered earth-works command them admirably, and stout machine gunners might be depended on to hold up and destroy advancing waves of infantry.

Yet our men passed safely and with celerity over this dangerous ground, the villages were swept clear with almost amazing rapidity, and before nine o'clock – four hours after the first group had vanished into the fog – they were nearly everywhere up to the railway. I believe that they have since gone further. As I write I hear that tanks and infantry have passed the embankment and penetrated some hundreds of yards beyond. . . .

Very few details are procurable yet of this capture of the other villages. Ablainzeville seems to have fallen without a murmur of protest. Courcelles Le Comte held sundry pockets of machine guns, and some resistance was shown, but it could not have been great, as word came back before the fog lifted that it had been occupied. Good news came fragmentarily of the progress of the tanks around Achiet-le-Petit, where stiff fighting had been looked for. The village is said to have been taken before nine o'clock. . . .

Our own fire died down in a most surprising way after the initial barrage, and for some time the batteries paused, waiting for the fog to lift. The silence was almost uncanny. Walking wounded, strolling in twos and threes across old No Man's Land, stopped to talk to troops waiting to go forward, their casual conversation made it difficult to realise that a battle was in progress over the next ridge.[10]

Beach Thomas reported from the town of Albert on 23 August.

Last night helped by the harvest moon, this morning aided by a low mist, and this noon in full sunlight two British armies again attacked the enemy, recovered many French villages, and refilled cages with prisoners at various points on a front of 30 miles, from the Cojeul River, about 5 miles south of Arras, away nearly to Lihons, north of Roye.

Where we struck we won, and what we have taken we hold. One could go freely into Albert this morning, and away to the north end of the Hindenburg Line was already close and clear. More than this, our shrapnel was winking away behind the hills that guard and threaten Albert and 5.9 shells were falling in quick rotation at points nearly a mile on the German side of the town. This was at 11 a.m. At the same time, both north and south, above the Ancre and along the Somme drumfire announced yet more onslaughts. . . .

So far I have written only of the fighting north of Albert and have taken this section first only because I have more personal knowledge of it, but bigger things happened further south, both this morning and yesterday. After our great success of yesterday morning in entering Albert and pushing up the Albert–Bray road the enemy, as above the Ancre, threw in a fresh division the 25th for a counter-attack. It was more fortunate than the 52nd, and, indeed, gained one considerable local success, punishing the English troops in what is called 'Happy Valley', a deep, bare scoop in this bare chalk ridge dividing the Ancre from the Somme, and drove back our advanced line some distance. But the check was purely local and at no time crucial. We held firm on both sides, and a little later pushed forward well along the Albert–Bapaume road, once again mined by the enemy, and seem to have taken Tara Hill.[11]

By 27 August it had become clear that the Germans were on the retreat. On a 55 mile line in the Somme region there began a 10 mile retirement, while two days later evacuations were also taking place in Flanders, the Aisne and the Lys salient. The Germans were on the defensive and moving back to hold the Hindenburg line. However, even at this stage the Allies and Home Front did not envisage an end to the war in 1918, and the plans for offensives in 1919 were already being drawn up in Britain and France.

Just a month later in September the German commanders Ludendorff and Hindenburg were trying to cut their losses and both agreed that Germany needed to request an immediate armistice. On 4 October Germany telegraphed Washington to request an armistice from President Wilson. The slow process of making peace would take another month to complete and the fierce fighting continued without abatement. Pressure was applied to the Hindenburg line and the war correspondents were still reporting strong resistance from the German troops. Fighting extended all along the British line.

From W. Beach Thomas, Wednesday
A brief storm, clamorous with every sort of shell, including smoke, phosgene, shrapnel, and high-explosive, from gun, howitzer, and trench mortar, announced at dawn this morning the latest phase of battle that opened with a gallop of men and tanks and cavalry on August 8.
    Many of the same English and Australian troops that then broke the German line have continuously followed up and fought his rearguards and this morning assaulted the stronger forces he had thrown in to keep us at a safe distance from his Hindenburg line and the great tunnel beneath it. . . .
    Reports confirm my estimate of prisoners, who now exceed 3,000. Villeret [9 miles north-north-west of St. Quentin] is in our hands, as well as a most important spur in front of Le Verguier, known as Ascension Farm, for which there has been hard fighting. All reports indicate great numbers of German dead. Many garrisons, especially in the south, fought to the death.[12]

The distances that the war correspondents now had to travel during a day's work and the pace of the advance were so great that they had little time to write about the events witnessed. Beach Thomas had this problem in early October, after a trip to Flanders.

I left the southern battle, in spite of its overwhelming interest, to visit that part of Flanders from where day after day last autumn we watched the British Army wade with its guns, slow stride by slow stride under full observation up the ridge and alongside that Houthulst Forest which Marlborough said was the citadel of Belgium.

Later
Distances are so great that I have returned to the south too late to give or hear any consecutive account of the battle, but certain things stand out in such completeness that the briefest tale is perhaps sufficient.[13]

In September 1918 the war correspondents had to contend with the issue of naming troops in Haig's weekly dispatches. Fighting troops involved in the battles against the retreating enemy were now identified by their regiments in official communiqués and to Philip Gibbs this presented a dilemma.

It would take a volume, or rather many volumes, to narrate the history of all the divisions named by the Commander-in-Chief, the old British divisions of English, Scottish, Welsh, and Irish battalions – all too few Irish battalions – who

British soldiers at home in German dugouts.

throughout this war have been the solid backbone of our Army, who, again and again, have fought themselves almost to a finish, until new drafts came along to learn the spirit of the older men, and who have planted a forest of graves, a forest of little white crosses, where their heroic dead lie over all these battlefields of France. They have not had much publicity. Often it has been necessary to hide the names of their battalions and divisions to prevent the enemy knowing our order of battle, because they are in smaller units than the Australians and Canadians, who fight in corps and are quickly identified. That has been rough on them, and rough on the correspondents who want to give them their honour; but when the full history of this war is written the names of their battalions will be in every chapter, and their glory and agonies and sacrifice and courage will never be forgotten.[14]

In October Germany accepted President Wilson's conditions for an armistice as the British moved their attentions to Flanders as well as the Somme. Cambrai was taken and the Hindenburg line completely broken by 9 October. By late October all the Belgian coast was in Allied hands, only a year after Haig's first attempt at the Third Battle of Ypres. Beach Thomas and Percival Phillips had both been into what was left of Cambrai. For the Home Front these types of dispatches illustrated the destructive power that the war had had on towns and villages in the battle zone.

Cambrai has fallen and two German armies are in retreat. The British front is sweeping eastward with such speed, releasing villages and their joyful inhabitants, and endeavouring to retain contact with the enemy rearguard, that it is impossible to estimate the full extent of this victory.

Cambrai was entered by the Canadians at four o'clock this morning. They advanced cautiously to the canal banks which enclose the town on the west, and had no trouble crossing to the inner quays. The town was deserted. Crossing the Boulevard Jean Bart on the west and skirting the old Chateau de Selles, they pushed past the barracks and up the main thoroughfare leading to the cathedral and Place d'Armes. The western half of the town showed little signs of damage, but beyond the central square were great gaps among the buildings, while fires still smouldered in the blackened ruins, and other fires of recent origin burned in the by-streets.[15]

On 15 October Percival Phillips reported from Flanders on the recapture of Passchendaele.

Allied troops attacked the Hun in Flanders to-day. They rose out of the dead battlefields beyond Messines Ridge and Passchendaele before the sun had pierced the mist, and bore down upon the waiting Germans of General von Armin's 4th Army. They are advancing this afternoon on firmer ground, their guns moving with them out of the desert, and the whole front from the Yser marshes by Dixmude down to the Lys Canal at the foot of Messines is slowly bending eastwards.[16]

During the last weeks of the war in November Germany's Home Front was in revolt and on the Western Front events had turned full circle. On 10 November Canadian troops entered Mons, which had witnessed the first engagements between British and German forces in August 1914. It was a fitting end to the war, and those who had fought for Mons in 1914.

The armistice signed on 11 November appeared from the dispatches of the war correspondents to have brought little comfort to the troops at the Front. Celebrations were sparse and the Army continued with the job in hand. It was a time to reflect on what had happened to Europe in the past four years and to begin to think of what the future might bring. For Perry Robinson it must have been a time of personal disappointment that he had not witnessed the coming of peace to the Western Front. Just a few days before the armistice he had been taken ill and on the 11th November was in England recovering. Percival Phillips recounted his whereabouts at 11 o'clock on that momentous day.

Just at eleven I came into the little town of Leuze, which had been one of the headquarters nearest the uncertain front. In the market-place were British troopers on their horses, drawn up in a hollow square – 3rd Dragoons, Royal Dragoons, and 10th Hussars, of the 6th Cavalry Brigade, all in fighting kit. In the centre was the 1/4th Battalion of the King's Own, Barrow men of the 51st Division, thrown across the square, their Colonel at the head and the Old Mayor of Leuze beside him. From the windows of all the houses round about, and even from the roofs, the inhabitants looked down on the troops and heard uncomprehendingly the words of the Colonel as he read from a sheet of paper the order that ended hostilities.

A trumpeter sounded the 'stand fast'. In the narrow high-street at one end of the little square were other troops moving slowly forward, and as the notes of the bugle rose clear and crisp above the rumble of the gun-carriages these men turned with smiles of wonder and delight and shouted to each other 'The war's over'.

The band of the Barrow men played 'God save the King'. None heard it without a quiver of emotion. The mud-stained troops paused in the crowded street, the hum of traffic was stilled. A rippling cheer was drowned in the first notes of the Belgian hymn; the 'Marseillaise' succeeded it, and the army of each ally was thus saluted in turn. I do not think that any one heard the few choked words of the old mayor when he tried to voice the thanks of Belgium for this day of happiness.

The Army 'carried on' briskly, as though a little ashamed of the emotion which had seized us all for one unforgettable moment. People shook hands in an embarrassed way and said to each other: 'Well, it's finished,' and the harassed traffic man at the corner resumed his weary task with even greater ferocity. Some one fired a Verey pistol into a field, and silver balls of light drifted over the heads of the troops – and that was the only outward sign of rejoicing.

The armies 'carry on' to-night as though many weeks of war lie before them – they try to imagine the wonderful scenes in London and Paris, and, indeed, throughout the world of the Allies. But for them there is still much work to be done, and the 'stand fast' only marks the end of a long nightmare and the beginning of a new day.[17]

The *Daily News* correspondent reported that the troops were ordered to unfix their bayonets at 11 a.m. and that the expected announcement was silently received.

The news that the armistice was to come into effect was got forward to our far-flung patrols and batteries with great promptitude, and a great silence fell upon the land after eleven o'clock.

There can be no harm now in saying that the message had been generally expected for hours beforehand, and therefore there had been ample time to arrange for signalling the news beyond the points where telegraph and the telephone cease. Our scattered troops were told to unfix bayonets and unload magazines and to stand to for further orders. No attempt was to be made to fraternise with the enemy. I believe there was some demonstrativeness on the German side, and I hear of German troops being seen trying to break their rifles or throwing them away. But on the whole the great tidings appear to have been taken pretty quietly.[18]

Again Beach Thomas witnessed little change after the armistice order was given to the troops.

A General I saw this morning a few minutes after the news of the armistice had come in issued an order that his men were to occupy certain high ground before

11. So, with an inspired sense of historic fitness, the Canadians swore to be in Mons while the war lasted, even if it cost life. They owed its capture to the spirit of the Old Contemptibles. . . .

I saw this morning, from corps to battalion, how the British Army received the news at 7.41. The 3rd Corps in Tournai, whom King Albert had visited and thanked them the night before, received the following telegram:

'Troops will stand firm on the positions reached at 11 a.m. A line of outposts will be established and reported to Army Headquarters. The remainder of the troops will be collected ready to meet any demand. All military precautions will be preserved and there will be no communication with the enemy. Further instructions will be communicated. Acknowledge.'

The men looked happy and proceeded with their business.[19]

Philip Gibbs' dispatch was the exception among the war correspondents as it did not portray the armistice in a subdued light.

Our troops knew this morning that the Armistice had been signed. I stopped on my way to Mons outside brigade headquarters, and an officer said, 'Hostilities will cease at eleven o'clock'. Then he added, as all men had in their hearts, 'Thank God for that!' All the way to Mons there were columns of troops on the march, and their bands played ahead of them, and almost every man had a flag on his rifle, the red, white, and blue of France, the red, yellow, and black of Belgium. They wore flowers in their caps and in their tunics, red and white chrysanthemums given them by the crowds of people who cheered them on their way, people who in many of these villages had been only one day liberated from the German yoke. Our men marched singing, with a smiling light in their eyes. They had done their job, and it was finished with the greatest victory in the world.

The war ended for us at Mons, as it had begun there. When I went into this town this morning it seemed to me a most miraculous coincidence and a joyful one. Last night there was a fight outside the town before our men forced their way in at ten o'clock. The Germans left many of their guns in the gardens before they ran. This morning Mons was full of English cavalry and Canadian troops, about whom there were crowds of townspeople, cheering them and embracing them. One old man told me of all they had suffered in Mons, but he wept only when he told me of the suffering of our prisoners. 'What shame for Germany,' he said. 'What shame when these things are known about your poor men starving to death. Our women tried to give them food, but were beaten for it, and fifteen days ago down there by the canal one of your English was killed because a woman gave him a bit of bread.' Little children came up to me and described the fighting in Mons in August 1914, when the 'Old Contemptibles' were there and fought their battle through the town, and then on their way of retreat outside.

All that is now a memory of the past. The war belongs to the past. There will be no flash of gun-fire in the sky to-night. The fires of hell have been put out, and I have written my last message as war correspondent. Thank God![20]

Gibbs' believed that the war belonged to the past, but to the people who had experienced war it was just the beginning of a journey to try and come to terms with all that had happened. This is why most of the dispatches from the fighting Front contrasted sharply with the celebrations throughout Britain. The Home Front could forget and look to the future because they had not experienced at first hand the hell that was the Western Front. The soldiers, however, had to cope with that nightmare for the rest of their lives. They had witnessed the dark side of human nature, their values and morality had been stripped from them and they were left wondering how a civilized world could stoop so low.

NOTES

1. The *Daily Mail*, Wednesday, 14 August 1918 (London).
2. B. Thomas, *A Traveller in News* (Chapman & Hall, 1925), p. 195.
3. The *Daily Express*, Friday, 9 August 1918 (London).
4. The *Daily Mail*, Friday, 9 August 1918 (London).
5. The *Daily Express*, Saturday, 10 August 1918 (London).
6. The *Daily Mail*, Friday, 9 August 1918 (London).
7. The *Daily News and Leader*, Friday, 9 August 1918 (London).
8. The *Daily News*, Saturday, 10 August 1918 (London).
9. The *Daily Mail*, Wednesday, 21 August 1918 (London).
10. The *Daily Express*, Thursday, 22 August 1918 (London).
11. The *Daily Mail*, Saturday, 24 August 1918 (London).
12. The *Daily Mail*, 19 September 1918 (London).
13. The *Daily Mail*, Tuesday, 1 October 1918 (London).
14. P. Gibbs, *Open Warfare, The Way to Victory* (Heinemann, 1919), p. 411.
15. The *Daily Express*, Thursday, 10 October 1918 (London).
16. The *Daily Express*, Tuesday, 15 October 1918 (London).
17. The *Daily Express*, Tuesday, 12 November 1918 (London).
18. The *Daily News*, Tuesday, 12 November 1918 (London).
19. The *Daily Mail*, Tuesday, 12 November 1918 (London).
20. The *Daily Chronicle*, Tuesday, 12 November 1918 (London).

AFFIRMING THE MYTH

The armistice in November 1918 was far from the end of the road for the British accredited correspondents who had chronicled the actions of the British Army for nearly four years. The fighting might have stopped, but the terms of peace had still to be finalized as the British and Allied troops moved into German territory across the Ruhr. Perry Robinson rejoined the press camp after his illness and with his fellow war correspondents accompanied the British force until the conclusion of the peace terms in June 1919 when they reached Cologne.

At the conclusion of peace, standing on the Hohenzollern Bridge in Cologne, the band of accredited correspondents stood together for one of the last times and listened to a speech from Sir Douglas Haig. Philip Gibbs described the special day.

> It was a recognition by the leader of our armies that, as chroniclers of war, we had been a spiritual force behind his arms. It was a reward for many mournful days, for much agony of spirit, for hours of danger – some of us had walked often in the ways of death – and for exhausting labours which we did so that the world might know what British soldiers had been doing.[1]

Soldiers observing the guns fire from the Hohenzollen bridge, Cologne, Peace Day, 28 June 1919.

The war correspondents had done the job the military wanted them to do – to inform the general public of their Army's progress on the Western Front. They had willingly become part of a propaganda machine which had produced patriotic and over-optimistic dispatches which lacked details of the true horror of war and could now go their separate ways to report from and travel around the post-war world. For their services to the Allied cause they were awarded the Chevalier of the Legion of Honour in 1919 by the French and five war correspondents received knighthoods in 1920. Gibbs had a moment of conscience about receiving his knighthood and said

> I was not covetous of that knighthood, and indeed shrank from it so much that I entered into a compact with Beach Thomas to refuse it. But things had gone too far, and we could not reject the title with any decency.[2]

Philip Gibbs embarked on a lecture tour of the USA for the rest of 1919, resigned from the *Daily Chronicle* in 1920 and wrote a book on his experiences of the First World War entitled *Realities of War*. He became a freelance writer of fiction, publishing nearly fifty novels in his lifetime and during the Second World War he again went to the USA on a lecture tour for the Ministry of Information. Before his death in 1962, with failing eyesight he completed his account of his professional recollections, which he had first started in 1925.

Percival Phillips accompanied the Prince of Wales on many Royal tours to other countries including Canada (1919), India and Japan (1921–2), and Africa (1928) and reported from many trouble spots, revolutions and uprisings around the world until his death in 1937.

Herbert Russell also accompanied the Prince of Wales on his tour of India and Japan with Percival Phillips in 1921, before beginning to write novels and books on his vast knowledge of naval matters. He died in 1944.

Perry Robinson, the eldest British war correspondent in 1919 at the age of sixty, retired from journalism to pursue his passion for natural history and golf until his death in 1930.

In 1922 William Beach Thomas went on a tour of the world for the *Daily Mail* and *The Times* newspapers. He then settled down writing regular newspaper articles and books on country matters and nature. He died in 1957.

The Fleet Street proprietors, who had achieved social rank and political influence through war profiteering and following the Government line, saw their influence decline with the end of the war. Any worries that Parliament might have had about being controlled by these men soon disappeared. Lord Beaverbrook resigned from the Ministry of Information in October 1918 due to ill health, and Lord Northcliffe (who was created a viscount as a reward for services to the British War Mission in the USA) resigned as Director of Enemy Propaganda the day after the armistice. Lloyd George had managed to exploit their power during the war because they all shared the same common aim of seeing Britain victorious.

After the war the Fleet Street newspaper proprietors returned to their pre-war roles of trying to manipulate mass opinion and influence the political situation. During the war the press had played a major part in closing all options open for a long-lasting peace and had helped commit Britain to achieving total victory over Germany at any cost. With peace in sight the Northcliffe presses embarked on another campaign to bring the Kaiser to trial and make Germany pay for the war. This issue was also taken up by Lloyd George in his election manifesto.

During 1914 propaganda had been employed to change a society's morality so that it could understand and accept warfare. War and a country's reasons for fighting have always been given the veneer of a moral crusade and this was certainly true of the First World War. A new set of principles and words come into play in wartime – the enemy is seen as evil and we are the righteous, the liberators, fighting for freedom. War is justified under the guise of a moral stand to maintain the foundations of civilization.

'A war to end all wars' was a common belief and a far-reaching image. It was emphasized that this could be the last chance men might have of fighting in a war. For the soldiers who sacrificed themselves it was for a better, peaceful world with no more war. During the First World War lost lives were seen as a small price to pay for eternal peace.

In 1914 Britain was in the midst of its own internal wars: the Irish conflict was escalating into civil war, the suffragette movement became a war of sexual equality, and class consciousness was rising in the form of trade-union action and strikes. What was needed was a 're-creative war' that would clear away the conflicts at home and reintroduce the abandoned concepts of Edwardian conduct that had built the great Empire.

However, in November 1918 the major concerns on the political and social agenda were not the ideals of a long and lasting peace but how to make Germany pay for the suffering that the British people had experienced. This meant the Home Front had to reject the optimistic dispatches of victories and successes of the British Army produced by the war correspondents and focus solely upon the slaughter, horror and destruction of battle which Germany had created. Propaganda was already creating a new image of war as John Terraine explained.

> The Government's failure to acknowledge and convey to the public, at the time, the supreme achievement of the British Army in 1918 was never corrected, and was fatal. The sense of having won a major victory in the field over a mighty enemy, obtained by absolute military prowess, hard-won professionalism, remained lacking. Propaganda stories of gallant deeds could not be a substitute. Soon they would, in any case, begin to be supplanted by the literature and propaganda of denigration and 'disenchantment'. The horrors of the Somme and Passchendaele made better 'copy' than the 'Hundred Day's Campaign' of 1918 with its nine cumulative victories.[3]

If the War Office, Army and war correspondents had provided the Home Front with a more realistic view of battle during the war, instead of the imbalance towards 'over-optimism' and patriotism, it might have prevented the backlash of disillusionment which began in November 1918. One extreme view of war had been replaced with another. Sacrifice changed to slaughter and the full horror of war was over-emphasized to create a new image of utter doom and destruction over peace and victory. This style, which was no closer to the reality of war than the war

The reality of war in Northern France.

correspondents' dispatches, forms much of the image of the First World War held today.

The soldiers returned to Britain and tried to make sense of what was happening in a world where justice and reason appeared to have faded away and indeed expired. All that was left was a sense of overriding loyalty to their dead comrades. Society had a growing feeling of grief, anger and an affirmation of the injustice of war. People were turning away from the celebration of peace in search of the other reality of war and when no more could be extracted from German war guilt the blame needed to be laid at somebody's feet. Their young had been sacrificed by the old men; the people who had had the power to send these men to their deaths were the politicians, generals and admirals. The victory of war and the great battles listed in substantial detail in the general war histories were rejected in favour of the image of the individual victimized figures found in warfare.

By 1928 ideas about the war had radically altered, as had the morality and language surrounding it, in order to reflect the disillusionment the country felt at the end of the First World War.

> They would go without dreams of glory, expecting nothing except suffering, boredom and perhaps death – not cynically, but without illusions, because they remembered a war: not the Great War itself, but the myth that had been made of it.[4]

Books such as Edmund Blunden's *Undertones of War*, Robert Graves' *Goodbye to All That*, Siegfried Sassoon's *Memoirs of George Sherston* and Erich Maria

Remarque's *All Quiet on the Western Front* became the new myth of war replacing the over-optimistic ideas prevalent between 1914 and 1918. Philip Gibbs wrote a book in this style focusing largely on the horrors of war which he had been unable to report at the time. Samuel Hynes explained this.

> Here, after the war, a journalist who had made his reputation out of heightened and emotive language comes to a soldier's style. Gibbs' realities, the things that could now be told, were first of all the grotesque details of death and devastation that the censors would not have tolerated while the war was going on. Not detail of actual fighting, of course – correspondents were not allowed to witness that – but of what was left after battle, the faceless corpses, the scattered limbs, the heaped-up bodies and the stench of death.[5]

The withholding of information by the War Office and press created two types of war out of one event.

The soldiers on the Western Front who were part of a situation beyond comprehension had witnessed the darker side of human nature rationalized as a fight to save civilization. They could not relate their experiences of battle to the same war which the Home Front encountered. Accounts of war such as Private Woodhead's diary were in contrast to the newspaper reports from the war correspondents. An image and reality problem had been born, caused by the use of propaganda, which still affects our views of past events today. This problem was illustrated by Siegfried Sassoon's observation of a war report which bore no resemblance to the war which he had been part of.

> . . . As I opened a daily paper one morning and very deliberately read a dispatch from 'War correspondents' Headquarters.'
> 'I have sat with some of our lads, fighting battles over again, and discussing battles to be,' wrote some amiable man who had apparently mistaken the war for a football match between England and Germany.[6]

These two groups, the Home Front and returning soldiers, had one serious difficulty with the war which went on to shape the post-war age – neither group could comprehend or really wanted to know what the other had experienced. In the book *Birdsong* a conversation between a soldier on leave called Weir and his father highlighted this impasse.

> 'It's been terrible,' said Weir. 'I've got to tell you, it's been –'
> 'We've read about it in the paper. We all wish it would hurry up and finish.'
> 'No, it's been worse. I mean, you can't imagine.'
> 'Worse than what? Worse than it says? More casualties, are there?'
> 'No, it's not that. It's . . . I don't know.'
> 'You want to take it easy. Don't get yourself upset. Everyone's doing their bit, you know. We all want it to end, but we just have to get on with things meantime.'[7]

The Home Front had played their part in the war effort and to them this was as valuable as the soldiers' fighting role at the Front. By the time society had realized the true nature of the fighting, the circumstances had entered history and become buried in the past. How are we to learn from our past mistakes if the truth becomes clouded by myth, lies and propaganda?

By the time Ponsonby's book[8] was published in 1928 and the film *All Quiet on the Western Front*[9] was released the perception had dawned that war still lingered as a major threat, an ever-present fear to civilization. A new myth of war had been accepted, but had society learnt anything from its experiences?

From the last moments of the war itself, its human suffering was embedded in the fabric of societies upon which its perpetuation had depended. The wounded men of all nations were to be a legacy of war which ended only with their deaths, or with the deaths of those who had lived with them and guarded their broken bodies or minds or both.[10]

NOTES

1. P. Gibbs, *Realities of War* (Heinemann, 1920), p. 25.
2. P. Gibbs, *Adventures in Journalism* (Heinemann, 1923), p. 256.
3. J. Terraine, *Impacts of War, 1914 & 1918* (Leo Cooper, 1993), p. 210.
4. S. Hynes, *A War Imagined* (Pimlico, 1992), p. 473.
5. Hynes, *A War Imagined*, p. 284.
6. S. Sassoon, *Memoirs of an Infantry Officer* (Faber & Faber, 1930), p. 176.
7. S. Faulks, *Birdsong* (Vintage, 1994), p. 231.
8. A. Ponsonby, *Falsehood in Wartime* (George Allen and Unwin, 1928).
9. Erich Maria Remarque, *All Quite on the Western Front* (1928). It was released as a film in 1930.
10. M. Gilbert, *First World War* (HarperCollins, 1995), p. 541.

EPILOGUE

The purpose of a war correspondent, is the ideal of an informed public. We are in democracies and democracies function because governments have the approval, the consent to govern. We as war correspondents have the responsibility to go out and make sure even in times of national crisis and war that the public are informed about what's really going on.[1]

This is the view of Peter Arnett, a contemporary war correspondent. In 1914 a letter to *The Nation* by H.F. Prevost Battersby, an experienced war correspondent of the time, set out the importance of having independent observers with an army at a time of war.

Their testimony may often be of importance to the soldiers themselves, and they form an acceptable link with the civil population of their country. Amongst millions of men, all too absorbed in the struggle for life to notice side issues, they alone are in a position to make a report, unbiased by military training and unprejudiced by personal concern. Let such men be selected with the greatest care, let the most stringent regulations safeguard their immediate utterances, but let them be allowed freedom of movement and the use of their eyes. They are the representatives of democracy, and the commanders of a democratic force must learn to put up with them.[2]

Both definitions of the role of the war correspondent, although almost eighty years apart, have the same fundamental understanding of the ideal role. They are representatives of democracy, a safeguard which keeps the public fully informed on war in an impartial manner.

If we relate these two definitions to the role of the war correspondent during the First World War then we may come to the conclusion that rather than informing the public and protecting democracy it was the job of the war correspondent to mislead, confuse and above all to promote a sense of patriotic duty in the Home Front. Sassoon in his book *Memoirs of an Infantry Officer* asked why war had to be reported in this way.

I wonder why it was necessary for the Western Front to be 'attractively advertised' by such intolerable twaddle. What was this camouflage war which was manufactured by the press to aid the imaginations of people who had never seen the real thing?[3]

Propaganda in warfare is a weapon used by governments intentionally to twist information to form images which will cajole the Home Front, attract allies and outwit the enemy. However, this process is incomplete without agents to convey these distorted pictures to the Home Front, allies and enemy. During the First World War correspondents were needed to fulfil this role, to fill the information void which existed between the military leadership and the general public. The generals and those in charge of the Army in France passed on to the war correspondents deliberate lies, exaggerated truth or used censorship to conceal the truth, which in turn the war correspondents willingly wrote into their dispatches. At the time war correspondents were identified as representatives of public interest, but in reality it would seem that this was not the case. War correspondents had become a passive tool in the propaganda process, the major communication link between the warring generals on the Western Front and the news-hungry Home Front.

A conversation between an editor of the *Unconservative Weekly* and Sherston in *Memoirs of an Infantry Officer* plainly illustrated how censorship and propaganda were viewed by those in power.

> With regard to what I suggested in my letter, he explained that if he were to print veracious accounts of infantry experience his paper would be suppressed as prejudicial to recruiting. The censorship officials were always watching for a plausible excuse for banning it, and they had already prohibited its foreign circulation. 'The soldiers are not allowed to express their point of view. In war-time the word patriotism means the suppression of truth,' he remarked. . . .[4]

The results of the propaganda process were at first enormously positive for the generals who wanted a complete victory, but the Home Front, starved of information, were almost treated as an enemy themselves.

It is inconceivable that the war correspondents knew nothing about the magnitude of killing during the First World War. However, it is more probable that they elected not to report these darker horrors until after the war, when it became too late for the Home Front to act. Philip Gibbs reflected that

> we saw the whole organisation of that great machine of slaughter . . . the effects of such a vision, year in, year out, can hardly be calculated in psychological effect unless a man has a mind like a sieve and a soul like a sink.[5]

As the war correspondents were not doing the job the public had entrusted them with, to report what was really happening on the Western Front, the military were able to exploit fear and patriotic duty in the Home Front. The generals now had a direct line of communication through which to influence public opinion and boost morale with the aim of total victory against the German Army. However, at what cost?

The war correspondents yielded to military pressure and became a propaganda tool. They had betrayed the trust of their readership, and this is a legacy never completely shaken off in peace time. Ethical questions concerning their role in the suppression of truth no doubt did cross the minds of the war correspondents, but they decided to accept the military approach to shaping public opinion of the war, arguably making peace impossible without a total victory.

After the war, it appears odd that out of the five accredited war correspondents rewarded with knighthoods for their services, only Philip Gibbs and William Beach Thomas wrote about their experiences and roles within the British Army. The other three chose to remain silent. Philip Gibbs felt it necessary to defend his role and believed he did a good job as a war correspondent.

> On the whole we may claim, I think, our job was worth doing, and not badly done. Some of us, at least, did not spare ourselves to learn the truth and to tell it as far as it lay in our vision and in our power of words. During the course of the battles it was not possible to tell all the truth, to reveal the full measure of slaughter on our side, and we had not right of criticism. But day by day the English-speaking world was brought close in spiritual touch with their fighting men, and knew the best, if not the worst, of what was happening in the field of war, and the daily record of courage, endurance, achievement, by the youth that was being spent with such prodigal unthrifty zeal.[6]

The First World War witnessed the end of a golden age of war reporting with the correspondent at the centre of a great adventure, free to report what he wanted, and saw the foundations laid for an organized structure within which the correspondent would be manipulated by governments for the national interest. After the war Henry Nevinson compared the two types of reporting.

> In the old days of 'scoops' and 'beats', I have sat at meals with a group of correspondents all silent for fear of giving away some piece of information which we all knew. But during the Great War a complete change was developed. We all lived in one château (there were only half-a-dozen of us) and went out to some point of the front line separately with one of our excellent censors, who were officers seconded for wounds. Returning about 1.30, we pooled our knowledge and submitted our composite reports to the body of censors to be dispatched by special messenger. We lived chirping together like little birds in a nest, and thought of the weary days when a war correspondent spent half his time in seeking food and shelter for himself, his horse, and his man, or wandering far and wide in search of a censor and telegraph office.[7]

It would be interesting to know how much of the system established in the First World War is still in operation today.

Max Hasting, a war correspondent who reported from the Falklands in 1982, likened the conditions of the trenches around San Carlos Bay to the misery of Passchendaele during the First World War. Trenches full of water created conditions associated with the First World War such as exposure, dysentery and trench foot and became all too familiar to the soldiers of 1982.

> They slept in the bitter cold and damp of their trenches, with only spasmodic chances of a night in a shearing shed to dry their clothing. At dawn each day, after the ritual of 'Stand to', when men manned their weapons until the light had cleared, . . .[8]

If the war correspondents of the First World War had witnessed the land fighting during the Falklands crisis they would have come to the conclusion that little had changed to the face of battle since their own time. What had also changed little was the conflict between the war correspondent and the military over censorship regulations.

At the beginning of the Falklands conflict the Royal Navy had no room for the media on their ships, but however had to bow to public pressure. As the task force set sail only fifteen war correspondents were assigned to it and again they were bound by the Defence of the Realm Act. Replacing the 'Eyewitness' reports of Colonel Ernest Swinton from the First World War, daily briefings were conducted by Ian McDonald at the Ministry of Defence. These meetings provided official stories of the battles for use by the media which, as before, concealed the reality of the events from the public. Again, because of the strict control of news from the war zone, there developed an information gap between the Home Front and the fighting troops in the South Atlantic. The bulk of the news from the Falklands consisted of optimistic reports which stressed patriotic duty just as the newspapers of 1914 had done.

Patrick Kettle, a sailor who had served on HMS *Sheffield*, explained this situation which was brought about by the lack of credible news.

I felt as if I wanted to pick them up and shake them and say: 'Look, there is a war going on, people are getting killed.' I felt for them war was something that happened at eight o'clock in the morning on the radio, or at nine o'clock at night when the TV news came on . . .

Throughout the Falklands conflict the Press were constantly being extremely jingoistic with banner headlines. There were large cheering crowds. To me it was just a reminder of August 1914. War is something that sometimes has to be done, but it doesn't have to be done in that state. I don't think until the Sheffield was hit people realised that we were really in a killing war . . .

I found it very difficult to speak to my wife about my experiences. The only way I could ever let her know how I felt was actually to tell the story to other people but to make sure that she was within earshot, and I consciously did this on several occasions . . .

I was left with the feeling of the absurdity of war. It's a message that has been said many times before. War is hell, believe me.[9]

For the war correspondents it was a frustrating time as their dispatches had to travel over 8,000 miles back to Fleet Street via defence communication channels. There was no other means of transporting copy and the military made no provision for live television pictures which meant that news from the Falklands' battlefields could be delayed by anything up to three weeks. Again the war correspondents attached to the task force had their own Ministry of Defence press officers who censored any explicit stories and film footage deemed to be damaging to Home Front morale and the distrust between media and military first witnessed during the First World War had not diminished. Trevor Royle summed up this situation.

It was the same old story: was the war correspondent to consider himself a propagandist for his own side or was he to be an objective reporter at the cost of criticizing the army he was accompanying?[10]

During the Vietnam War Irma Kurtz, a war correspondent, commented that

War is a devilish hard place to find a story. I used to gather most nights with other reporters in Saigon, in bars or restaurants, where we hunched over maps and talked offensives, some of us scribbling notes, playing soldiers with the guys and mostly desperately trading rumours with no more real knowledge of what the blazes was going on than the Generals had or the poor grunts flailing around in alien swamps.[11]

This description of war reporting in Vietnam sounds woefully similar to that of the explanations used by war correspondents in the First World War. It begs the question, just how much of the truth of present-day wars do we actually know or are likely to find out? Has anything changed?

Even in the most media-friendly war in the Gulf in 1991 many images of the events had little connection with the reality on the battlefield. As we slept safely at night in the knowledge that the American Patriot missile was there to stop the enemy Scud rockets falling on Allied territory, five years later the truth slowly appeared. In fact this just was not the case and the Patriot missile success rate was far from favourable, but through the media the world was led to believe in an image in order to maintain the morale and support for an ongoing war. If the truth about the failings of the Patriot weapon had been common knowledge the generals believed it could have broken up the fragile Allied coalition and have been used as a valuable source of propaganda material by Saddam Hussein. The same excuses were being employed as had been during the First World War.

Ultimately the question arises as to why we have not learnt our lesson and still find war necessary? Could it be that the power of propaganda distorts the true picture of war with its great losses in human life so much that when the truth is revealed it can only be assigned to the past and forgotten.

It may be right to attack the military leaders, they held the responsibility . . . But it is difficult to avoid the suspicion that they have become whipping posts or scapegoats. The Somme battle, as indeed the whole of the Great War, was ultimately the responsibility of the people of Europe and the United States, who permitted conditions to come to such a pass.[12]

NOTES

1. Interview with Peter Arnett, CNN war correspondent, *This Morning* (ITV), 8 March 1994.
2. The *Nation*, 19 September 1914 (London).
3. S. Sassoon, *Memoirs of an Infantry Officer* (Faber & Faber, 1930), p. 176.
4. Sassoon, *Memoirs*, p. 184.

5.   P. Gibbs, *Adventures in Journalism* (Heinemann, 1923), as cited in P. Knightley, *The First Casualty* (Quartet Books Limited, 1982), p. 93.

6.   Gibbs, *Adventures*, p. 253.

7.   H.W. Nevinson, *Anywhere for a News Story. Being the Personal Narrative of Thirteen Men who have Adventured in Search of News* (John Lane, 1934), p. 12.

8.   M. Hasting and S. Jenkins, *The Battle for the Falklands* (Michael Joseph Ltd, 1983), p. 221.

9.   P. Kosminsky and M. Bilton, *Speaking Out: Untold Stories from the Falklands War* (Andre Deutsch, 1989), p. 54.

10.   T. Royle, *War Report* (Grafton Books, 1989), p. 280.

11.   Irma Kurtz, on *Fourth Column* (Radio Four), 30 June 1995.

12.   Farrar-Hockley, A.H., *The Somme* (B.T. Batsford, 1964), p. 212.

BIBLIOGRAPHY

Badsey, S.D. 'Battle of the Somme; British War Propaganda', *Historical Journal of Film, Radio and Television*, vol. 3 (1993)

Barker, P. *Regeneration*, Penguin, 1993

——. *The Eye in the Door*, Penguin, 1994

——. *The Ghost Road*, Viking, 1995

Barnett, C. *The Sword Bearers*, Hodder & Stoughton, 1986

Beaver, P. *The Wipers Times*, Papermac, 1988

Beaverbrook. *Politicians and the War, 1914–18*, New York, 1928

Bell, M. *In Harm's Way*, Hamish Hamilton, 1995

Berry, P. and Bostridge, M. *Vera Brittain, a Life*, Pimlico, 1995

Bishop, A. *Chronicle of Youth, Vera Brittain's War Diary, 1913–1917*, Victor Gollancz, 1981

Blake, R. (ed.). *The Private Papers of Douglas Haig 1914–1919*, Eyre & Spottiswoode, 1952

Blakeway, D. *The Falklands War*, Sidgwick and Jackson, 1992

Blunden, E. *Undertones of War*, Penguin, 1982

Bond, B. *The First World War and the British Military History*, Clarendon Press, 1991

Bond, R.C. *The King's Own Yorkshire Light Infantry in the Great War 1914–1918*, vol. III, Percy, Lund, Humphries and Co., 1928

Bourke, J. 'Masculinity, Men's Bodies and the Great War', *History Today*, vol. 46 (2) (Feb, 1996)

Brittain, V. *Testament of Youth,* Virago Press, 1978

Brooke, R. *If I Should Die*, Phoenix, 1996

Brown, M. *The Imperial War Museum Book of the First World War*, Sidgwick & Jackson, 1993

——. *The Imperial War Museum Book of the Somme*, Sidgwick and Jackson, 1996

Buchan, J. *A History of the First World War*, Lochar Publishing, 1991

——. *Memory Hold-the-Door*, Hodder and Stoughton, 1940

Buitenhuis, P. *The Great War of Words*, B.T. Batsford, 1989

Carmichael, J. *First World War Photographers*, Routledge, 1989

Charteris, Brig-Gen J. *At G.H.Q.*, Cassell, 1931

Clark, A. *The Donkeys*, Pimlico, 1991

Clarke, B. *My Round at the War*, Heinemann, 1917

Coate, L. *The Somme 1914–18*, Tressell, 1983

Commonwealth War Graves Commission. *Introduction to the Register of the Thiepval Memorial, France*, Commonwealth War Graves Commission, 1978

Coombs, R.E.B. *Before Endeavours Fade. A Guide to the Battlefields of the First World War*, Battle of Britain Prints International Limited, 1983

Crernie, R.B. *A Short History of the King's Own Yorkshire Light Infantry 1755–1965*, The Wakefield Series, 1965

Dyer, G. *The Missing of the Somme*, Hamish Hamilton, 1994

Eddy, P. et al. *The Falklands War*, Sphere, 1982

Edmonds, J.E. *The Official History of the Great War; Military Operations, France and Belgium, 1914*, Macmillam, 1933

——. *The Official History of the Great War; Miltary Operations, France and Belgium, 1915*, vol. 4, Macmillam, 1928

——. *The Official History of the Great War; Military Operations France and Belgium. December 1915–July 1st 1916*, Shearer, 1986

——. *The Official History of the Great War; Military Operations, France and Belgium, 1917, Volume II*, HMSO, 1948

Farrar-Hockley, A.H. *The Somme*, B.T. Batsford, 1964

Faulks, S. *Birdsong*, Vintage, 1994

Fletcher, D. *Tanks and Trenches*, Sutton Publishing, 1996

Fussell, P. *The Great War and Modern Memory*, Oxford University Press, 1975

Fyfe, H. *The Making of an Optimist*, Leonard Parsons, 1921

Gibbs, P. *The Souls of War*, Heinemann, 1915

——. *The Battles of the Somme*, Heinemann, 1917

——. *Open Warfare, The Way to Victory*, Heinemann, 1919

——. *Realities of War*, Heinemann, 1920

——. *Adventures in Journalism*, Heinemann, 1923

——. *From Bapaume to Passchendaele*, Cedric Chivers, 1965

Gilbert, M. *First World War*, HarperCollins, 1995

Graves, R. *Goodbye to All That*, Penguin, 1960

Griffith, P. *Battle Tactics of the Western Front. The British Army's Art of Attack, 1916–18*, Yale University Press, 1994

Groot, G.J. *Douglas Haig 1861–1928*, Unwin Hyman, 1988

Haig, D. *Cavalry Studies, Strategical and Tactical*, Hugh Rees, 1907

Harris, R. *GOTCHA! The Media, the Government and the Falklands Crisis*, Faber & Faber, 1983

Hart-Davis, R., (ed.). *Siegfried Sassoon, The War Poems*, Faber & Faber, 1983

Haste, C. *Keep the Home Fires Burning*, Allen Lane, 1977

Haythornthwaite, P.J. *The World War One Source Book*, Arms and Armour Press, 1992

Hemingway, E. *A Farewell to Arms*, Arrow, 1994

Hibberd, D. (ed.). *Poetry of the First World War*, Macmillan, 1981

Holmes, R. *The Little Field-Marshal: Sir John French*, Jonathan Cape, 1981

——. *Riding the Retreat: Mons to the Marne 1914*, Pimlico, 1996

Holt, T. and V. *Battlefields of the First World War*, Pavilion, 1995

Hynes, S. *A War Imagined*, Pimlico, 1992

Keegan, J. *The Face of Battle*, Penguin, 1978

Knightley, P. *The First Casualty*, Quartet Books Limited, 1982

Kosminsky, P. and Bilton, M. *Speaking Out: Untold Stories from the Falklands War*, Andre Deutsch, 1989

Laffin, J. *British Butchers and Bunglers of World War One*, Alan Sutton Publishing, 1988

——. *A Western Front Companion, 1914–1918*, Sutton Publishing, 1994

Liddell Hart, B.H. *History of the First World War*, Pan Books, 1972

Liddle, P.H. *The Soldier's War, 1914–1918*, Blandford Press, 1988

Livesy, A. *Great Battles of World War I*, Marshall, 1981

Low, R. *The History of British Film, 1914–1918*, George Allen & Unwin Ltd, 1948

Lytton, N. *The Press and the General Staff*, W. Collins Sons & Co., 1920

McCarthy, C. *The Somme, the Day-by-Day Account*, Arms and Armour Press, 1993

Macdonald, L. *Somme*, Papermac, 1984

——. *They Called it Passchendaele*, Papermac, 1984

——. *1915, The Death of Innocence*, Headline, 1993

Marwick, A. *The Deluge*, second edition, Macmillan, 1991

Messenger, C. *The Century of Warfare. Worldwide Conflict from 1900 to the Present Day*, HarperCollins, 1995

Messinger, G.S. *British Propaganda and the State in the First World War*, Manchester University Press, 1992

Middlebrook, M. *The First Day of the Somme*, Penguin Books, 1971

——. *The Fight for the 'Malvinas'*, Penguin, 1990

Middlebrook, M. and M. *The Somme Battlefields*, Penguin Books, 1994

Miles, W. *History of the Great War. Military Operations France and Belgium, 1916. 2nd July to the End of the Battles of the Somme*, Macmillan, 1938

Mundy, H. *No Heroes, No Cowards*, People's Press of Milton Keynes, 1981

Nevinson, H.W. *Anywhere for a News Story*, John Lane, 1934

Northcliffe. *At the War*, Hodder & Stoughton, 1916

Owen, W. *The Pity of War*, Phoenix, 1996

Ponsonby, A. *Falsehood in Wartime*, George Allen & Unwin, 1928

Prior, R. and Wilson, T. *Command on the Western Front*, Blackwell, 1992

Read, D. *The Power of News, The History of Reuters*, Oxford University Press, 1992

Reeves, N. 'Film Propaganda and its Audience', *Journal of Contemporary History* vol. 18, no. 3 (1983)

——. 'The Power of Film Propaganda, Myth or Reality?', *Historical Journal of Film, Radio and Television*, vol. 13, no. 2 (1993)

Remarque, E.M. *All Quiet on the Western Front*, 1928

Repington, C. *The First World War, 1914–1918, Personal Experiences*, vol. I, Constable & Company, 1920

Robbins, K. *The First World War*, Oxford University Press, 1984

Roberts, A. *Churchill: Embattled Hero*, Phoenix, 1996

Robinson, H.P. *The Turning Point: The Battle of the Somme*, William Heinemann, 1917

Royle, T. *The Kitchener Enigma*, Michael Joseph, 1985

——. *War Report*, Grafton Books, 1989

Sanders, M.L. et al. *British Propaganda During the First World War 1914–1918*, Macmillan Press, 1982

Sassoon, S. *Memoirs of an Infantry Officer*, Faber & Faber, 1930

——. *Siegfried's Journey*, Purnell & Sons, 1947

——. *Sherston's Progress*, Faber & Faber, 1983

Short, K.R.M. *Feature Films as History*, Croom Helm, 1981

Smith, J.A. *John Buchan, a Biography*, Rupert Hart-Davis, 1965

Smither, R. '"A Wonderful Idea of the Fighting": the Question of Fake in "Battle of the Somme"', *Historical Journal of Film, Radio, and Television*, vol. 13, no. 2 (1993)
——. *The Battles of the Somme and Ancre*, Imperial War Museum, 1993
Stedman, M. *Battleground Europe: Somme, Fricourt-Mametz*, Leo Cooper, 1997
Stroud, J. *Special Correspondent*, Ward Lock & Co., 1969
Swinton, E.D. *Eyewitness*, Hodder & Stoughton, 1932
Taylor, A.J.P. *The First World War*, Penguin Books, 1966
——. *English History, 1914–1945*, Oxford University Press, 1992
——. *The Trouble Makers*, Pimlico, 1993
Terraine, J. *The First World War, 1914–1918*, Papermac, 1984
——. *White Heat. The New Warfare, 1914–1918*, Leo Cooper, 1992
——. *Impacts of War, 1914 & 1918*, Leo Cooper, 1993
Thomas, W.B. *With the British on the Somme*, Methuen, 1917
——. *A Traveller in News*, Chapman & Hall, 1925
Travers, T. *The Killing Ground. The British Army, the Western Front & the Emergence of Modern Warfare, 1900–1918*, Routledge, 1993
Westwood, J. *Railways at War*, Osprey, 1980
Winter, D. *Death's Men: Soldiers of the Great War*, Penguin, 1979
——. *Haig's Command, a Reassessment*, Penguin, 1992
Winter, J.M. *The Great War and the British People*, Macmillian, 1986
Wolff, L. *In Flanders Fields*, Penguin, 1979

UNPUBLISHED MATERIAL

War Diaries of the 21st Division. WO-95/2130 130666 (July 1916) (Public Record Office, Kew)
War Diaries of the 64th Brigade. WO-95/2159 130677 (July 1916) (Public Record Office, Kew)
War Diaries of the 9th & 10th Battalion, the King's Own Yorkshire Light Infantry. WO-95/2162 124235. (Public Record Office, Kew)
Woodhead, B. *Life in France* (1916)

FILMS

Mallins, G. and McDowell, J.B. *The Battle of the Somme* (WO Films Committee, 1916)
Urban, C. *Britain Prepared* (Urban/Vickers, 1914)

INDEX